AF484924

The Accents of Faith

THE ACCENTS OF FAITH

Why Morality Is Older Than God, and What That Means for All of Us

Michael Carroll

Copyright © 2026 Michael Carroll

All rights reserved. No part of this publication may be reproduced, distributed, or transmitted in any form or by any means, including photocopying, recording, or other electronic or mechanical methods, without the prior written permission of the author.

First paperback edition, 2026

ISBN: 979-8-9954519-2-1

For Paul, Tom, Allen, Dan, and Claire.

*And for my parents, who drove me to serve 7 a.m. Mass
and sent me to Catholic school.*

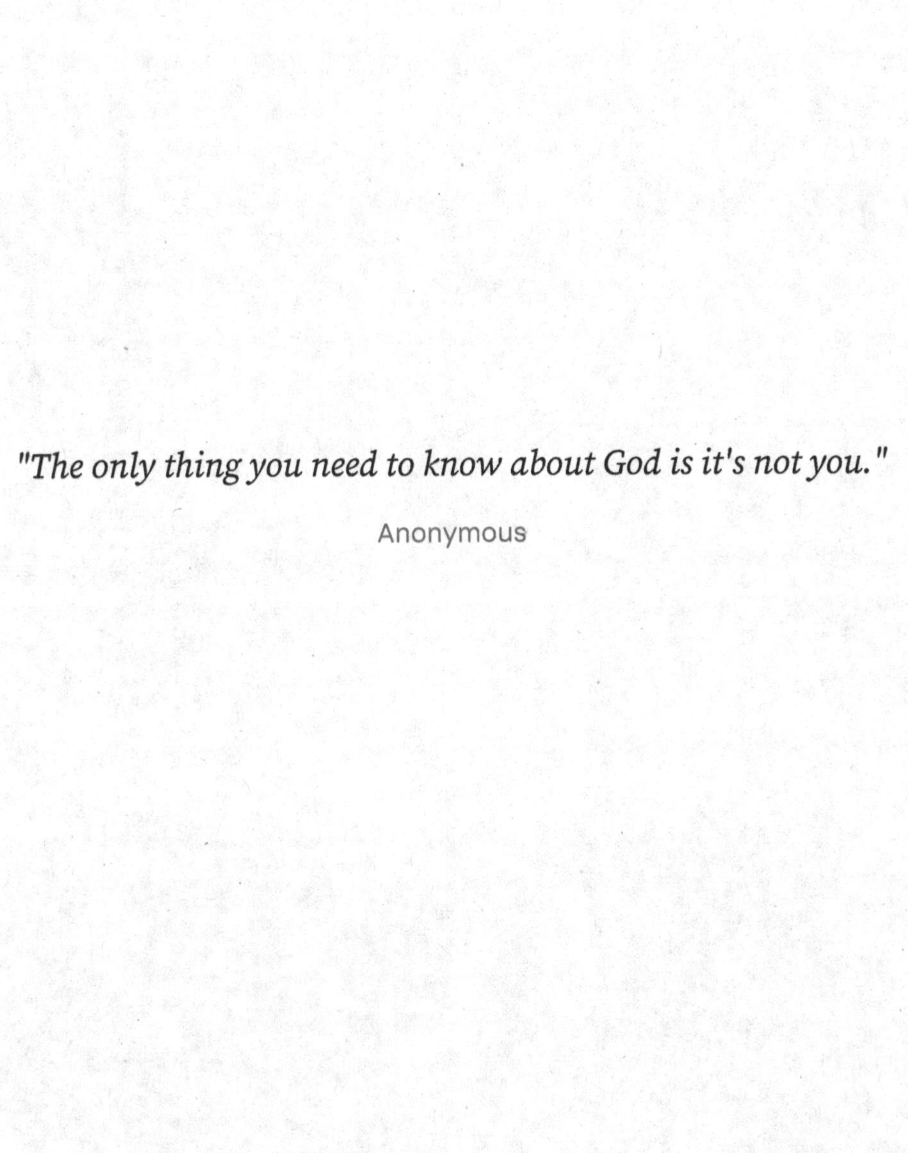

"The only thing you need to know about God is it's not you."

Anonymous

Contents

Introduction: The Language Beneath the Words

Five Cities, Five Moments

It's dawn in Istanbul, and the call rises from a minaret above Sultanahmet. The muezzin's voice, amplified now but unchanged in its melodic arc for fourteen centuries, begins with the phrase that opens every prayer: *Allahu Akbar*. God is greater. In apartments and streets below, men and women pause. They turn toward Mecca, fold their hands below their navels, and begin. The words come in Arabic, a language most of them don't speak in daily life but know by feel, the syllables worn smooth with repetition. The body leans forward, then prostrates fully, forehead to the ground. Then stillness. Then, from somewhere in the chest, the breath slows. The world outside the mind grows quiet.

Three thousand kilometers to the west, in Rome, an elderly woman kneels in a pew near the back of a side-chapel in Santa Maria Maggiore. She's not attending Mass. She's alone, holding a rosary between her fingers, lips moving just slightly as she counts through the beads. Each decade is ten Hail Marys and one Our Father, and she's done this so many times that the prayers run almost below conscious thought. What remains is the rhythm: a slow, steady cycling of breath and whisper, ten seconds forward, pause, ten seconds forward, pause. Her shoulders drop. The candlelight in front of a painted Madonna becomes the only thing in the room that matters.

In Kyoto, in the predawn quiet of a Zen temple, a monk sits on a cushion in a position he'll hold for an hour without moving. He's not reciting anything. He's not asking for anything. He's attending to breath itself, watching thoughts arrive and leave without attachment, the way a river watcher observes a current. The hall smells of cedar and incense. Another monk, seated six feet away, is in the same posture, attending to the same breath, thinking his own thoughts about nothing in particular. The silence between them isn't empty. It's a texture, the texture of shared attention, two people inhabiting the same still space.

On the western edge of Jerusalem, in a synagogue on a Friday evening, a congregation rises and turns toward the door as the Shabbat prayer begins. The cantor's voice opens the Lecha Dodi, a sixteenth-century poem welcoming the Sabbath as a bride. The congregation joins on the chorus, dozens of voices in loose, overlapping harmonies that would horrify a conductor but feel, to the people singing, like something alive and larger than any individual voice. Children who are too young to understand the words stand on pews to see better. Old men with beards close their eyes. For a moment, the hundred ordinary worries of a hundred ordinary lives go quiet, replaced by something that doesn't have an easy name in the secular vocabulary: presence, maybe, or the sense of being held inside something that holds together.

And in a Buddhist temple in Chiang Mai, Thailand, on a Tuesday morning that's ordinary in every other respect, a middle-aged woman places offerings of jasmine and rice at the feet of a gilded figure. She speaks softly, not in supplication exactly but in acknowledgment, the way you might speak at the grave of someone you loved. She doesn't believe the statue can hear. She believes the practice of speaking matters nonetheless. She lights incense, bows three times with her palms together, and sits for a while in what looks to an outside observer like simple quietness.

Five cities. Five traditions. Five entirely different accounts of who or what is being addressed, what is owed, what comes after death, what the rules are for a good life, and what the cosmos is made of. And yet: if you were to compress these five moments into a single scene, the body language would be nearly interchangeable. The downcast or closed eyes. The deliberate regulation of breath. The repetitive words or movements, pared down to their essentials. The physical posture of receptiveness, whether it's a prostration, a bow, a stillness, or an upturned palm. The slowing of the pulse. The quieting of mental noise. The sense, reported independently and consistently across all these traditions, of being less alone.

What is happening here? What is really happening, underneath the theology and the language and the competing claims about the divine?

That's the question this book is about.

After fifty years of increasingly sophisticated science across evolutionary biology, neuroscience, developmental psychology, and anthropology, we now have a remarkable answer. Religion didn't invent human morality. Human morality is older, deeper, and wider than any religion. What religion did, and what it continues to do, is organize, amplify, and ritualize moral instincts that were already present in the species long before the first written scripture, the first temple, or the first priest. Religion is one of the most powerful instruments humanity has ever developed for shaping moral behavior. But it's an instrument. The music was already in us.

Notice what the question isn't asking. It's not asking which of these five people has it right. It's not asking whether there's a God to receive their prayers.

The question is narrower, and more interesting: what is happening in human beings when these practices occur? What do evolution, neuroscience, developmental psychology, and anthropology tell us about why human beings in every known culture develop practices that look like these, and what those practices do to the people who engage in them? That's a question science can make progress on. The answers, accumulated over the past several decades from laboratories and fieldwork sites and cross-cultural surveys around the world, turn out to be both illuminating and, for some readers, unexpected.

The Question Underneath

The easy answer is wrong. The religious answer, in one of its forms, might be that what's happening is encounter with God, or ultimate reality, or the Dharma, and that the similarities between traditions are evidence of a common divine source that all humans reach toward in their different ways. The secular dismissal, in one of its forms, might be that what's happening is nothing more than a kind of self-hypnosis, a pleasant but in the end illusory state that people mistake for transcendence. Both answers close the question too quickly. They don't explain the specific patterns: the universality of body postures, the convergence on similar breathing rhythms, the same neurological signatures in the brains of Franciscan nuns and Tibetan monks, or the fact that human infants, months before any religious instruction, already prefer helpers over hinderers.

The question this book takes seriously isn't: which religion is right? That question is outside the reach of science, and this book doesn't pretend otherwise. The question is: what does the scientific study of human evolution, neuroscience, developmental psychology, and anthropology tell us about why religion exists, why it's so powerful, and what it's actually doing in human moral life?

Decades of research across multiple disciplines confirm it: religion didn't create morality. It inherited morality, and built upon it, with extraordinary skill and consequence.

The Accent Metaphor

There's a useful way to hold all of this in mind throughout the chapters ahead, and it's the metaphor of language.

Every human being, wherever they're born, learns to speak. The capacity for language is built into the species. A child born in Tokyo and raised in Buenos Aires will speak Spanish as fluently and naturally as a child born there. A child born in São Paulo and raised in Tokyo will speak Japanese the same way. The underlying cognitive machinery, the capacity for grammar, for syntax, for the acquisition of vocabulary, is universal. What varies is the particular language, and within that, the particular accent, the local, historical, culturally specific way of pronouncing and inflecting that universal capacity.

Morality works the same way.

The evidence from evolutionary biology, developmental psychology, and cross-cultural anthropology converges on the same basic picture: human beings come into the world equipped with a moral sense. It's not complete. It's not perfect. But it's real, and it's there from the beginning. Infants prefer helpers to hinderers before they can sit up. Toddlers show a sense of fairness before they have language to describe it. The great apes reconcile after fights, console one another, and discriminate between intentional and accidental harm. Across the enormous diversity of human cultures, certain moral intuitions recur so consistently that they look less like cultural inventions and more like features of the underlying human architecture: care for children and close kin, fairness and reciprocity, sanctions against unprovoked violence, the importance of trustworthiness.

This is the moral language. It's shared, species-wide, the foundation beneath all the variation.

Religions are accents.

Each major world religion, and each local tradition within those religions, is a particular way of speaking that underlying moral language. It's shaped by history, by geography, by the specific problems a particular community faced over centuries, by the specific teachers and prophets who gave it form, by the institutions that preserved and transmitted it. Catholicism and Islam and

Buddhism and Judaism and Hinduism and the other major traditions pronounce the same underlying words, the words about harm, care, fairness, loyalty, and the sanctity of life, in recognizably different ways, with different emphases and different ritual forms. None of them invented the moral language. They all inherited it from somewhere much older than any of them.

The implications run in several directions at once.

First, no single religious accent has a monopoly on moral meaning. The Catholic tradition's account of human dignity isn't more or less fundamental than the Buddhist tradition's account of compassion, or the Jewish tradition's account of justice, or the Islamic tradition's account of submission to a moral order larger than the self. These are different pronunciations of the same deep commitment to taking other people's suffering seriously. A person raised in one tradition and encountering another isn't, at the deepest level, encountering a foreign moral language. They're encountering a different accent. This doesn't mean all practices within all traditions are equally good or that nothing can be criticized. Accents can develop habits that distort the underlying language. Some pronunciations make the meaning less clear, or shade it in ways that exclude people who ought to be included. The accent metaphor makes room for both genuine difference and genuine common ground.

Second, and equally important: secular ethics is another accent in the same conversation. The tradition of secular moral philosophy, from Aristotle's account of virtue and human flourishing to Enlightenment accounts of human rights to contemporary utilitarian ethics, draws on the same underlying moral language that religious traditions draw on. It simply pronounces it without reference to the divine. This isn't a deficiency. It's a different inflection. The same moral intuitions that drove Martin Luther King Jr.'s religious case against racial segregation also drove the secular case made by the civil rights lawyers, the journalists who documented the injustice, and the philosophers who articulated equal human dignity without reference to God. They were all speaking the same language in different accents.

A second metaphor is worth introducing alongside this one, working at a slightly different level: the relationship between an operating system and the applications that run on top of it. The moral operating system, the evolved human capacity for empathy, fairness, cooperation, and norm enforcement, runs beneath all the applications. Religion is one of the most powerful applications ever developed. It bundles together moral guidance, ritual practice, community structure, cosmic meaning, and identity in a single package that has proven extraordinarily effective for millions of people across thousands of years. Secular ethics, mindfulness practices, civic institutions, and humanitarian movements are other applications running on the same underlying system. The operating system analogy captures something the accent metaphor doesn't: different applications can accomplish similar functions by very different means. What matters is whether the application helps the underlying system work well, making cooperation more stable, suffering less, and human dignity more real.

What Science Can and Cannot Tell Us

A note about what science is doing in this book, and what it's not doing.

Science can describe. It can measure how prayer affects the autonomic nervous system. It can trace the evolutionary origins of moral emotions. It can use brain imaging to show what happens in the minds of people in states of religious ecstasy or deep meditation. It can map, across cultures, the moral intuitions that appear to be universal and those that vary. It can show, using economic game experiments, how religious belief affects cooperation among strangers. It can chart the historical record of when moralizing gods first appeared in human cultures, and why they appeared when they did.

What science can't do is decide whether any of this is, in the end, evidence for or against the existence of God. The question of God's existence isn't a scientific question in the same way that the question of the Earth's age is. Science works by observing, measuring, and constructing falsifiable hypotheses about the natural world. The question of whether there's a transcendent reality underlying the natural world is, by definition, outside the scope of what scientific methods can resolve. This book takes that boundary seriously. The scientific findings reported here aren't offered as proof that religion is an illusion, nor as proof that it's a vehicle for genuine divine encounter. They're offered as evidence about how human beings function, what they need, and how religion fits into that picture.

This means that a deeply committed Catholic or Muslim or Buddhist reader can accept everything in this book and remain exactly as committed to their faith. The findings don't threaten faith. They describe it from the outside, the way a musicologist can describe the physics of a violin without diminishing the beauty of the music. What the reader may find is that the scientific account illuminates aspects of faith that are easy to overlook from the inside, the way understanding the physics of light doesn't make a sunset less beautiful, but does make it more interesting.

By the same token, a thoroughgoing secularist who has no sympathy for organized religion can accept everything in this book and remain exactly as secular. The finding that religion is a powerful and in many respects effective moral technology doesn't require admiring or endorsing any particular religion's truth claims. It simply requires taking seriously the evidence about what religion does, and asking honestly whether what it does is worth understanding.

A Map of the Journey Ahead

The book moves in four parts, each taking on a different layer of the question.

Part One asks: where does morality come from? The answer turns out to be older than any civilization and older than any religion. The moral sense is an evolutionary inheritance, built into the human genome by millions of years of social life among beings for whom cooperation was survival. Infants as young as six months old show preferences for helpers over hinderers, a finding that emerged from developmental psychology laboratories at Yale University. The great apes from whom we're descended show empathy, reconciliation, and rudimentary fairness. The moral emotions, guilt, shame, indignation, compassion, aren't cultural additions to an otherwise amoral species. They're core features of the species, shaped by natural selection because they made cooperation possible in groups, and groups that cooperated outcompeted groups that didn't. This part also examines the specific shape of human moral intuitions, the foundations that appear across cultures, and the ways they vary. Morality, before religion, was already complex, already contested, and already consequential.

Part Two asks: what does religion do with the moral architecture it inherits? Religion functions as cultural technology: a bundled system of practices, narratives, rituals, institutions, and beliefs that channels, amplifies, and organizes human moral instincts in specific directions. Religion activates the social brain through ritual and communal practice. It manages death anxiety. It extends the circle of moral concern beyond kin and immediate neighbors to include fellow believers, and sometimes, at its best, all of humanity. It encodes moral rules in stories and commandments that are easier to transmit and remember than abstract philosophical principles. It creates the felt experience of belonging to something larger than the self. These aren't trivial achievements. For most of human history, and for most people on earth today, religion has been the primary infrastructure for moral life. Part Two also examines what happens when the moral accents develop in particular directions: how religious language has been used to expand the circle of moral concern, as in the abolitionist and civil rights movements, and how it's been used to shrink that circle, as in the Inquisitions and many instances of religiously sanctioned violence. The same psychological machinery that produces solidarity and compassion can, under different conditions, produce exactly the opposite. Understanding how the machinery works in both directions isn't an attack on religion. It's the most honest way to understand it.

Part Three asks: how do we speak the moral language when traditional religious frameworks are unavailable or unconvincing? This is a pressing question for a world in which religious affiliation is declining in many wealthy democracies even as the need for moral community, guidance, and existential meaning remains entirely undiminished. The evidence here is more tentative, but not discouraging. Secular societies can and do function with high levels of moral health. The philosophical traditions of virtue ethics, care ethics, and secular humanism offer coherent and rigorous frameworks for moral reasoning without supernatural grounding. The practices that religion has developed over centuries, contemplation, ritual, communal belonging, charitable service, aren't the exclusive property of religious institutions. They can be, and are being, adapted for secular contexts. What this part also shows, honestly, is that the adaptation isn't free: the community structure, the shared narrative, the felt sense of meaning and purpose that religion packages together aren't easy to replicate. The evidence suggests that living spiritually in isolation, without either traditional religion or secular community, is associated with worse outcomes for mental and physical health than either committed religious practice or committed secular community membership. The moral of this finding isn't that everyone should go back to church. It's that the communal and ritual dimensions of religion are meeting real human needs, and those needs don't disappear when the theology does.

Part Four turns to a question that has become urgent in the twenty-first century: where are people actually finding moral community outside traditional religion? The answer leads into football stadiums, CrossFit gyms, Alcoholics Anonymous meetings, parent groups, and the quiet revolution of parkrun, a free, weekly, global gathering that has become, without anyone planning it, one of the closest things to a secular congregation the modern world has produced. These are places where secular communities are developing moral accents of their own. Some are surprisingly effective. Others reveal, by their limitations, just how much religious congregations have been doing all along. The question isn't whether secular community can exist. It plainly can. The question is whether it can do the full work that religion has done, and what it takes to build something that lasts.

The Heart of the Argument

Before moving into the evidence, it's worth stating the core argument directly.

Human beings need moral guidance. They need belonging. They need meaning. These aren't optional features of a well-functioning human life. They're structural requirements of the kind of animal we are, an intensely social primate with a large prefrontal cortex that can contemplate its own death, project itself into the futures of others, and ask, with genuine anxiety, whether it's living well.

Religion is one powerful way of meeting those needs. It's not the only way. It's probably the most thoroughly tested way, having been refined by millions of people over thousands of years through a relentless practical process of figuring out what helps people live together with some decency and hold themselves together under suffering. That's not nothing. That's an extraordinary legacy.

But religion's power to meet those needs doesn't depend on any religion's particular account of the cosmos being literally true. A person can be sustained by the practice of prayer without believing in the metaphysics of the tradition the prayer comes from, as the research on the physiological effects of rhythmic breath-regulation makes clear. A person can be morally formed by the stories of a tradition without accepting every doctrinal claim the tradition makes.

A person can be nourished by belonging to a community organized around shared values without sharing every belief that community espouses. And a person can live an exemplary moral life with no religion at all, drawing on secular traditions of ethics and on communities organized around shared values other than theological ones. None of this diminishes religion. All of it puts it in a larger frame.

That larger frame is what this book is about.

The path through Istanbul and Rome and Kyoto and Jerusalem and Chiang Mai doesn't lead to the same theological destination. But the people walking those paths are, in their depth, asking the same questions and feeling the same pull toward the same things: to be less alone, to be more good, to make something of the brief and astonishing fact that they exist at all.

That shared pull is where this book begins.

A note on citations: this book weaves together findings from evolutionary biology, neuroscience, developmental psychology, anthropology, and philosophy. Where specific studies are referenced in the text, sources are provided in the notes at the end of each chapter. Two findings are worth flagging at the outset because they recur throughout the book in different forms. The first is the 2001 study by Luciano Bernardi and colleagues, published in the British Medical Journal, which found that reciting the Catholic rosary and a Hindu yoga mantra produced virtually identical cardiovascular effects, slowing breathing to approximately 6 breaths per minute and producing striking improvements in heart rate variability, the same beneficial rhythm in both cases, achieved through cadence alone, not through theology. The second is the body of research emerging from Yale University's infant cognition laboratory, which demonstrated that infants as young as six months show preferences for characters who help rather than hinder others, suggesting that the roots of moral evaluation run deeper in human development than any religious or cultural instruction could reach. Both findings, drawn from entirely different research traditions, point in the same direction: the machinery underneath the faith is older, stranger, and more deeply human than the faith itself.

PART I

MORALITY BEFORE RELIGION

Chapter 1

What Humans Needed Before Gods

The Hunt

Picture the scene as precisely as the evidence allows. East Africa, roughly 70,000 years ago. A band of perhaps thirty people has been following a herd of wildebeest for two days across a dry, thorn-scrub landscape. The hunters are tired and thirsty. This morning their patience finally paid off: two animals are dead, their carcasses already drawing vultures in lazy circles overhead.

The men who made the kills are Kato and his brother-in-law, Sule. Kato drove the first wildebeest into a marsh where it bogged down and could be dispatched. Sule took the second at a distance with a throwing spear, a difficult shot that most men would have missed. Both men are breathing hard, streaked with dust and blood, standing over a combined 600 kilograms of meat.

Now comes the problem.

The rest of the band is approaching. Thirty people, including women carrying infants, children, two elders too old to run, and a young man, Jonah, who twisted his ankle badly on the first day of the hunt and has been limping behind on a makeshift crutch ever since. Jonah contributed nothing to this kill. He may never be a reliable hunter again.

What happens next isn't obvious. Kato and Sule could claim the meat for themselves and their immediate families. Every calorie matters in a world without refrigeration. A wildebeest carcass will rot within two days in the heat. They could eat to fullness, render and carry what they can, and leave the rest for the vultures and hyenas. On strict nutritional grounds, this is rational.

But Kato doesn't do this. Neither does Sule. Without deliberation, without consulting a rulebook, without invoking any god, they begin dividing the carcass. The choicer pieces go to the elders, who have knowledge and counsel to offer even when their legs fail. The nursing mothers receive cuts that will sustain their milk. Jonah gets a portion, too, smaller than the hunters' but enough. Children eat alongside adults. The band settles around the meat in an arrangement so orderly it looks, to an outside eye, like it was planned.

It wasn't planned. It was felt.

This is where morality begins: not in a divine commandment, not in a written law, not in a philosophical argument about the good life, but in the almost automatic pull of obligation that a social animal feels toward the members of its group. The pull is real, and it's very old. It predates agriculture, cities, writing, and organized religion by tens of thousands of years. Understanding where it came from, and how it works, is the first task of this book.

Why Cooperation Was Not Obvious

To understand what evolution accomplished in the human moral system, it helps to first appreciate what it was working against.

Natural selection operates on individual reproductive success. Genes that help their carrier survive and reproduce spread through a population. Genes that don't, fade out. From this perspective, generosity looks like a problem. If you share your food with someone who didn't help you acquire it, you're transferring calories you might have used for your own children to another person's children. Why would genes for generosity persist?

This isn't a new question. Charles Darwin himself recognized the puzzle. In *The Descent of Man* (1871), he observed that any tribe containing many members who are "always ready to give aid to each other and to sacrifice themselves for the common good" would be victorious over most other tribes. But the mechanism behind such selfless behavior was unclear for nearly a century after Darwin wrote those words.

The answers began arriving in the 1960s and 1970s, and they transformed biology, psychology, and eventually our understanding of religion. Two insights stand out.

Research Finding 1: Reciprocal Altruism and the Emotional Architecture of Fairness

In 1971, the biologist Robert Trivers published a paper that would become one of the most cited works in evolutionary science. Titled \"The Evolution of Reciprocal Altruism,\" its core argument was elegant: altruism between unrelated individuals can evolve when individuals interact repeatedly, when each can help the other at low cost, and when cheaters are reliably identified and punished.

The logic isn't complicated. Think of two neighbors who take turns watching each other's children. If I watch your child today when you need to work, and you watch mine next week, we both benefit. The exchange works over time because we live near each other and will keep encountering each other. If one of us consistently takes but never gives, the other will stop cooperating and tell everyone else about the unreliable neighbor.

What made Trivers' paper genuinely groundbreaking was a second step in his argument. He proposed that the psychological system regulating this kind of exchange could explain a wide range of emotions that feel distinctly moral: friendship, gratitude, suspicion, guilt, moral indignation, and various forms of dishonesty and hypocrisy. These emotions, in Trivers' account, aren't accidents of culture. They're adaptations. Gratitude motivates us to return favors. Guilt motivates us to repair relationships we've damaged. Suspicion motivates us to monitor potential cheaters. Moral indignation motivates us to punish those who violated the unspoken contract of mutual aid.

Think about the last time you felt guilty. Perhaps you promised to help a friend move and then canceled at the last minute. Or you snapped unkindly at someone who had done nothing to deserve it. The guilt that followed wasn't pleasant. It wasn't supposed to be. In Trivers' account, guilt exists precisely because it motivates repair: it makes you apologize, explain, compensate, demonstrate that you're still a trustworthy partner. Guilt is a social glue, and it evolved because individuals who felt it were better at maintaining the alliances they needed to survive.

The same logic applies to outrage. When you see someone take advantage of a vulnerable person, when a colleague claims credit for work they didn't do, when a free-rider drains a shared resource without contributing, something in you activates quickly, involuntarily, and powerfully. You feel that something wrong has occurred, and you feel motivated to do something about it. That feeling doesn't wait for a theological opinion. It arrives on its own, urgent and clear, because our ancestors who felt it and acted on it were more successful at maintaining the cooperative groups they depended on.

Trivers provided the first rigorous scientific grounding for moral emotions as adaptations. The emotions themselves are the mechanism. Morality, at its deepest level, isn't a set of rules that minds follow. It's a set of feelings that minds generate, and those feelings evolved because they solved the cooperation problem.

This is the foundation. Now consider the family.

Research Finding 2: Kin Selection and Why Charity Begins at Home

Seven years before Trivers published his paper, the biologist W.D. Hamilton had already provided a partial answer to Darwin's puzzle about selfless behavior among relatives. Hamilton's insight, published in the *Journal of Theoretical Biology* in 1964, is now known as Hamilton's Rule, and it can be stated in a single inequality:

r times B is greater than C

Here, r stands for the genetic relatedness between two individuals (siblings share on average 50 percent of their genes, first cousins share 12.5 percent), B stands for the benefit to the recipient, and C stands for the cost to the actor. The rule says: an act of sacrifice is favored by natural selection when the genetic relatedness between actor and recipient, multiplied by the benefit to the recipient, exceeds the cost to the actor.

The evolutionary biologist J.B.S. Haldane captured the intuition famously: "I would lay down my life for two brothers or eight cousins." This isn't cynicism. It's mathematics. Two full siblings carry the same total number of my genes as I do, statistically speaking. So if I die to save them, my genes don't go extinct. They persist. The calculation is, of course, not one that anyone consciously performs. It runs in the background, shaping the emotions we call love, loyalty, and family obligation.

This matters enormously for understanding moral life. The deep human pull toward protecting family members, the visceral horror at harm done to a child, the special weight we assign to the suffering of people we love: these feelings aren't cultural constructs. They're ancient. They're shared with other mammals. And they explain a great deal of everyday moral behavior, from parents sacrificing sleep and career advancement for their children to the nepotism (favoritism toward relatives) that appears in every known human society.

Hamilton's Rule also explains why in-group morality, the fierce care for "us," tends to coexist with indifference or hostility toward "them." The calculation changes dramatically with genetic distance.

For most of human evolutionary history, people lived in small bands composed largely of relatives and long-term partners. Strangers were genuinely dangerous, competing for the same scarce resources. Moral concern naturally tracked social distance.

This creates a recurring theme in this book: morality as the language of social life has a range, and the range has historically been short. Expanding it to cover strangers, foreigners, and enemies has always required additional mechanisms, cultural scaffolding built on top of the biological foundation. Religion has often been one of those mechanisms. But it built on something that was already there.

Research Finding 3: Altruistic Punishment and the Emotional Engine of Social Norms

In 2002, the economist Ernst Fehr and his colleague Simon Gächter published a paper in *Nature* that delivered an experimental shock to standard economic theory. The finding was simple to describe and difficult to explain: people will pay a personal cost to punish a cheater, even when they have nothing to gain and will never interact with that person again.

Fehr and Gächter demonstrated this using a public goods game. Participants were given money and asked to contribute to a shared pool. Whatever was contributed would be multiplied and shared equally among the group. This creates a free-rider incentive: the rational self-interested move is to contribute nothing while others' contributions multiply. But when everyone reasons this way, the pool empties and everyone gets nothing. Free-riding corrodes cooperation.

Here is the key result: when participants were given the option to pay a small fee to punish free-riders, reducing the free-rider's payoff at cost to themselves, they did so with remarkable consistency. They punished free-riders even in one-shot games where they'd never encounter the person again. They punished free-riders even when this hurt their own final payoff. They reported feeling angry at free-riders, and the strength of their anger predicted how much they were willing to pay to punish.

Fehr called this "altruistic punishment" because it benefits the group by deterring future free-riding, at personal cost to the punisher, with no direct benefit to the punisher. Classical economic models, which assume self-interested maximizing agents, can't explain it. But evolutionary models can. Fehr's conclusion was blunt: "The evidence indicates that negative emotions toward defectors are the direct cause of altruistic punishment."

In plain terms: moral outrage is the engine that keeps social norms enforced. When you feel compelled to say something when a stranger is rude to a service worker, or when you feel physically uncomfortable sitting next to someone who bragged about cheating, you're experiencing the same mechanism Fehr documented in his laboratory. These feelings aren't voluntary, and they're not primarily rational. They're ancient alarms, evolved in environments where defection needed to be punished swiftly, consistently, and sometimes at personal cost, because groups that didn't punish defectors collapsed.

Research Finding 4: Cooperation's Five Engines and the Power of Reputation

The mathematician Martin Nowak at Harvard devoted his career to a single question: how does cooperation evolve in a world that tends to reward selfishness? In a landmark 2006 paper in *Science*, he synthesized the research into five rules for the evolution of cooperation.

Three of these rules, kin selection, direct reciprocity, and group selection, were already familiar from the work described above. Two others are particularly relevant for understanding morality.

The fourth rule is network reciprocity. Cooperation can persist when cooperators tend to cluster together spatially or socially. Cooperators help their neighbors, and those neighbors help them. Defectors, isolated from the cooperative network, lose out. This is why human communities form neighborhoods, parishes, and social clusters where norms are shared and enforced locally.

The fifth rule changed everything: indirect reciprocity. Unlike direct reciprocity, where I help you and you help me and we keep score, indirect reciprocity works through reputation. I help you. Someone else observes this. My reputation rises. That observer is now more likely to help me when I need it, because they know I'm the kind of person who helps. I help you knowing that my generosity will be broadcast and that strangers I've never met will treat me better because of it.

Nowak put this in stark terms: "The evolution of cooperation by indirect reciprocity leads to reputation building, morality judgment and complex social interactions with ever-increasing cognitive demands."

Consider what indirect reciprocity requires. I must track the reputations of many individuals I've never personally interacted with, form judgments about the moral quality of their behavior, broadcast information about my own behavior credibly, and navigate a social world in which everyone else is simultaneously tracking me. This is cognitively demanding. It requires sophisticated memory, theory of mind, and language to circulate reputation information.

Language, in this account, evolved in part because reputation-based cooperation required it. Before you could trust a stranger, you needed to know about their history with others. That knowledge had to be transmitted verbally. The conversations humans have had for hundreds of thousands of years about who did what to whom, who can be trusted, who took more than their share: this isn't idle gossip. It's the information system on which large-scale cooperation runs.

And here a connection to religion begins to take shape, though we'll develop it fully in Chapter 3. If cooperation depends on reputation, and reputation depends on being observed, then a mind evolved for cooperation would naturally wonder: who else is watching? The answer that supernatural belief provides, across almost every culture, is: someone always is. But before that belief became formalized into religion, the band itself was watching.

Christopher Boehm and the Band as Moral Community

The anthropologist Christopher Boehm spent decades studying hunter-gatherer societies, and what he found challenged a common assumption about human prehistory. We tend to imagine our pre-agricultural ancestors living under the rule of the strongest, alpha-male hierarchies where the most powerful individual took first and most. This picture fits some other primates reasonably well. It doesn't fit most human hunter-gatherer societies.

Boehm described what he called "reverse dominance hierarchies." In band after band, across cultures as different as the San of the Kalahari and the Inuit of the Arctic, he found the same pattern: when an individual began claiming more than a fair share, demanding deference, or attempting to monopolize women or resources, the rest of the band responded collectively. They gossiped. They ridiculed. They stopped cooperating. In severe cases, they ostracized or executed the offender.

The rank and file acted together to suppress would-be tyrants. The mechanism isn't physical strength but coalition. Any single individual challenging the dominant bully is likely to lose. But when the entire group unites, the calculus changes entirely. As Boehm put it: "In effect, the band keeps a dossier on every individual, noting positive and negative points."

The implications for moral evolution are significant. Boehm's evidence suggests that for most of our species' 300,000-year existence, and for much of the two million years before that, human societies maintained shared behavioral norms enforced by collective sanction. They had moral rules. They punished violators. They maintained what Boehm calls "moral communities," groups held together by shared expectations and the willingness to enforce them.

This moral community preceded any formal religious institution by tens of thousands of years. The band's dossier on each member is the original moral accounting system. The outrage that motivates altruistic punishment (Fehr) and the reputation system that makes indirect reciprocity possible (Nowak) combine here into something recognizable as moral life: a group of people who know each other, watch each other, judge each other, and hold each other accountable.

What this means for the central argument of this book is worth stating plainly: the moral community came first. The gods came second.

The archaeological evidence supports this sequence. Studies of comparative hunter-gatherer religion, summarized by Ara Norenzayan and Azim Shariff at the University of British Columbia, show that the most ancient religious traits across cultures are shamanism, belief in an afterlife, and ancestor worship. Moralizing "big gods," the kind that actively monitor human behavior and punish transgressors, are a recent development. They appear most robustly as societies grew too large for face-to-face reputation systems to function, roughly coinciding with the rise of agriculture and urban civilization over the past 10,000 years.

This doesn't mean that religion was irrelevant to morality, or that it's been merely parasitic on something that already existed. Religion found ways to extend, amplify, and encode moral norms in powerful ways that we'll explore in later chapters. But the sequence matters. Morality isn't something that religion installed in an otherwise indifferent species. Morality was the operating system. Religion, when it developed, found an environment it hadn't created.

Guilt, Shame, Empathy, Outrage: The Moral Emotions

The emotional architecture that makes all of this work deserves closer attention.

Guilt, as Trivers understood, motivates repair. When we harm someone we depend on, or violate a norm that holds our group together, guilt is the internal signal that says: the damage you've done may be recoverable, but only if you act. Guilt motivates apology, compensation, and behavioral change. Evolutionary game theory models, developed in part by the philosopher of biology Cailin O'Connor, show that guilt-prone individuals are measurably more likely to maintain valuable cooperative relationships. They defect less, apologize more, and signal trustworthiness more credibly.

Shame is a related but distinct emotion. Where guilt focuses on a specific act, shame focuses on the self: not "I did something wrong" but "I'm the kind of person who does wrong things." Shame is more debilitating and harder to recover from. The threat of public shame has historically been one of the most powerful behavioral regulators human societies have deployed. Exposure in the village square, public censure in the town meeting, the whisper network of a community that knows you've behaved badly: these mechanisms have enforced moral norms in every society for which we have records.

Empathy, the capacity to feel something of what another person is feeling, is the cognitive and emotional bridge that makes moral concern for others possible. The neurological foundation of empathy, including a class of neurons that fire both when an animal performs an action and when it observes the same action in another, sometimes called mirror neurons, appears throughout the mammalian family. Frans de Waal, whom we'll meet in depth in the next chapter, documented empathy in chimpanzees, bonobos, and elephants. When a young chimpanzee falls and cries, its companions gather around it, touching and grooming it, displaying what looks very much like concern. The capacity to care about another's pain isn't uniquely human. It's an ancient feature of social mammalian life.

Outrage, Fehr's altruistic punishment mechanism, is the enforcement arm of the moral system. It motivates punishment of norm-violators even at personal cost. It's the emotional fuel of justice, and it doesn't require instruction. Small children display moral outrage at age two and three, long before they can articulate why something is unfair or why it matters. The feeling arrives first.

Together, these emotions constitute a pre-linguistic moral operating system. They don't form a philosophy. They don't articulate principles. But they regulate social behavior with remarkable effectiveness, maintaining cooperation, punishing free-riders, repairing damaged relationships, and keeping the group's dossier on each member up to date.

Think of morality as a language: the structures and patterns through which humans organize collective life, communicate obligation, and coordinate behavior. Every known human society speaks this language. The grammar is remarkably consistent. The content can vary enormously from culture to culture.

Religion, in this metaphor, is an accent. It shapes how the language is pronounced, which words are emphasized, which phrasings are considered polite or taboo. A religious tradition doesn't create the language of morality from nothing. It inherits the language and adds a distinctive character to it, one that marks membership in a particular community, encodes particular histories, and connects daily moral life to cosmic narratives of meaning and purpose.

The accent is real and significant. No one should dismiss it. But it's not the language itself. And the language was there long before any particular accent developed.

The Long View

This chapter has covered scientific territory ranging from evolutionary biology to economics to anthropology, but all of it points in the same direction. Human moral life didn't begin with a commandment. It began with need.

Early humans needed each other to survive. Cooperation wasn't optional. A band that failed to share food reliably collapsed. One that couldn't maintain trust disintegrated into conflict. One that allowed free-riders to drain shared resources found its cooperative infrastructure eroding until nothing was left. Bands that solved these problems outcompeted those that didn't, and over generations, the genetic and cultural traits that supported cooperation spread.

The emotional architecture that supported cooperation, guilt, gratitude, outrage, empathy, shame, is ancient. It predates Homo sapiens. It predates language. It's what Jonah and Kato and Sule brought to that carcass on the East African plain, long before anyone had a word for fairness or a god to enforce it.

Religion would arrive later. It would find this architecture already in place and build magnificently on top of it, adding new stories to explain why the rules mattered, new rituals to cement group identity, and new concepts of divine surveillance to extend moral accountability beyond the band where reputation systems could operate directly. All of this deserves serious examination in the chapters ahead.

But none of it invented what was already there.

Morality is the operating system. Religion is one of the most powerful applications ever developed to run on it. That operating system, the evolved human capacity for empathy, fairness, cooperation, and norm enforcement, was already running when religion arrived. It didn't install new hardware. It found the hardware already in place, and built something extraordinary with it.

For Reflection

Take a moment with the following questions. They're not designed to challenge your beliefs but to help you observe your own moral life more precisely.

The next time you feel guilty about something, pause before you dismiss the feeling. What relationship does the guilt point to? What repair does it suggest? Notice that the feeling arrived before any conscious reasoning, and that its direction is toward the other person, not away from them. Trivers would recognize what you're experiencing.

The next time you feel outrage at something that has nothing directly to do with you, a news story about a powerful person abusing a vulnerable one, a stranger being treated dismissively, an obvious lie being told without consequence, notice how quickly the feeling arrived and how little you had to think about it. Fehr would recognize that feeling too. Your ancestors paid personal costs to act on it, because groups that contained people like them were more successful than groups that didn't.

And when you feel a pull of loyalty toward your family that feels different from your concern for strangers, notice that too. Hamilton would note the gradient. The question worth sitting with isn't why you feel more for those close to you, that's deeply natural, but how the circle of genuine moral concern might be extended, and what mechanisms, cultural, institutional, perhaps spiritual, make that extension possible.

The moral instincts you carry aren't gifts from any particular god, though particular religious traditions have given them names, stories, and sacred weight. They're inheritances from ancestors who, like Kato and Sule on the African plain, looked at the people around them and felt, without needing to think about it, that those people deserved a share.

That feeling is where we begin.

Sources for this chapter: Robert Trivers, \"The Evolution of Reciprocal Altruism\", Quarterly Review of Biology, 1971; W.D. Hamilton, \"The Genetical Evolution of Social Behaviour\", Journal of Theoretical Biology, 1964; Martin Nowak, \"Five Rules for the Evolution of Cooperation\", Science, 2006; Nowak and Sigmund, \"Evolution of Indirect Reciprocity\",

Nature, 2005; Ernst Fehr and Simon Gächter, \"Altruistic Punishment in Humans\", Nature, 2002; Christopher Boehm, Hierarchy in the Forest, Harvard University Press, 1999; Boyd and Richerson, \"Culture and the Evolution of Human Cooperation\", Philosophical Transactions of the Royal Society B, 2009; Ara Norenzayan et al., \"Hunter-Gatherers and the Origins of Religion\", Human Nature, 2016.

Chapter 2

The Moral Instinct

A Six-Month-Old and a Puppet Show

The room is quiet, and the room is small. A baby sits in an infant seat angled toward a small wooden stage, roughly the size of a television screen. The baby is six months old. She can't sit up without support. She has no language. She's been alive for approximately 180 days, and roughly 120 of those days have been spent sleeping.

The puppet show begins.

A round yellow character, cheerful-looking, appears at the bottom of a gentle hill. It begins trying to climb. It struggles. It slides back. It tries again. From stage left, a triangular character appears. It gets behind the round one and pushes, gently and persistently, helping it up the hill. The round character reaches the top.

The baby watches.

The show resets. The round character is at the bottom of the hill again, trying to climb again, struggling again. This time, from stage right, a square character appears. It pushes the round one back down. It blocks its path. It actively prevents the climb.

The baby watches.

Now the stage is cleared and two objects are placed in front of the baby: the triangle that helped, and the square that hindered. The experimenter holds them equidistant from the baby's reaching hands.

The baby reaches for the triangle.

She does it again. And again. And so does virtually every other baby tested in this model. The helper is preferred. The hinderer is rejected. A six-month-old, who can't walk or talk, who has had less than six months of any experience at all, is making what can only be described as a moral evaluation. She's assessed the social and ethical quality of a character's behavior toward a third party, and she's chosen accordingly.

This is the Yale Baby Lab, and what the researchers found there reshaped the scientific conversation about the origins of morality.

Research Finding 1: Babies Know Right from Wrong (Before They Know Anything Else)

The landmark 2007 study was led by developmental psychologist J. Kiley Hamlin, working alongside Karen Wynn and Paul Bloom at Yale University. Their central finding was both simple and startling: infants as young as six months old prefer helpful agents over unhelpful ones, and they make this judgment based on third-party interactions they've merely observed, not experienced.

This matters enormously. It means the infant isn't simply responding to which character has been nice to her. She's watched one character help another character, and she prefers the helper. She's making, in the language of moral philosophy, an impartial judgment about the quality of an act between two parties who aren't herself.

The results held robustly across the age range studied. At six months, preference for helpers was clear. At ten months, infants showed more sophisticated evaluations: they preferred not only helpers over hinderers, but also characters who punished hinderers over characters who rewarded them. An eight-month-old already has an intuition that punishment of wrongdoers is appropriate.

The researchers were careful in their language, but their conclusion was direct. In the published paper, they wrote: "This capacity may serve as the foundation for moral thought and action, and its early developmental emergence supports the view that social evaluation is a biological adaptation."

A biological adaptation. Not a cultural lesson. Not a rule absorbed from parents. Something built into the developmental program of human beings, expressed before language, before walking, before the first real social relationships are fully established.

A 2024 large-scale replication study involving multiple laboratories raised questions about the size of the effect in certain specific conditions of the hill-climbing model. Science proceeds by testing and revising findings, and that's how it should work. But the broader picture from decades of infant research, using diverse stimuli and methods, is consistent: within the first year of life, human infants show systematic preferences for helpers over hinderers, for fair distributors over unfair ones, and for those who respond appropriately to antisocial behavior. The moral sense is part of the human developmental package from very early on.

What we're looking at in that New Haven laboratory is the same system Trivers described as the emotional regulator of reciprocal altruism, the same system Fehr showed motivates costly punishment of cheaters, expressed in its earliest form: a baby, six months old, reaching for the good one.

This connects directly to the metaphor at the heart of this book. If morality is a language, then what the Yale Baby Lab found is that human beings are born with the capacity for this language already activated. We don't need to be taught to distinguish helpers from hinderers. We arrive with that distinction pre-loaded. What culture, community, and religion provide is the vocabulary, the specific words and rules and stories through which that basic capacity gets elaborated, extended, and directed. The capacity to speak comes first. The specific accent comes later.

Research Finding 2: The Six Foundations of Moral Life

Jonathan Haidt spent years doing something unusual for a psychologist: he traveled. He interviewed people in Brazil, India, and the United States, studied the moral arguments of political conservatives and progressives, and read widely in cultural anthropology and evolutionary biology. What he found was that the model of morality he'd absorbed in graduate school, the view that morality is really about harm and fairness, was radically incomplete.

In *The Righteous Mind* (2012), Haidt presented Moral Foundations Theory: the argument that human moral psychology has at least six distinct foundations, each with its own evolutionary history, each sensitive to a different class of moral events, each generating its own emotional reactions.

The six foundations are worth understanding individually.

The Care and Harm foundation concerns protecting vulnerable individuals from suffering. It evolved around the demands of caring for dependent offspring, and its emotional signature is compassion when someone suffers and outrage when someone causes needless pain.

The Fairness and Cheating foundation concerns the monitoring of reciprocal exchanges. It evolved, as Trivers and Fehr showed, to detect free-riders and cheaters. Its emotional signature is the sense of injustice when someone takes more than their share, and satisfaction when contributions are proportional to rewards.

The Loyalty and Betrayal foundation concerns group cohesion and coalition maintenance. It evolved for the challenges of intergroup competition, when groups that held together survived and groups that fractured didn't. Its emotional signature is pride in the group, and fury or disgust when members defect.

The Authority and Subversion foundation concerns navigating social hierarchies. It evolved to regulate relationships between those with more and less power, managing the negotiation between deference and resistance. Its emotional signature is respect for legitimate authority and contempt for those who abuse it.

The Sanctity and Degradation foundation concerns purity, contamination, and the integrity of the body and the sacred. It evolved from the disgust system that motivated avoidance of disease vectors and spoiled food, and has been extended by virtually every known culture to cover moral violations with nothing to do with physical contamination: betrayal of the sacred, desecration of revered objects, behavior that "taints" a person or community.

The sixth foundation, Liberty and Oppression, concerns resentment of coercion and defense of individual freedom. It evolved as part of the reverse dominance hierarchies Boehm described: the collective resistance to would-be tyrants and bullies.

Haidt's research, conducted across dozens of countries, showed that all six foundations appear across all cultures, but that their relative weighting varies enormously. Western, educated, industrialized, rich, and democratic populations tend to weight Care and Fairness heavily while weighting Loyalty, Authority, and Sanctity lightly. Most other populations weight all six more evenly. Political conservatives in Western countries weight Loyalty, Authority, and Sanctity much more strongly than progressives do.

This finding has a direct implication for understanding religion. Religious moral traditions, in Haidt's analysis, aren't simply intensified versions of Care and Fairness. They speak powerfully to all six foundations. They address loyalty through narratives of community, covenant, and belonging. They address authority through hierarchies of sacred texts and clergy. They address sanctity through rituals of purity, sacred spaces, and taboos about what must not be touched or profaned. This is partly why religious moral arguments can feel, to secular people weighted toward Care and Fairness, like a different language entirely. It's not that religious people fail to understand morality. They're tuned to a wider frequency spectrum of the same underlying signal.

Haidt also made a controversial but well-supported claim about moral reasoning: moral judgment is primarily emotional, and moral reasoning is primarily a justification for judgments already made. "The emotional dog wags its rational tail," as he put it. We decide quickly and intuitively that something is wrong, then construct arguments to defend that judgment. This matters because changing minds on moral questions rarely succeeds through argument alone. It requires engaging the emotional foundations, not just the logical superstructure.

The implication is uncomfortable for secular progressives and religious conservatives alike. Secular liberal moral psychology, on average, isn't broader or more sophisticated than religious conservative moral psychology. It's more restricted. Liberals feel morality most powerfully on two foundations. Most of the world's religious traditions engage all six. Secular moral psychology isn't more evolved. It's more narrow. That's not a comfortable thing to say, but the data say it plainly, and this book takes the data seriously.

Research Finding 3: The Moral Grammar

In 2006, the Harvard psychologist Marc Hauser published *Moral Minds*, developing a striking analogy. The linguist Noam Chomsky had argued that children acquire language through a combination of innate universal grammar and specific cultural input. No child has to be taught that sentences have structure, that words can function as nouns or verbs, that questions have different forms than statements. These structural features are part of the built-in cognitive package for language. What the child learns from its environment is the specific vocabulary, rules, and sounds of the language spoken around it.

Hauser argued that morality works the same way. Humans possess what he called "moral grammar": an innate, largely unconscious set of principles for generating moral judgments. Just as children produce sentences they've never heard and immediately recognize sentences that "sound wrong," people make confident moral judgments about situations they've never encountered and recognize when a moral rule has been violated, even when they can't articulate why.

The cross-cultural evidence is compelling. People in radically different cultures, with radically different explicit moral beliefs, make the same structural distinctions when presented with moral dilemmas. They distinguish sharply between harm that's a direct means to an end, using someone's death as a tool, and harm that's an unintended side effect of achieving a good outcome. They find the first more morally objectionable even when the outcomes are identical. They make this distinction consistently across cultures, across age groups, and across wide variations in formal education.

One disclosure is warranted: in 2010, a Harvard investigation found that Hauser's laboratory had engaged in data manipulation in his research on non-human primate cognition. This misconduct was unrelated to the moral psychology findings cited here, which have been independently replicated.

The distinction between moral grammar and moral vocabulary is exactly the distinction between the universal structure of moral cognition and the specific content that cultures fill it with. Every culture has rules about harm. What counts as harm, who counts as a moral patient deserving protection, what circumstances justify it, which rituals mark the transition from permissible to impermissible: these are the vocabulary. Religion is one of the most powerful forces in human history for developing, encoding, and transmitting this vocabulary.

To return to the central metaphor: the grammar is the deep structure of the language of morality, the universal patterns in how humans think about right and wrong. The accent is the specific pronunciation that a community brings to that language. A New Yorker and a person from rural Georgia speak the same grammar of English. The accents are unmistakable. Neither is speaking wrong. They're speaking the same language from within different histories, communities, and identities.

When a devout Catholic and a practicing Buddhist and a secular humanist all agree that cruelty to children is wrong, they're speaking the same grammar. When they disagree about the moral status of an embryo, the ethics of eating certain foods, or the obligations owed to strangers versus community members, they're often expressing different accents: the same underlying moral concern rendered through different cultural vocabularies, different narrative traditions, and different sacred reference points.

Research Finding 4: Two Systems, One Brain

In 2001, the Harvard psychologist Joshua Greene published a study in *Science* using functional magnetic resonance imaging, which measures blood flow in the brain to indicate neural activity, to watch people's brains as they wrestled with moral dilemmas. What he found illuminated the deep structure of moral cognition in a way that pure behavioral research couldn't.

The classic dilemma used in this tradition comes from moral philosophy. Imagine a runaway trolley heading toward five people on the tracks who will certainly die if nothing is done. You're standing near a switch. If you throw the switch, the trolley will divert to a side track, where it will kill one person instead of five. Should you throw the switch?

Most people say yes. They find this uncomfortable but acceptable. Five lives saved at the cost of one seems like the right arithmetic.

Now change the scenario. The trolley is heading toward five people, but there's no switch. You're standing on a footbridge above the tracks, and next to you is a large man whose body, if it fell onto the tracks, would stop the trolley. Should you push him off the bridge?

Most people say no. Absolutely not. Even though the arithmetic is identical, one death to prevent five deaths, the act of pushing a person to their death with your own hands feels categorically different from throwing a switch.

Greene's brain imaging data showed why. The footbridge scenario, in which the harm is direct, physical, and personal, activated brain regions associated with emotional processing: the medial prefrontal cortex, the posterior cingulate, and the amygdala. These are regions involved in empathy, visceral aversion, and social emotion. The switch scenario, in which the harm is impersonal and mediated by a mechanism, recruited regions associated with abstract reasoning and working memory.

Two different neural systems are at work. One is old, social, and emotional. It evolved in environments where moral decisions were made face to face, where your own hands were the instrument of action, where the person you might harm was someone whose face you could see. This system generates strong intuitions: don't harm this person in front of you. Don't use a person as a mere tool. It produces what philosophers call deontological intuitions, rules about what may not be done regardless of consequences.

The other system is newer, more abstract, and more deliberately rational. It calculates outcomes. It asks how many lives are saved. It reasons about aggregates rather than individuals. It produces what philosophers call utilitarian intuitions, judgments based on maximizing overall welfare.

The tension between these two systems is, as Greene argues in *Moral Tribes* (2013), the engine of many of the deepest moral disagreements within and between human communities. Arguments about when violence is justified, about the moral weight of statistics versus identified individuals, about whether the suffering of many strangers outweighs the obligation to a single person before you: in many cases these aren't arguments between people using the same system to different conclusions. They're arguments between the two systems themselves.

Religion tends to speak primarily to the older, emotional, personal system. Sacred texts and traditions are full of stories about specific individuals, face-to-face encounters, embodied acts of mercy and cruelty. They're not, in general, treatises on aggregate welfare. This is one reason why religious moral reasoning can feel alien to those trained in utilitarian or policy frameworks: they're literally using different cognitive hardware to think about moral questions.

Neither system is superior. Both reflect real aspects of moral life. Morality requires both the visceral refusal to harm the person before you and the reasoned concern for populations of people you'll never meet. The history of moral progress is partly the history of extending the emotional system, which naturally concentrates on the nearby and familiar, with the reasoning capacity that can hold distant and statistical lives in the same moral register.

What Chimpanzees Teach Us

Frans de Waal spent decades studying primates at the Yerkes National Primate Research Center and elsewhere, and his findings make a simple but powerful argument: the raw materials of morality aren't unique to humans. They're present in other social mammals, most clearly in our closest relatives, the chimpanzees and bonobos.

De Waal documented emotional contagion in chimpanzees: the tendency to feel distress when a group member is distressed, and to respond with consoling behavior, touching, embracing, sitting close to the upset animal. He found that chimpanzees reconcile after conflicts, returning to opponents with kisses and embraces that repair the relationship. He documented prosocial preferences: given a choice between a task that rewards only themselves and one that rewards both themselves and a partner, chimpanzees frequently prefer the prosocial option.

In capuchin monkeys, de Waal and his colleague Sarah Brosnan found something even more striking: a rejection of unequal treatment. When one monkey received a grape as reward for completing a task while the other received only a cucumber slice, the cucumber-receiving monkey was likely to reject it and sometimes throw it at the experimenter. The monkeys were protesting unfairness, not simply expressing food preference, because they accepted cucumbers happily when no grape-receiving partner was visible.

De Waal's core argument is what he calls the "bottom-up" view of morality: moral behavior didn't arrive in humans from outside, as a set of rules imposed by culture, philosophy, or divine command on an amoral animal. It grew from within, from building blocks that are visible across the mammalian family: empathy, reciprocity, consolation, reconciliation, fairness intuitions, community concern. *The Age of Empathy* (2009) makes this case with detail drawn from decades of observation.

This doesn't mean human morality is just animal behavior with better vocabulary. Human moral life is vastly more complex, more extended, more abstract, and more self-reflective than anything observed in other species. We have moral philosophy. We have sacred texts. We have legal systems and human rights frameworks. We hold each other responsible for moral failures in ways that require language, memory, and social institutions that no other animal has developed.

But the foundation, the raw emotional capacity to feel another's distress, to register unfairness, to want to help and to resist being cheated, isn't a human invention. It's an inheritance. This is one more way in which morality is the language: it's spoken with a human accent, with all the richness and complexity that human cognitive capacity enables, but it runs on vocal architecture that we share with every social mammal.

A Word About Empathy's Limits

This chapter would be incomplete without a counterpoint. In 2016, the Yale psychologist Paul Bloom published *Against Empathy: The Case for Rational Compassion*. Its argument deserves serious consideration.

Bloom's claim isn't that empathy is bad. It's that empathy, understood as the direct emotional experience of another's suffering, is a poor guide to moral action. Empathy is powerfully activated by identifiable, nearby, visible individuals and barely activated by statistics. The death of one child, photographed and named, moves millions of people. The death of a million in a distant famine, represented as a number, moves far fewer. Empathy tracks narrative vividness more reliably than moral importance.

This bias has real consequences. Empathy leads us to prioritize people we can see and imagine over people we can't. It leads us to overweight the suffering of individuals who resemble us. It can fuel the very tribalism that moral progress requires us to overcome. The passionate empathy that groups feel for in-group members has historically been one of the most reliable drivers of violence against out-group members, because the vividness of "our" suffering justifies terrible acts against those who cause it.

Bloom isn't arguing for indifference. He argues for what he calls rational compassion: genuine concern for others' wellbeing, expressed through reasoned judgment about how to help most effectively, rather than through emotional identification that may mislead. The distinction is important, and it resonates with the earlier point about Greene's two moral systems. Empathy is powerful but parochial. It needs to be extended and disciplined by the more abstract reasoning capacity that can hold distant strangers in moral regard.

Bloom's counterpoint also clarifies something about religion's moral role. Religious traditions have historically amplified in-group empathy dramatically. The love of the community, the willingness to sacrifice for fellow believers, the solidarity of shared suffering: these are genuine moral goods that religion has reliably produced. But religious traditions have also, with similar reliability, generated the logic that places out-group members outside the circle of full moral concern. The history of religion includes both saintly compassion and horrifying violence, often motivated by the same underlying psychology: intense empathy for those inside the community, and a corresponding dehumanization of those outside it.

This isn't an argument against religion. It's a description of a psychological pattern that religion inherits from the evolutionary history of in-group/out-group cognition. Every tradition that has expanded the circle of moral concern, and many have done so, has done so by extending the accent metaphor: finding ways to pronounce the moral language so that "us" becomes larger, more inclusive, more willing to accommodate those who sound different.

The Language and Its Speakers

By now the outline of the moral instinct should be clear. It's not a single thing. It's a complex system built from several subsystems, each with its own evolutionary history and its own emotional signature.

There's the evaluative capacity that allows a six-month-old to reach for the helper. There are the six moral foundations that structure adult moral intuitions across cultures. There's the moral grammar that generates consistent structural distinctions across radically different cultures. There are the two neural systems that produce emotional and deliberative moral judgments, sometimes pulling in different directions. And there's the empathic capacity that motivates concern for others, chastened by Bloom's reminder that empathy isn't the whole of morality.

All of this was in place before any organized religion existed. The Yale baby was born with the evaluative capacity. The Moral Foundations were assembled by evolution over millions of years. The moral grammar appears in hunter-gatherer societies as surely as in modern urban ones. The dual neural systems were shaped by a brain architecture that predates our species.

What religion provided, when it developed, wasn't this system itself. It provided a way of organizing and elaborating the system, giving it narrative form, embedding it in community, connecting it to accounts of what the universe is and why the rules matter. This is an extraordinary contribution, and we'll examine it in detail in the chapters ahead.

But it's a contribution to an existing structure. It's an accent on an existing language. The language was already being spoken.

For Reflection

Here are three questions worth carrying into the coming chapters.

The first: when was the last time you felt moral outrage? Perhaps it was at something in the news, or in a conversation, or at a memory of something that happened to you or someone you care about. Did that feeling need a theological justification to arrive? Did it come with a scripture attached, or did it arrive on its own, fast and full? If it arrived first and the justification came later, Haidt's model is describing your experience accurately. What does that suggest about the relationship between the feeling and the explanation?

The second: do you notice that different moral issues activate different emotional registers in you? Some things feel wrong in a visceral, physical way. Others feel wrong in a more abstract, reasoned way. Can you identify which of Haidt's six foundations might be active in each case? And can you imagine someone you respect, someone with genuinely good values, weighing those foundations differently than you do?

The third: the Yale babies weren't blank slates. They arrived pre-equipped with something. Whether you're a person of faith or not, whether you believe that moral sense was placed there by God or assembled by evolution, or both, in ways that aren't mutually exclusive, take a moment to wonder at it. The moral capacity is there from the very beginning of a human life. It's part of what it means to be born human. That's remarkable, by any account.

Sources for this chapter: J. Kiley Hamlin, Karen Wynn, Paul Bloom, \"Social Evaluation by Preverbal Infants\", Nature, 2007; replication context at PubMed; Jonathan Haidt, The Righteous Mind, Pantheon Books, 2012; Moral Foundations Theory overview at Wikipedia; Marc Hauser, Moral Minds, HarperCollins, 2006; linguistic analogy elaborated at Georgetown Faculty; Joshua Greene, \"An fMRI Investigation of Emotional Engagement in Moral Judgment\", Science, 2001; Moral Tribes, Penguin Press, 2013; Frans de Waal, Good Natured, Harvard University Press, 1996; \"Prosocial Primates\", Philosophical Transactions B, 2010; Paul Bloom, Against Empathy, Crown Publishers, 2016; PMC review of Against Empathy.

Chapter 3

Stories, Myths, and Shared Worlds

The Fire

The fire has been burning for an hour. Outside the circle of its light, the night is absolute. Earlier, the band made a good kill, and the meat has been eaten, and the children are drowsy and full. But no one is asleep yet, because the old man is talking.

He's not exactly telling a story about something that happened today. He's telling a story about his grandfather's grandfather, who encountered a spirit in the high country, a being that appeared as a man but moved wrong, too smooth, too fast, without the hesitation that a living body shows. The being told the great-grandfather something. It was a warning, or a commandment, or a gift of knowledge. What exactly was said, no one can be sure anymore. But the lesson survived: don't go into the high country in the dry season. Don't go alone. When the high country must be crossed, make the right offerings.

Everyone around the fire is listening. The children are most awake of all.

In some version, this scene has repeated itself every night for approximately 300,000 years, because Homo sapiens has been gathering around fires and telling stories since it became a species. The specific stories change. The participants change. The language changes beyond recognition. But the structure is constant: a group, a fire, a story with a moral, and attentive listeners who'll remember it and eventually tell it again.

This is humanity's oldest technology for transmitting values. Before writing. Before schools. Before scripture. Long before any institutional religion. The story came first, and it worked.

Understanding why it works, and why the most powerful stories have so often been religious ones, requires looking at three things: what stories do for human minds, why certain agents appear across all cultures, and why the invisible, powerful, morally concerned agents we call gods aren't random inventions but predictable products of how the human mind works.

Research Finding 1: The Storytelling Animal

Jonathan Gottschall, a literary scholar at Washington and Jefferson College, opens his 2012 book *The Storytelling Animal* with an observation that ought to be astonishing but feels obvious: human beings devote an extraordinary proportion of their lives to fiction. We read novels. We watch films and television. We go to the theater. We dream, which is the brain producing narrative involuntarily for six to eight hours every night. Children play imaginative games from the moment they can walk. Without formal instruction, children the world over invent stories with the same basic structure: a character with a goal, an obstacle, an attempt.

Gottschall argues that this near-universal behavior, universal across human cultures and absent in other species at anything like the same scale, isn't accidental. It reflects a function. Stories are, in his phrase, "flight simulators for the mind." They allow humans to practice navigating complex social and moral situations without the costs of real-world failure. In the story, you can betray your friend and see what happens. You can face the monster and discover whether you survive. You can make the hard decision and watch the consequences unfold. You accumulate something like experience without acquiring the risks.

The problem-simulation hypothesis explains why stories are structured the way they are. A narrative without conflict isn't a story. It's a description. The problem structure, character, predicament, resolution, is the functional core of the device, not an aesthetic convention. The brain needs to rehearse solving problems, and it finds the rehearsal compelling enough to seek it out voluntarily, for entertainment.

Gottschall also makes a point crucial for understanding religion: stories enforce morality. Across cultures and genres, fiction is intensely moral. Villains are punished. Heroes are rewarded. Betrayal is portrayed as a catastrophe. Loyalty as beautiful. This pattern pervades adventure tales, romance, and comedy as reliably as fables and parables. Gottschall writes: "Story binds society."

Research by the Dutch scholar Jèmeljan Hakemulder found measurable positive effects on moral development and empathy in people who read extensively. Stories don't merely reflect moral norms. They actively reinforce them, creating and maintaining the "just-world" expectations that social life requires.

What this means for religious narrative is significant. Sacred stories are the most moralized stories human culture produces. They're stories in which the stakes are cosmically high, the moral lessons are explicit and repeated across generations, and the audience is expected to internalize the narrative as a guide not just for appreciating what happened but for living. The Exodus story doesn't merely describe a historical event. It instructs a community about who they are and how they should treat the vulnerable. The parable of the Good Samaritan doesn't merely illustrate kindness. It expands the definition of "neighbor" beyond ethnic and religious boundaries. The story of the Buddha's renunciation doesn't merely chronicle a prince's choices. It models the relationship between desire, suffering, and liberation.

These stories are powerful because narrative is what the human brain evolved to process and retain. Principles are forgettable. Rules are forgettable. Stories aren't. A rule that says "care for strangers" is easily ignored. A story in which a stranger is cared for at personal cost, and in which the care makes all the difference, lodges in memory and activates the same emotional systems that moral action requires. Religion learned, very early, that the story is the delivery mechanism for the value.

Research Finding 2: Gossip, Language, and the Superhuman Storyteller

In 1996, the British psychologist and anthropologist Robin Dunbar published a book with an unusual central claim. *Grooming, Gossip and the Evolution of Language* argued that language didn't evolve primarily to describe the physical environment or to coordinate technical tasks. It evolved as social technology: a way of maintaining bonds in groups that had grown too large for physical grooming, the mammalian default for social bonding, to manage.

Dunbar's research on primates had established that social cohesion in other species is maintained largely through touch: grooming, huddling, and physical contact. Grooming takes time, and it's one-to-one. As group size increases, the proportion of time required for grooming eventually exceeds what's physically possible. Dunbar hypothesized that language, which allows one person to "groom" several others simultaneously, evolved as a higher-bandwidth alternative.

The supporting evidence came from studying what people actually talk about. Dunbar and his colleagues conducted observational studies of naturally occurring conversation in multiple cultures and contexts. The finding was consistent: approximately two-thirds of human conversation concerns social topics, meaning information about people. Who is doing what with whom. Who behaved well or badly. Who is trustworthy and who isn't. This is what Dunbar calls gossip, and he uses the term neutrally, as a description of a category of information exchange rather than as a pejorative.

Gossip is reputation information, and as Chapter 1 established, reputation is the fuel on which large-scale cooperation runs. Nowak's model of indirect reciprocity requires that information about who helped and who cheated circulates reliably through a community. The conversations around the fire aren't idle entertainment. They're the information system that keeps the moral community functioning: maintaining the band's dossier on each member, as Boehm described, through the constant exchange of social information.

Dunbar's extension of this argument to religion is the insight that matters here. If gossip is conversation about the reputations and behaviors of social agents, then sacred stories are what he calls "super-gossip": stories about the most powerful agents in the social world. In a small band, the most consequential agents are the most powerful humans. Stories about these people regulate behavior by broadcasting reputation information.

Scale this up. Imagine that the most powerful agent in the world isn't a human but a being who sees everything, who knows everything, who created everything, and who cares deeply about whether you followed the rules. Stories about this being aren't just gossip. They're gossip about the agent with unlimited power and unlimited knowledge of your behavior. They're the ultimate reputation management information.

This is why religious narratives so often focus on observation and accountability. The God who counts every hair on your head, who records every thought and deed, who will judge each soul in the final accounting: this being solves the cooperation problem that Nowak identified as requiring ever-increasing cognitive demands. You can't defect in private when the most powerful agent in the universe is always watching. Whether or not anyone else knows what you did, someone does. The reputation mechanism extends infinitely, to cover even the private, the hidden, and the unwitnessed.

The story became the enforcement mechanism. The superhuman storyteller became the ultimate reputational authority.

Research Finding 3: Seeing Faces in the Smoke

Here's a question about your own experience. Have you ever been alone in an unfamiliar place at night, heard an unexpected sound, and felt a surge of alertness before you even consciously registered what you heard? Have you ever seen a face in a cloud formation, or in the grain of a wood panel, or in the pattern of shadows on a ceiling? Have you ever had the sudden conviction, passing and irrational, that someone is watching you?

These experiences are near-universal. They're also very informative about how the human mind is built.

The cognitive scientist Justin Barrett proposed an explanation he called the Hyperactive Agency Detection Device. This agency detection system is a cognitive mechanism that monitors the environment for signs of intentional agents: beings with desires, beliefs, and plans that might affect you. In evolutionary terms, the most important agents in your environment are predators, which might eat you, rivals, which might harm you, and allies, which might help you. The ability to detect these agents quickly and respond appropriately was enormously important for survival.

The critical asymmetry is in the error costs. If you miss a real predator, you may die. If you falsely detect a predator that isn't there, you waste a few seconds of alertness and then relax. The cost of the false negative vastly exceeds the cost of the false positive. Evolution therefore calibrated the system to err on the side of over-detecting agents.

Barrett's proposal is that this system is hyperactive: it fires on insufficient evidence, detecting intentional agents behind events that are actually random, mechanical, or natural. Thunder doesn't require a cause with intentions. But a mind built to detect intentional agents will generate the hypothesis of an agent behind the thunder, because that hypothesis has historically been cheaper to investigate than to ignore.

This is the seed of supernatural belief. When the agency detection system fires on ambiguous stimuli, the mind generates the concept of an invisible agent. And then, because the same mind has a highly developed capacity for attributing mental states to other agents, it immediately begins asking: what does this invisible agent want? Why did it act? What will appease or please it?

Barrett was careful to note that the hyperactive agency detection system is one factor among several in the cognitive origins of religion, and that subsequent research has continued refining the model. A 2025 critical review raised questions about the directness of the empirical evidence for the mechanism specifically, proposing that "motivated mentalizing," the desire to explain events through intentional agents, might be a simpler account. The debate continues, which is how science should work. But the broader claim has strong support: human minds apply intentional agent frameworks to non-agents, including weather, illness, coincidence, and cosmic events. This generates supernatural beliefs as a cognitive by-product.

Barrett's own position is interesting. He's a devout Christian, and he's argued that his research is compatible with religious belief: the ready generation of God-concepts from human cognitive architecture might be evidence that we were built to find God, rather than evidence that God is merely a cognitive error. This book takes no position on that theological question. What matters here is the scientific observation: the human tendency to see agents in the world, to attribute minds and intentions to forces that may not have them, is deep, automatic, and cross-cultural. It's part of the same perceptual architecture that lets us read faces instantly, detect social cues from tiny behavioral signals, and build complex theories of what other people are thinking.

Anthropologist Stewart Guthrie made the same case in his 1993 book *Faces in the Clouds*: religion is at its core anthropomorphism applied to the cosmos. The face you see in the clouds, the agent you sense behind the thunder, the cosmic judge who monitors your behavior: all are products of the same face-recognition and mind-reading machinery that evolved to navigate a world dense with other human beings, the most important and most dangerous agents in the ancestral environment.

Research Finding 4: Why Gods Are Memorable

If the agency detection system generates the hypothesis of invisible agents, it doesn't explain why certain kinds of supernatural agents persist across cultures while others fade. Why do gods across radically different cultures share so many structural features? Why are they typically invisible but possessing sight? Eternal but capable of anger? All-knowing but interested in human moral behavior? Why not simply random?

The cognitive anthropologist Pascal Boyer, working at Washington University in St. Louis, developed one of the most influential answers in the cognitive science of religion. His 2001 book *Religion Explained* argued that religious concepts are constrained by the architecture of human memory and inference.

Boyer identified what he called minimally counterintuitive concepts. The human mind organizes its knowledge about the world into categories with associated expectations. An animal breathes, moves, eats, and dies. A tool doesn't move on its own, doesn't eat, and doesn't have preferences. A person has thoughts, desires, relationships, and a lifespan. When an object conforms perfectly to the expectations of its category, it's uninteresting and forgettable. When an object violates a small number of category expectations while conforming to the rest, it's memorable and surprising in a productive way.

A ghost that can walk through walls (violating expectations about solidity) but still remembers people, gets angry, has preferences, and can communicate (conforming to all expectations about persons) is a minimally counterintuitive agent. It's memorable because it's surprising. It's cognitively rich because it conforms to enough person-expectations to generate a cascade of inferences about its behavior. You know how to think about its motives. You can reason about what might offend it or please it. You can tell stories about it.

Compare this to a purely arbitrary supernatural entity: an agent that has no desires, no memory, no relationship to humans, and behaves in completely random ways. Such an entity would be difficult to remember, difficult to reason about, and impossible to build a story around. It wouldn't survive cultural transmission.

The gods that survive, the ones that spread across communities and generations, hit the sweet spot: one or two counterintuitive properties, invisible, immortal, omniscient, combined with a full suite of person-typical properties, desires, emotions, relationships, moral concern. This combination makes them maximally memorable and maximally inference-generating. You can build a rich narrative around such a being. You can ask what it wants, what it commands, how it can be approached.

The gods we first imagined in campfire smoke are the gods we still argue about today. Not because we're gullible, but because story is the oldest technology in the human toolkit.

Boyer's argument isn't that religion is false. It's that the concepts of religion aren't arbitrary. They're predictable products of human cognitive architecture. Given minds like ours, given how human memory and inference work, these particular kinds of concepts were always likely to arise, spread, and stabilize across cultures. They're, in a precise sense, what the human mind tends to generate when it applies its person-reasoning systems to the cosmos.

This is consistent with a theme that runs through all three chapters of Part I. Religion emerged as a natural, predictable extension of the cognitive systems that evolved to navigate social life. The moral grammar described in Chapter 2 needed stories to transmit itself across generations. The reputation systems described in Chapter 1 needed a watching agent to extend their reach into the private and unwitnessed. The narrative mind needed characters with intentions. The agency detection system generated the invisible agent. Boyer's work explains why that invisible agent looks the way it does across cultures: not arbitrary, but constrained, predictable, and cognitively powerful.

The Hero and the Journey

There's another dimension of storytelling that connects sacred narrative to deep cognitive structures, identified most clearly not by a scientist but by a mythologist.

Joseph Campbell, a scholar at Sarah Lawrence College, spent decades comparing myths across the world's cultures, from ancient Greek epic to Hindu scripture to Native American legend to Norse mythology. What he found, published most accessibly in his 1949 book *The Hero with a Thousand Faces*, was a structural pattern so consistent across unrelated cultures that it couldn't be explained by cultural borrowing alone.

Campbell called the pattern the monomyth, or the hero's journey. It's three phases: the departure, in which a character receives a call to venture beyond the familiar world. The initiation, in which the hero faces trials, undergoes transformation, and acquires a special insight or boon. And the return, in which the hero brings that boon back to the community, usually at some personal cost.

This pattern appears in the stories of Odysseus, Gilgamesh, the Buddha's enlightenment, the Exodus of Moses, and the life of Jesus Christ, as well as in the vast majority of popular films and novels today. Star Wars. The Lord of the Rings. Every coming-of-age story. Every conversion narrative.

Campbell's claim was that the monomyth reflects something universal in human psychological experience: the structure of initiation, the encounter with mortality, the transformation that identity requires to move from one stage of life to another. These aren't merely cultural conventions. They map onto the architecture of human experience at points that matter universally: leaving home, encountering the limits of what you know, being changed by what you encounter, and returning altered.

The scientific follow-up to Campbell's intuition has been provided by researchers like Gottschall: the hero's journey recurs because it's the strongest form of the problem-predicament-resolution structure that human narrative cognition generates. It also maps onto real psychological processes of development, transition, and transformation that every human undergoes. Stories in this structure feel true because they resemble, at the level of form, the shape of actual human experience.

Religious narratives that follow the hero's journey structure aren't using a technique. They're deploying a universal resonance. Character receives call, enters unknown territory, undergoes trial and transformation, returns with life-altering knowledge. The story feels profoundly true because the structure resonates with something the mind already knows.

The Person Behind the Storm

The research on anthropomorphism, the attribution of human characteristics to non-human entities, fills in the last piece of this picture.

In 2007, the psychologists Nicholas Epley, Adam Waytz, and John Cacioppo published a theoretical framework for understanding when and why people anthropomorphize. They identified three motivating conditions.

The first is the sociality motivation. When people are lonely, isolated, or socially excluded, they're more likely to attribute minds and intentions to pets, to inanimate objects, and to supernatural beings. The social cognition system is hungry, and when it can't find real social partners, it generates social partners from available material. Pets become confidants. Cars become personalities. God becomes a companion.

The second is the effectance motivation: the need to understand and predict the environment in order to exert some control over it. Random, mindless events are genuinely harder to deal with than events caused by intentional agents. An agent with intentions can potentially be reasoned with, appealed to, placated, or at least understood. A mindless disease process, an arbitrary storm, a senseless accident: these offer no purchase. Perceiving an agent behind these events restores the possibility of understanding and influence. Praying to a god who sent the storm isn't irrational if you believe the storm was sent. It's the logical next step.

The third is cognitive accessibility: the more habitually active our social cognitive systems are, and for social animals like humans, they're extremely active, the more readily we apply them to non-social stimuli.

Guthrie's synthesis is that religion is, at its most fundamental level, systematic anthropomorphism. Faces in the clouds. A mind behind the thunder. An agent who loves, commands, and judges. The systems that allow humans to read strangers' emotions with extraordinary speed, infer a competitor's plans from subtle cues, or understand what a crying infant needs from the quality of its cry: turned outward toward the cosmos, these systems generate gods.

This isn't a dismissal of religious experience. The fact that religious experience is generated by identifiable cognitive systems doesn't settle the question of whether the gods those systems point toward are real. Humans have color vision because evolution equipped us with light-sensitive cells. That evolutionary explanation doesn't mean that colors are illusions. The cognitive science of religion describes the machinery. It doesn't adjudicate the output.

But for understanding the universality of religious belief, the cognitive account is powerful. Gods and spirits aren't arbitrary cultural constructs that some societies happened to invent. They're predictable products of minds like ours, built to see agents, to tell moral stories, to maintain reputations, to detect the watcher even in the dark. The landscape of religious belief across human history looks the way it does because the minds that created it were built the same way.

Every Family Has Its Stories

Near the end of every family gathering in every culture there's a recognizable moment. The older people start talking about the way things used to be. Someone tells a story about a grandparent or great-grandparent, usually one that doubles as a moral: about sacrifice, or courage, or foolishness, or faithfulness. The children listen. The adults listen too, even when they've heard the story before. Especially when they've heard the story before.

These stories don't describe events that everyone in the room witnessed. Many of the protagonists are long dead. The precise details are probably not perfectly accurate. Memory isn't a recording device, and every retelling adjusts the edges slightly. None of that diminishes their function.

Family stories answer two questions every human being needs answered: who are we, and how do we behave? They establish identity by connecting present-day members to a lineage with specific values, specific sacrifices, and specific ways of meeting hardship. They transmit behavioral norms not as abstract rules but as concrete demonstrations: this is what a person from this family does when tested.

Religion does the same thing on a larger scale. The congregation, the denomination, the tradition: these are communities unified by shared stories that answer the same two questions at a collective level. Who are we? The people of the covenant. The followers of the Way. Those who have surrendered to the will of God. Those who seek enlightenment. How do we behave? In accordance with what the story teaches: what the ancestors did, what the sacred figures modeled, what the tradition requires.

The power of religious narrative isn't separate from the cognitive systems described in this chapter. It's the product of their convergence. The narrative mind described by Gottschall is engaged. The social cognition that creates memorable persons and agents, constrained by Boyer's minimally counterintuitive principle, is satisfied. The agency detection system is activated. The moral enforcement system is extended to cover even the private and unwitnessed. The hero's journey structure gives the story its emotional depth.

Religion, in this view, isn't an arbitrary cultural artifact. It's the most cognitively powerful form of the most cognitively powerful human technology: narrative. It deploys the full range of human mind-generating, meaning-making, morality-enforcing capacity simultaneously.

That's why it's been so durable. And that's why it matters, whether or not you're a believer, to understand it.

A Necessary Caution

This account might seem to imply that religious stories are merely cognitive confections, beautiful but empty productions of a mind that can't help itself. That's not the claim being made here, and it's important to be clear about this.

Describing the psychological mechanisms that generate and sustain religious belief doesn't answer the deeper question of whether the beliefs are true. Science explains how we process and generate religious concepts. It doesn't explain them away. A person of faith who accepts everything in this chapter can reasonably respond: yes, the cognitive systems that generate religious belief are exactly what you'd expect from a God who designed them to be capable of finding and responding to the divine.

What the cognitive science of religion does establish is that religious moral instruction arrives in minds already morally prepared to receive it. The story about caring for strangers lands in a mind that already has an evolved care-harm foundation (Chapter 2). The narrative about betrayal lands in a mind that already has a loyalty-betrayal foundation. The account of divine observation and judgment lands in a mind already built to worry about reputation and to behave better when watched.

The accent settles onto a voice already capable of speech.

What this means for the relationship between believers and non-believers, between secular moralists and religious ones, should be productive rather than divisive. The moral language you speak is recognizable across that divide. The accent is different. The stories are different. The sacred reference points are different. But the underlying grammar, care for others, resist injustice, maintain trust, punish betrayal, extend the circle of concern, is the same grammar that appears in every culture and every tradition, because it's written into human cognitive architecture deeper than any culture reaches.

The question worth asking isn't whether we need stories. We do, without question. The better question is what we do when the stories of one tradition claim exclusive access to moral truth. The cognitive science suggests that claim is harder to sustain than it might appear. The same cognitive architecture that generates one tradition's sacred stories generates them all. The same minimally counterintuitive structure that makes one tradition's divine beings memorable makes all of them memorable. The same hero's journey that structures one founding narrative structures them all.

This doesn't mean all stories are equally wise, or that all traditions are equally successful at producing moral behavior. Evidence matters. Outcomes matter. Some stories have been used to justify terrible things. Others have inspired extraordinary acts of courage, compassion, and justice. Specific moral traditions should be evaluated carefully, on the evidence, not dismissed wholesale.

But the claim that only one accent speaks real morality, that only one tradition has access to the language itself: that claim is what the cognitive science challenges most directly. The language belongs to the species. The accent belongs to the community.

For Reflection

Every family carries its own myths, the stories that define who you are and how you behave. Some of these stories are explicit: the grandparent who walked away from wealth on principle. The ancestor who survived something terrible. The relative whose failure became a cautionary tale passed down through generations. Others are implicit, woven into habits and reactions that you may not have examined closely.

Here are three questions to sit with.

What are the stories, sacred or familial or cultural, that most powerfully shaped your sense of how you're supposed to behave? Not the rules you were taught explicitly, but the stories that showed you what a person like you does when tested. Who were the heroes in those stories? What did they sacrifice?

If those stories were told by someone from a completely different tradition, a different religion, a different culture, a different family background, what would they recognize in them? Where would the moral grammar be the same, even if the vocabulary and the sacred reference points were entirely different?

And finally: the old man around the fire in East Africa told a story that kept his band alive for another generation. He didn't know he was doing evolutionary work. He was just telling the truth as he understood it, making it vivid, making it memorable, making it carry.

What stories are you telling? And what do they say about who you are and how you behave?

Sources for this chapter: Jonathan Gottschall, The Storytelling Animal, Houghton Mifflin Harcourt, 2012; Scientific American interview; Robin Dunbar, Grooming, Gossip and the Evolution of Language, Harvard University Press, 1996; Wikipedia summary; \"Gossip in Evolutionary Perspective\", Review of General Psychology, 2004; Justin Barrett, Why Would Anyone Believe in God?, AltaMira Press, 2004; Secular Frontier explanation of HADD; 2025 critical review; Pascal Boyer, Religion Explained, Basic Books, 2001; Wikipedia summary; Joseph Campbell, The Hero with a Thousand Faces, Pantheon Books, 1949; Wikipedia summary; Epley, Waytz, Cacioppo, 'On Seeing Human: A Three-Factor Theory of Anthropomorphism,' *Psychological Review*, 2007; Stewart Guthrie, Faces in the Clouds, 1993; discussed at Patheos.

Chapter 4

The Gods We Left Behind: Why Religions Die

But cognitive architecture alone doesn't explain what happens to the moral content when the religion it carried disappears. To understand that, we need to visit some ruins.

I. The Silence at Karnak

Stand in the hypostyle hall of the Temple of Amun-Ra at Karnak and you'll feel the weight of the world pressing down on you. There are 134 sandstone columns here, the tallest rising to seventy-nine feet, each one carved and painted in colours that still blush faintly after thirty-three centuries. The hall was designed to make human beings feel small, and it succeeds. The ceiling, once decorated with stars and wheeling birds, represented the sky itself. The columns, carved with lotus and papyrus motifs, recreated the marsh from which, Egyptians believed, the world had first emerged. To walk this space was to walk inside a cosmology. It was to inhabit, physically, a story about the origin and meaning of all things.

When Karnak was at its height, during the New Kingdom period roughly spanning 1550 to 1070 BCE, this was the most important religious complex on earth. Known in ancient times as *Ipet-isut*, "The Most Select of Places," it was the earthly dwelling of Amun-Ra, the king of the gods. Priests lived here permanently. Workshops produced the sacred vessels and garments used in daily rituals. A sacred lake reflected the pylons and obelisks. Twice each year the god's image was carried in procession down an avenue of ram-headed sphinxes toward the temple at Luxor, three kilometres to the south, and crowds of tens of thousands lined the route, pressing forward, seeking a glimpse of the divine.

Today there are tourists where the crowds once stood. There are guidebooks where there were once prayers. The god whose name was spoken here a million times isn't spoken here now, except in footnotes.

Amun-Ra is gone. So is Ra, and Osiris, and Isis, and the whole brilliant, elaborate, morally serious civilization of faith that built this hall and maintained it for three thousand years. They didn't go quietly, and they didn't go all at once. They faded, slowly, across centuries, as the world changed around them and the institutional structures that held them in place one by one gave way.

The story of why gods die isn't a simple story. It's not merely a story of conquest, or of superior argument, or of people finally seeing through a delusion. It's a story about the relationship between religious traditions and the social, political, and ecological conditions that sustain them. It's a story, in the end, about what religion actually is and what it does.

And because this book argues that morality is older and deeper than religion, the story of dead gods is also, paradoxically, a story about moral persistence. The temples fell. The priests scattered. The sacred languages became dead languages. But the moral insights those traditions encoded, the ideas about justice and reciprocity and care and judgment, didn't vanish with them. They migrated. They were absorbed, often without acknowledgment, into the religions that replaced them. The accent changed. The language survived.

II. The Gods That Ruled the World

Before we can understand why religions die, we need to appreciate what was lost, and how much was at stake.

Egypt: Three Thousand Years of the Sacred

Egyptian religion is one of the longest-running experiments in organized human spirituality on record. It ran, in recognizable form, for roughly three thousand years, from the unification of Upper and Lower Egypt around 3150 BCE until the final closure of the last pagan temple at Philae by the Byzantine emperor Justinian I in approximately 537 CE. That span of time is so vast it nearly defeats the imagination. It's longer than the distance between Julius Caesar and the present day. Rome itself, as a recognizable civilization, barely approaches it.

At its centre stood a cast of deities of extraordinary psychological richness. Ra, the sun god, crossed the sky each day in his solar barque and descended each night into the underworld, where he battled the serpent Apep in darkness before rising again at dawn. His victory wasn't guaranteed. It required the cooperation of the deceased, the prayers of priests, the maintenance of cosmic order. Osiris, murdered by his brother Set and resurrected by his wife Isis, was the god of the dead and of resurrection, presiding over the judgment of souls in the afterlife. Isis herself became, over centuries, a goddess of such universal appeal that her cult spread across the entire Roman Empire, with temples from Palmyra in Syria to Londinium, what is now London.

What's most striking about Egyptian religion, from the perspective of this book's argument, is the degree to which it was morally structured. At the heart of the Egyptian afterlife stood the concept of Ma'at: truth, justice, cosmic order. Ma'at wasn't merely a god. She was a principle, the animating force that held the universe together. And the fate of every human soul was determined by whether or not that person had lived in accordance with her.

The ritual of the Weighing of the Heart made this explicit in a way that remains startling even now. After death, the heart of the deceased, understood as the seat of moral conscience, was placed on one side of a scale, and the feather of Ma'at on the other. If the heart was light, if the person had lived justly, the soul passed into the Field of Reeds and eternal life. If the heart was heavy with wrongdoing, it was devoured by Ammit, a terrifying composite creature, and the soul was annihilated. Presiding over this judgment was Anubis, the god of the dead, and the forty-two Assessors of Ma'at, before whom the deceased recited the Negative Confessions: "I have not committed robbery with violence. I have not told lies. I have not stolen food. I have not slain men or women."

The Egyptologist E. A. Wallis Budge, who translated the Papyrus of Ani in 1895, was among the first modern scholars to note that this list of ethical prohibitions bore a striking resemblance to later moral codes, including the Ten Commandments. Whether there was direct influence remains a matter of scholarly debate, but the structural parallel is unmistakable. Thousands of years before the Abrahamic traditions articulated the idea of divine moral judgment, Egyptians had already encoded it in stone and papyrus. The moral instinct for accountability, for the idea that actions have consequences that outlast this life, wasn't invented by Christianity or Judaism. It was already ancient when those traditions were young.

Egyptian religion didn't die from intellectual inadequacy. It died when the infrastructure that supported it was dismantled. Wikipedia's analysis of the decline of ancient Egyptian religion identifies the collapse of institutional support as the central cause. As long as pharaohs and emperors built and maintained temples, as long as a professional priesthood was funded and protected, as long as the state identified itself with the old gods, the religion persisted. When that support was withdrawn, when Christian emperors decreed against pagan worship and Christian missionaries demolished shrines, the religion fragmented and localized. The last hieroglyphic inscription dates to 394 CE. The last demotic inscription, at Philae, to 452 CE. Yet active temple ritual continued at Philae even after the epigraphic record closed. The temple wasn't formally shuttered until Justinian's order forced its closure around 535 to 537 CE. The inscriptional record and the institutional life of the religion ended at different moments.

Three thousand years of theologically sophisticated, morally serious, institutionally elaborate religious life, ended in a matter of generations.

Mesopotamia: The Gods of the River Land

If Egypt represents one of history's longest religious traditions, Mesopotamian religion represents one of its most generative. The religious ideas that first developed in Sumer, the southernmost part of ancient Iraq, around 4500 BCE and were elaborated through successive Akkadian, Babylonian, and Assyrian civilizations, shaped the religious landscape of the entire ancient Near East for millennia and left fingerprints on every Abrahamic tradition.

The Mesopotamian pantheon was large and hierarchical. At its head stood the great gods: Anu, lord of the heavens. Enlil, who commanded the storms and breathed life into humanity. Ea, god of the fresh underground waters and of wisdom. And, from the second millennium BCE onward, Marduk of Babylon, who displaced the earlier order and was celebrated in the Babylonian creation epic *Enuma Elish* as the god who slew the chaos-monster Tiamat and built the world from her body. Inanna, known to the Akkadians as Ishtar, was the goddess of love, war, and the planet Venus, one of the strongest and most complex female divine figures in all of human religion.

The religious practices of Mesopotamia centred on the ziggurat: the stepped temple tower that rose above the flat alluvial plain like a mountain, a deliberate simulation of the sacred highlands where the gods were believed to dwell. Within the ziggurat's temple, daily rituals fed, clothed, bathed, and entertained the divine image as if it were a living monarch. The great Akitu festival, the Babylonian New Year celebrated each spring, dramatized Marduk's primordial victory over chaos and renewed the king's divine mandate to rule. Religion and governance were inseparable. The king was the god's representative. The god was the kingdom's ultimate sovereign.

Mesopotamian religion ended not with a single blow but through a slow withering. As a spoken language, Akkadian died out toward the end of the first millennium BCE. Yet the temple scribes continued for centuries, preserving the astronomical observations, omens, and ritual texts in cuneiform long after the living language had gone. According to Archaeology Magazine's account of the last cuneiform tablets, the last cuneiform tablets that can be positively dated were written in the late first century CE. Assyriologist Markham Geller of the Free University of Berlin argues that temple scribes continued working until the third century CE, when the Sassanian Empire seized Babylon and, in Geller's phrase, "shut the temples down and sent everyone home." When the last of those scribes died, the 3,000-year-old cuneiform record fell silent.

The Metropolitan Museum of Art's essay on Mesopotamian deities notes that the Mesopotamian pantheon itself had been contracting for centuries before that final silence, as smaller deities faded and the great gods absorbed their attributes. The process of absorption and simplification that would eventually lead to monotheism was already underway within the polytheistic tradition itself.

Greece and Rome: The Gods of the Forum and the Agora

The Olympian religion of ancient Greece, inherited and adapted by Rome, is perhaps the most familiar of the dead traditions to modern Western audiences, in part because it survived so completely in literature, art, and philosophy. Zeus, Athena, Apollo, Aphrodite, Poseidon: these are names that every educated person still knows. The Greek myths were preserved, discussed, and debated because they were embedded in texts, the works of Homer, Hesiod, Sophocles, Aristophanes, that were never fully abandoned, even when the gods they portrayed had been officially displaced.

Greek religion, at its height from roughly the seventh century BCE onward, wasn't primarily a system of private faith. It was a system of civic obligation. The gods were the gods of particular cities: Athena of Athens, Apollo of Delphi, Zeus of Olympia. To honour the gods was to honour the city. To neglect the gods was to endanger it. Socrates was tried and executed not for abstract theological dissent but for "impiety," for allegedly corrupting the young and failing to honour the gods the city honoured. Greek religion was, at its core, a technology of civic cohesion.

Roman religion inherited this civic character and systematized it further. The Romans absorbed Greek deities into their own pantheon (Zeus became Jupiter, Athena became Minerva, Aphrodite became Venus) with a thoroughness that reveals their thoroughly pragmatic attitude toward the divine. The Romans also introduced the concept of *pietas*, duty and reverence toward family, community, and the gods, as a central civic virtue. *Fides*, faithfulness to one's word, and *virtus*, the courage to serve the community, completed the moral vocabulary of Roman public life.

These values didn't vanish when Rome became Christian. They migrated. The historian and classicist Bret Devereaux, writing about Roman virtues, notes that *pietas* "involved a deep sense of duty, respect and affection toward one's family, elders, country and friends" and became the root of the Christian concept of "piety." *Fides* became the Latin word for faith itself, *fidelity*, the quality of keeping one's commitments. The Roman moral vocabulary was so thoroughly absorbed by Christianity that most Christians today have no idea that the moral categories they use to describe their obligations to God and neighbour were forged in a pagan civic tradition.

Roman polytheism ended, officially, with the Edict of Thessalonica in 380 CE, when the emperor Theodosius declared Christianity the only lawful religion of the Roman Empire. In practice, the process was far more gradual, and paganism persisted in various forms into the sixth century. But the institutional structures of the old religion, the state-funded priesthoods, the public sacrifices, the civic festivals, couldn't survive the withdrawal of imperial patronage. Without the state, there was no mechanism to sustain them.

Norse Religion: Gods on a Time Limit

Norse religion presents a distinctive case among the dead traditions: it was, uniquely, a religion that had built its own death into its theology. At the centre of Norse cosmology stood Ragnarok, the doom of the gods, a final catastrophic battle in which Odin, Thor, Freya, and most of the Aesir would die, the world would be consumed, and a new, renewed world would emerge. The gods of the Norse tradition were explicitly mortal. They were powerful, but not eternal. They fought. They feasted. They aged. They knew that their time would end.

Norse and Germanic religion, practiced by the Scandinavian and Germanic peoples, had roots extending back to the pre-Roman Iron Age, with the distinctively Norse tradition reaching its fullest articulation in the Viking Age from roughly the 8th to 11th centuries CE. Odin, the Allfather, was the god of wisdom, death, war, and poetry, a figure of cunning and sacrifice (he hanged himself from the world-tree Yggdrasil for nine days to win the runes). Thor, his son, commanded thunder and protected humanity with his hammer Mjolnir. Freya presided over love, fertility, and war, and was so beloved that she may share an etymological root with the English word "Friday," though most scholars trace that weekday name specifically to Frigg, Odin's wife. The two goddesses were possibly descended from a common Germanic figure.

Research on the Christianization of Scandinavia identifies the period of official religious change as approximately 950 to 1100 CE, varying by country. Denmark converted first, under Harald Bluetooth sometime around 960 to 965 CE. The exact date of his baptism is debated by scholars, with estimates ranging across that decade. Norway followed, through a mixture of royal pressure and coercion, during the early eleventh century. The Christianization of Iceland in the year 1000 CE is particularly well-documented: the Althing, Iceland's parliament, resolved the conflict between pagans and Christians through arbitration, with the law-speaker Thorgeir Thorkelsson, himself a pagan, decreeing that the whole country would be baptized while permitting private continuation of certain old practices.

This Icelandic resolution is instructive. The conversion of the Norse peoples wasn't primarily a theological event. It was a political and economic one. Christianity brought new trade networks, alliances with Christian courts in continental Europe, access to literate bureaucratic culture, and, crucially, the endorsement of kings with armies. The gods of the Aesir didn't lose a theological argument. They lost a political competition.

Zoroastrianism: The Diminished Flame

Zoroastrianism occupies a peculiar position in any survey of dead religions: it's not fully dead. Approximately 110,000 to 120,000 Zoroastrians survive today, mostly Parsis in India and a smaller community in Iran. But for a tradition that was once the state religion of the Persian Empire, the largest empire the world had yet seen, covering most of the known world at its height under Darius I and Xerxes I in the fifth century BCE, this represents an almost unimaginable decline.

Founded by the prophet Zarathushtra (the Greek transliteration is Zoroaster), whose dates are debated by scholars but generally placed somewhere between 1500 and 600 BCE, Zoroastrianism was the first religion to insist on a radical moral dualism: the universe as a battleground between Ahura Mazda, the Wise Lord, the source of all truth and goodness, and Angra Mainyu (later called Ahriman), the Destructive Spirit, the principle of evil and falsehood. Human beings weren't passive spectators of this cosmic conflict. They were its active participants, obligated to choose good thoughts, good words, and good deeds (*humata, hukhta, hvarshta*) in every moment of their lives.

The PBS NewsHour account of Zoroastrianism notes that the faith predates Christianity and Islam by many centuries. Its decline began with Alexander the Great's conquest of Persia in 330 BCE, which "largely displaced Zoroastrianism with Hellenistic beliefs," though the religion persisted and was eventually restored as the state religion under the Sassanian Empire (224 to 651 CE). The decisive blow came with the Arab Muslim conquest of Persia in the seventh century CE. Many Zoroastrians fled to India, where they were granted asylum and became the ancestors of today's Parsi community.

What Zoroastrianism contributed to the world's religious inheritance is incalculable. The dualistic framework, good versus evil, light versus darkness, cosmic struggle with a definitive outcome, entered Judaism during the Babylonian exile, when Jews encountered Persian Zoroastrian theology directly. A George Mason University analysis of Zoroastrian influence on Judaism and Christianity documents how ideas of Heaven and Hell, angels and demons, the resurrection of the dead, a final judgment, and a coming saviour figure were largely absent from pre-exilic Judaism and entered Jewish theology after sustained contact with Zoroastrian Persia. Christianity inherited all of these. The Satan of Christian theology, the Last Judgment, the idea of eternal damnation for the wicked and eternal paradise for the righteous: these are, in significant part, Zoroastrian ideas wearing Abrahamic clothing.

The Maya and Aztec Traditions: Calendars of Blood and Time

In the pre-Columbian Americas, the Maya and Aztec civilizations developed religious traditions of remarkable complexity, organized around a complex understanding of cyclical time, the cosmic stakes of human behavior, and the obligation of human beings to sustain the universe through sacrifice.

The Maya, whose civilization's roots extend to roughly 2000 BCE in the Preclassic period and which achieved its Classical flowering between approximately 250 and 900 CE, developed one of the most sophisticated calendrical and astronomical systems in human history. Mayan religion understood time as cyclical and hierarchical, composed of interlocking cycles of different lengths. The cosmos had been created and destroyed multiple times, and it was the obligation of human beings, through ritual, offerings, and sometimes bloodletting, to maintain the conditions necessary for its continuation.

The Aztec tradition, centered on the empire of the Triple Alliance, established in 1427, that dominated central Mexico across the fifteenth and into the early sixteenth century CE, shared this cosmological framework but intensified its sacrificial dimension. The Aztecs understood the sun itself as requiring constant nourishment in the form of human blood, because the current age (the fifth sun) had been created by the self-sacrifice of the gods at Teotihuacan and could only be sustained by reciprocal human sacrifice. This wasn't cruelty for its own sake. Within its own logic, it was a deep sense of cosmic obligation. The universe owed its existence to divine sacrifice, and human beings owed the universe their blood.

The end of these traditions came rapidly and violently. The Spanish conquistador Hernán Cortés entered Tenochtitlan in 1519 and captured the emperor Moctezuma II; the fall of the Aztec Empire was complete by 1521, according to the Encyclopaedia Britannica's account of the decline. In the Mayan region, the destruction was drawn out over decades, culminating in the infamous auto-da-fé conducted by the Franciscan bishop Diego de Landa in 1562, in which the Encyclopaedia Britannica's biography of Landa records that thousands of Maya sacred objects and nearly all of the surviving Mayan codices were burned. Landa, who was simultaneously one of the most acute observers of Maya civilization and one of its most destructive enemies, ordered the burning on the grounds that the books contained "nothing in which there was not to be seen superstition and lies of the devil."

The destruction wasn't complete. As the Encyclopaedia Britannica's account of the decline notes, many aspects of indigenous religious and moral life persisted, adapted, hidden, and preserved by generations of indigenous people. Elements of Mayan and Aztec cosmology survive in hybrid form in contemporary Mexican Catholic practice, in festivals, in oral traditions, in ways that are still being documented by anthropologists. The accent changed, dramatically and traumatically. The underlying moral and existential intuitions, about cosmic obligation, about the reciprocal relationship between human beings and the world they inhabit, were never entirely silenced.

III. Why Religions Die: Five Mechanisms

The deaths of these traditions weren't random or inexplicable. Looking across them, we can identify a set of recurring mechanisms, each of which operated with different force in different cases but which collectively explain why any given religious tradition eventually loses its grip on the societies that produced it.

1. Political Conquest and Forced Conversion

The most obvious mechanism is the simplest: the religion's political sponsors were defeated, and the victors imposed their own faith. This explains the Egyptian case most directly, the Norse case almost entirely, and the Mayan and Aztec cases with brutal clarity. When the Aztec empire fell, the institutional and political structure that maintained Aztec religion fell with it. The temples were literally demolished. The stones were frequently used to build Catholic churches on the same sites. Without state support, without the funding for priesthoods and rituals, without the social authority of the old religious specialists, there was no mechanism for transmission to the next generation.

This isn't primarily a story about ideas. It's a story about power and institutional infrastructure. The gods of the conquered didn't lose a theological debate. They lost the protection of armies and courts.

2. Loss of Institutional Infrastructure

Even without conquest, religions can die when the institutions that sustain them are dismantled or allowed to decay. The Wikipedia analysis of the decline of Egyptian religion is explicit on this point: the erosion of native Egyptian religion was traceable primarily to "the state of its infrastructure." When emperors stopped building and repairing temples, when the professional priesthood lost its funding and authority, when the centralizing authority of the pharaoh was replaced by the diffuse authority of distant Roman emperors, the religion "fragmented and localized." Local practices persisted for a while, but without the institutional backbone, they had no mechanism for coherent transmission.

The Assyriologist Markham Geller's account of the end of Mesopotamian religion tells essentially the same story from a different angle: the last practitioners of the tradition were temple scribes, professionals who kept the ritual and astronomical knowledge alive because they were employed to do so. When the Sassanian Empire shut the temples down in the third century CE, those scribes went home. When they died, no one had been trained to replace them. The knowledge died with them.

Harvey Whitehouse of Oxford University, whose work on the cognitive science of religion has examined how religious traditions are transmitted across generations, emphasizes that religious continuity depends on what he calls "routinized rituals," regular, collective practices that create shared identity and allow traditions to be transmitted to strangers and future generations. When those routines are disrupted, whether by conquest, institutional collapse, or simply the withdrawal of state support, the transmission chain breaks. Generations lose the ability to participate in a tradition that their grandparents understood fluently.

3. Cultural Assimilation and Syncretism

A third mechanism is more gradual and less violent: the tradition doesn't die so much as it dissolves into its successor, contributing elements to a new synthesis while losing its distinct identity. This is what happened to Greek religion within Rome, and to Roman religion within Christianity.

The Romans were systematic syncretists. They identified their own gods with those of conquered peoples, declared them equivalent, and incorporated local cults into the imperial religious framework.

Greek Apollo remained Apollo in Rome, but most Greek gods acquired Roman names and were absorbed into the Roman pantheon. When Christianity spread through the Roman Empire, it in turn absorbed elements of the civic and philosophical culture it encountered: Roman institutional structures (the diocese, the bishop's role as administrator), Greek philosophical vocabulary (the Logos, ousia, hypostasis), and Roman civic virtues became Christian virtues. The process wasn't seamless, and it generated centuries of fierce theological dispute, but the net result was that the moral content of the earlier tradition survived, clothed in new theological language.

The scholar Rodney Stark, in his influential theory of why religious movements succeed or fail, identifies one key success factor for new religions as "cultural continuity": the ability to retain as much of the existing religious culture as possible while offering new elements. Christianity was spectacularly good at this. It absorbed the moral vocabulary of Rome, the philosophical framework of Greece, the eschatological hopes of Judaism, and the cosmic dualism of Zoroastrianism, offering all of them under a single theological roof.

4. Competition from Religions with Better "Technology"

The fourth mechanism is perhaps the most intellectually interesting: some religious traditions outcompeted others because they offered a more effective social technology, a better mechanism for creating cooperation and moral community among strangers.

This is the central insight of the psychologist Ara Norenzayan of the University of British Columbia, whose 2013 book *Big Gods: How Religion Transformed Cooperation and Conflict* has become one of the most influential frameworks for understanding religious evolution. Norenzayan's argument, developed with colleagues including Joseph Henrich and summarized in a landmark 2016 paper in *Nature*, is that beliefs in "Big Gods," powerful, omniscient, moralizing deities who monitor human behavior and punish wrongdoing, solve a specific social problem: how to maintain cooperation among strangers in large, anonymous societies.

In small hunter-gatherer groups, cooperation is maintained by reputation, kinship, and direct reciprocity. Everyone knows everyone. Cheating is visible and punishable. But as societies grow larger and more anonymous, these mechanisms break down. The answer that many societies independently arrived at was an invisible, omniscient watcher: a god who sees everything you do, who cares about how you treat strangers, and who will punish you if you cheat. As Norenzayan's research puts it: "Watched people are nice people."

The gods of Greek and Roman polytheism were largely not Big Gods in this sense. The Olympians were interested in worship, sacrifice, and their own competitive dramas. They could be petty, vengeful, capricious. They weren't particularly interested in whether you cheated a stranger in the marketplace, as long as you honoured them with the correct rituals. Mesopotamian and Egyptian religion had developed more moralizing elements, particularly in their afterlife theologies, but neither scaled easily beyond the boundaries of its particular civilization.

Monotheism, by contrast, offered a god of genuinely universal scope: omniscient, omnipresent, deeply invested in human morality, and available to anyone regardless of ethnicity, geography, or social standing. Christianity's radical universalism, the insistence that the same God was equally accessible to slave and emperor, Roman and barbarian, wasn't just a theological position. It was a social technology of extraordinary power. Paul's declaration in Galatians that "there is neither Jew nor Greek, slave nor free, male nor female, for you are all one in Christ Jesus" was, among other things, a statement about the terms of moral community: universal, non-negotiable, and administered by a God who didn't respect the hierarchies of empire.

Islam offered something similar, with even greater structural clarity: a single God, a single community of believers (the *umma*), and an insistence on the formal equality of all Muslims before God. Historians have long noted that Islam spread with particular speed among populations where existing religious traditions offered stratified, exclusionary access to the divine.

Religions with Big Gods simply outcompeted religions without them, not because their theology was more philosophically sophisticated, but because their social technology was more effective. They created larger, more cohesive moral communities. Those communities were more successful in economic competition, military conflict, and demographic expansion. Over centuries and millennia, the religions that couldn't match this social scalability were absorbed, marginalized, or extinguished.

5. The Ecological Mismatch

A fifth, subtler mechanism deserves attention: some religious traditions were too tightly bound to the specific ecological, political, or social conditions that produced them to survive when those conditions changed.

Aztec religion was built around the specific cosmology of a particular empire in a particular valley. Its sacrificial theology was inseparable from the military structure that produced captives for sacrifice, from the agricultural calendar of the Valley of Mexico, from the architecture of Tenochtitlan. When all of that was destroyed in a single generation, the religion had nothing to stand on. Norse religion was similarly embedded in a particular martial culture and social structure. Christianity offered, among other things, a model of religious practice that could function in any social context: in slave quarters and palaces, in deserts and forests, in cities and farms. It was, in the vocabulary of engineering, more portable.

IV. What Survived: The Moral Core That Could Not Be Killed

Here is the paradox at the heart of this chapter. The gods died, but something else didn't.

Look carefully at what the surviving traditions absorbed from the traditions they replaced, and a pattern becomes visible. It's not the theological architecture that was preserved: not the specific claims about divine identity, not the ritual forms, not the mythology. What was preserved, again and again, was the moral content. The ethical intuitions that the dead religions had developed, tested, and refined over centuries or millennia were too useful, too deeply resonant with human nature, to be discarded even when everything else was thrown away.

The Egyptian concept of cosmic moral judgment entered Christianity through multiple channels. The image of the soul standing before a divine judge, having its deeds weighed, wasn't invented by Christianity. It was already thirty centuries old when the earliest Christian texts were written. The Egyptian afterlife theology, with its insistence that moral conduct in this life determines the fate of the soul in the next, is structurally identical to Christian eschatology. Scholars, including those whose work is collected in the UCLA Encyclopedia of Egyptology, have long noted the structural parallel between the forty-two Negative Confessions of Ma'at and the Ten Commandments, and between the Weighing of the Heart and the Christian Last Judgment. The theology differs, but the moral logic is the same.

Zoroastrian dualism entered Judaism during the Babylonian exile of the sixth century BCE, when Jews lived for decades under Persian Zoroastrian authority. Before that contact, the Hebrew God was the sole author of both good and evil (as Isaiah 45:7 states: "I form the light and create darkness, I bring prosperity and create disaster," though most Old Testament scholars read the Hebrew word *ra* here as "calamity" or "adversity" referring to divine judgment on nations, rather than moral evil in the dualist sense). After the exile, a distinct adversarial figure, the Satan, begins to appear in Jewish texts, and ideas of Heaven, Hell, bodily resurrection, and a final apocalyptic judgment enter the tradition. The George Mason University analysis concludes that the Jewish concept of the coming Messiah was itself influenced by the Zoroastrian expectation of a saviour (*Saoshyant*) who would defeat evil at the end of time. Through Judaism, these Zoroastrian moral and eschatological ideas entered Christianity and Islam. The moral framework of three of the world's major living religions carries, in its foundations, the intellectual legacy of a tradition now reduced to roughly 110,000 practitioners.

Roman civic ethics, the vocabulary of *pietas*, *fides*, *virtus*, and *humanitas*, was absorbed so completely into Christian moral language that most of the Latin-derived ethical vocabulary of Western civilization is in the end Roman in origin. When Thomas Aquinas synthesized Christian theology in the thirteenth century, he did so using Aristotelian philosophical categories and Latin civic moral vocabulary. The moral philosophy of Rome didn't die with Roman polytheism. It found new institutional expression in the Church that replaced it.

And then there's the Golden Rule. Perhaps no single moral principle better illustrates the point this chapter is building toward. The principle of treating others as you would wish to be treated appears independently in virtually every major moral and religious tradition that has existed. It's present in Confucianism ("Do not impose on others what you do not wish for yourself"), in Buddhism ("Hurt not others in ways that you yourself would find hurtful"), in Hinduism ("This is the sum of duty: do not do to others what would cause pain if done to you"), in Judaism (Hillel: "What is hateful to you, do not do to your fellow"), in Christianity (Matthew 7:12: "Do to others as you would have them do to you"), in Islam ("None of you truly believes until he loves for his brother what he loves for himself"), and in Zoroastrianism ("Do not do unto others all that which is not well for oneself"). The philosopher Derek Parfit, cited in a Cambridge University Press analysis of the Golden Rule, observed that "the Golden Rule was independently proclaimed and accepted in several of the world's earliest civilizations."

It was independently arrived at because it was independently discovered. The principle isn't a theological idea. It's a moral one, and it's one that human beings, reasoning from their own nature and their own social experience, reach again and again regardless of the specific theological framework they inhabit. The Golden Rule isn't a religious principle that survived the death of the religions that first expressed it. It's a moral principle that those religions recognized, articulated, and transmitted, and that would have existed whether they had recognized it or not. It's older than all of them.

V. The Accent Metaphor Revisited

There's something almost vertiginous about standing in the hypostyle hall at Karnak and contemplating what was there. Not merely the physical scale of it, though that's extraordinary. Not merely the artistic achievement, though the faint traces of original paint on those seventy-nine-foot columns are among the most moving things in human history. What's vertiginous is the realization that the people who built this place and worshipped in it for three thousand years weren't, in any morally meaningful sense, different from us.

They worried about justice. They worried about death and what came after it. They worried about the behavior of their children and the fate of their souls. They believed that how they treated other people mattered in the deepest possible way, that the universe kept score, that the scales would eventually be balanced. They were wrong about the specific theology. They weren't wrong about the moral instincts that theology expressed.

This is the central claim of this book, and this chapter has been building toward it from the opening scene. Morality isn't what religions invented. Morality is what religions found, already there, already operating in human social life, already generating the intuitions about fairness and harm and reciprocity and care that every functioning human community requires. Religion is the accent in which those intuitions were expressed: elaborate, culturally specific, institutionally sustained, adapted to the particular conditions of particular peoples in particular times and places.

When an accent dies, the language doesn't die with it. When we read the forty-two Negative Confessions of Ma'at ("I have not committed robbery with violence. I have not told lies. I have not slain men or women"), we aren't reading an alien moral system from a dead civilization. We're reading a recognizable statement of the same moral grammar that operates in every living tradition today. The specific theological framework, the specific deities, the specific ritual forms, those are the accent. The moral grammar is the language.

The gods of Karnak are gone. The last priest of Marduk died sometime in the third century CE in a city the Sassanians had already emptied. The last public sacrifice to Zeus was made sixteen centuries ago. Odin hasn't been worshipped at a public altar in more than a thousand years. The temples in which these gods lived have crumbled or been repurposed or been turned into tourist attractions. The languages in which their praises were sung have been dead for millennia.

But the children who were taught, in Egyptian, to place their hearts honestly on the scale. The Babylonian scribe who copied out the observations of the planets and believed that the god Marduk held the cosmos in order. The Athenian citizen who argued about justice in the agora under the aegis of Athena. The Norse farmer who trusted that there was a moral structure to the universe even though it would eventually end: all of them were speaking a moral language that you and I still speak today. They spoke it with different accents, in different vocabularies, with different stories. But the language was the same.

Dead religions aren't failures. They're experiments. And like all experiments, they generated data: about what moral intuitions human beings share across cultures, about what kinds of social technology most effectively translate those intuitions into cooperative communities, about what ideas prove strong enough to survive transplantation from one tradition to another, and what ideas prove too fragile or too locally specific to travel.

The silence at Karnak isn't the silence of an idea that turned out to be wrong. It's the silence of an accent that's no longer spoken. The language it carried is still alive, in forms those original speakers wouldn't recognize, but with a moral vocabulary they would understand.

The gods we left behind didn't take their moral insights with them. They left them here, for us, encoded in the traditions that replaced them. And that fact, more than anything else, suggests that those insights were never really the property of the gods at all.

They were always ours.

But while many accents have fallen silent, others have branched and multiplied. The following diagram traces the major living world religions back to their common roots, showing how a single disagreement about succession, scripture, or the nature of God can fracture a tradition into branches that diverge for centuries. The same moral grammar runs through all of them.

The Tree of Faith

How minor differences ripple through millennia

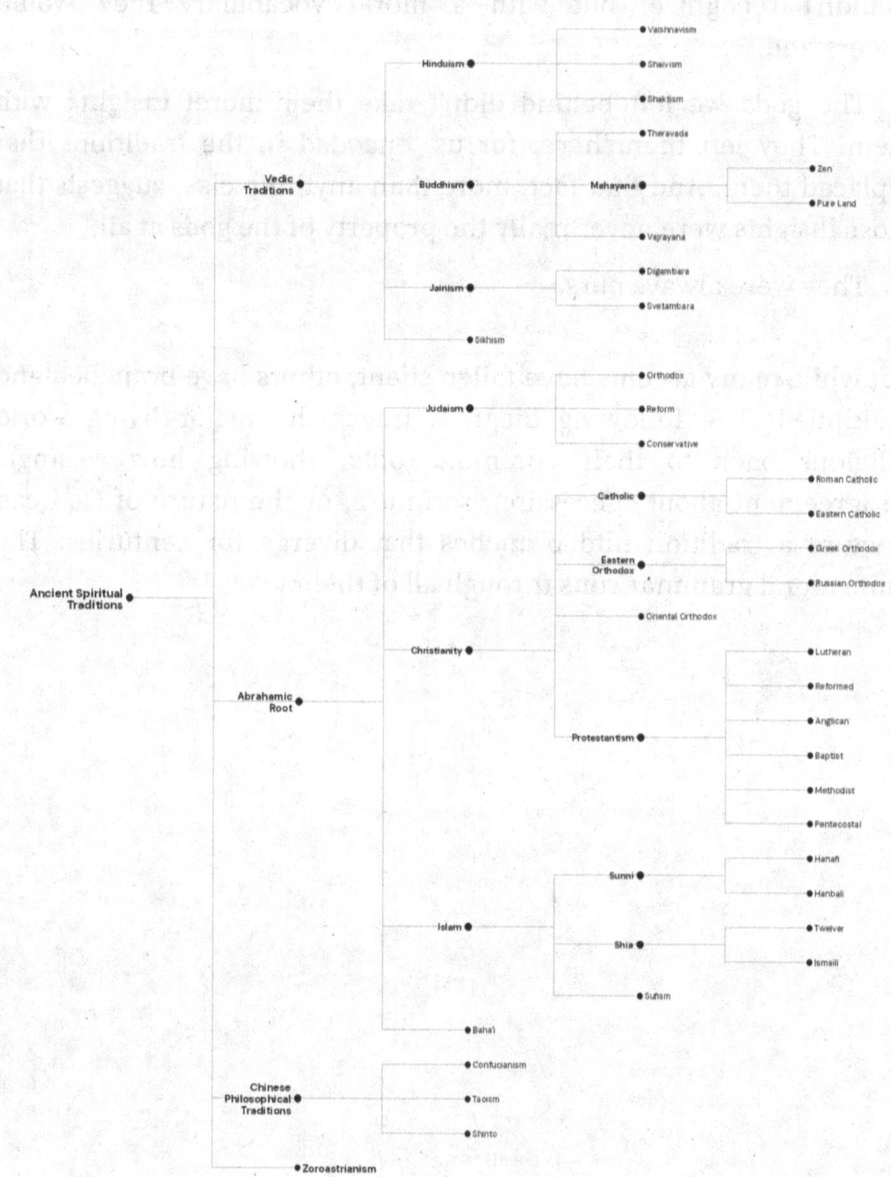

Figure 1. Major world religions and their historical branching points.

Figure 1. Major world religions and their historical branching points.

Sources cited in this chapter include: Wikipedia's analysis of the decline of ancient Egyptian religion; Ancient Egyptian religion (Wikipedia); the Smarthistory essay on the Temple of Amun-Re at Karnak; Archaeology Magazine on the last cuneiform tablets; the Metropolitan Museum of Art essay on Mesopotamian deities; Britannica on Mesopotamian religion; Wikipedia on Zoroastrianism; the PBS NewsHour on Zoroastrianism; the George Mason University analysis of Zoroastrianism, Judaism, and Christianity; the International Cognition and Culture Institute précis of Norenzayan's Big Gods; Purzycki et al., "Moralistic gods, supernatural punishment and the expansion of human sociality," Nature (2016); Wikipedia on the Christianization of Iceland; the Swedish Research Council study on the demise of Norse religion; the Rodney Stark paper on why religious movements succeed or fail; the UCLA Encyclopedia of Egyptology on judgment of the dead; and the Cambridge University Press analysis of the Golden Rule.

PART II

RELIGION AS CULTURAL TECHNOLOGY

Chapter 5

Prayer: The Shared Cadence of Calm

In 2001, a professor of internal medicine at the University of Pavia named Luciano Bernardi wasn't studying prayer. He was studying cardiovascular rhythms, specifically the way that slow breathing patterns synchronize with the body's own oscillatory systems. His research team had recruited volunteers to recite the Ave Maria in Latin, timing each repetition against measurements of blood pressure, heart rate, and respiratory rhythm.

Then his data showed him something that changed the question entirely.

The volunteers who recited the rosary were breathing at a rate of approximately 5.6 breaths per minute. This happened spontaneously: no one had told them to breathe at any particular rate. The prayer itself, through its syllabic structure and its traditional pacing, was guiding their respiration to a frequency that matched the body's own Mayer wave, a natural oscillation in blood pressure that cycles at approximately six times per minute. The rosary, without anyone intending it, was tuning the cardiovascular system like a metronome.

Bernardi's team then asked a separate group of volunteers to recite the yoga mantra 'om mani padme hum'. The breathing rate landed at 5.7 breaths per minute. The physiology was, within measurement error, identical.

Two contemplative practices from traditions separated by thousands of miles, thousands of years, and entirely different theological frameworks had converged on the same respiratory rhythm and produced the same cardiovascular response. Bernardi noted the finding with what can only be described as scientific understatement. The effect, he wrote, had occurred 'serendipitously.'

The rosary, it turned out, is a very old cardiovascular tool. And it's not the only one.

The Rhythm Beneath the Words

Bernardi's 2001 paper in the *British Medical Journal* did more than identify a cardiovascular curiosity. It pointed toward a pattern that turns out to be widespread across contemplative traditions.

The effect was produced not by the content of the words, not by the beliefs associated with them, not by the deity addressed, but by the rhythm. The prayer works because of its cadence, not its theology.

This is a remarkable thing to say about an ancient religious practice. It's also a deeply respectful one. It says that those who developed the rosary, over centuries of practice and reflection, weren't simply performing symbolic gestures. They were, unknowingly, discovering something real about the human body: that a particular pace of repetition unlocks a particular state of calm. They didn't have the vocabulary of heart rate variability, a key indicator of nervous system health, or baroreflex sensitivity, the body's automatic mechanism for regulating blood pressure. But they found the mechanism anyway.

What the Brain Does During Prayer

Around the turn of the millennium, a neuroscientist named Andrew Newberg began doing something that hadn't been done before: he scanned the brains of people while they were actively praying.

Newberg used a brain imaging technique called Single Photon Emission Computed Tomography, commonly referred to as SPECT, which measures blood flow through the brain as a proxy for neural activity. He worked with Franciscan nuns who agreed to pray inside the scanner and with Buddhist monks who meditated in it. He found a consistent pattern across both groups.

Two things happened. First, the frontal lobes, the regions associated with attention, deliberate focus, and concentration, showed increased activity. The praying person was concentrating deeply, and the brain was working hard to sustain that concentration. Second, a region toward the top of the brain called the superior parietal lobe, which Newberg called the orientation association area, went quiet. This region constructs our sense of where our body ends and the world begins. It's the part of the brain that knows you are you and not the chair you're sitting in.

When that region grows quiet, the felt sense of where the self ends changes. The boundary between self and world becomes less defined. This is the neurological basis, Newberg argued, of the mystical sense of "oneness" or "presence" that practitioners in many traditions describe. The Catholic nun who reports feeling the presence of God. The Buddhist monk who describes the dissolution of the separate self. They're not speaking metaphorically, or at least not only metaphorically. They're describing a measurable shift in brain activity.

This finding doesn't tell us whether God exists. It doesn't adjudicate between theological claims. The experience people associate with prayer has a physical correlate in the brain, and that correlate is strikingly similar across traditions as different as Franciscan Christianity and Tibetan Buddhism.

The frontal lobe activation matters too. Sustained attention is one of the most therapeutically valuable mental states a human being can cultivate. Rumination, which involves repetitive looping through worry and regret, involves a different network altogether, one that runs on autopilot when the mind isn't given something deliberate to do. Prayer, by demanding focused attention, interrupts that loop. It gives the mind a specific object, a phrase, a bead, a breath, a presence, and holds it there. This is why prayer often feels clarifying even when nothing in the external situation has changed. The situation hasn't changed. The attentional state has.

The Body's Quieting System

To understand what prayer does to the nervous system, it helps to understand the two modes the nervous system operates in.

The first mode is the sympathetic response, commonly known as fight-or-flight. When the brain perceives a threat, real or imagined, it triggers a cascade of physical changes: heart rate increases, breathing becomes shallow and rapid, stress hormones including cortisol flood the bloodstream, digestion slows, and muscles prime for action. This system evolved to handle acute physical danger, and it does that job extremely well. The problem is that modern human anxieties, financial worry, social embarrassment, anticipation of failure, loneliness, are often chronic rather than acute. The fight-or-flight response wasn't designed for problems that can't be resolved by running or fighting.

The second mode is the parasympathetic response, sometimes called rest-and-digest. This mode slows the heart rate, deepens the breath, reduces cortisol, promotes digestion, and signals to the brain that the threat has passed. Activating this system isn't merely comfortable. It's physiologically restorative. Chronic sympathetic dominance, the state of being perpetually in low-level fight-or-flight, is associated with inflammation, cardiovascular disease, impaired immune function, and disrupted sleep.

The key player in shifting between these two modes is the vagus nerve. Its name comes from the Latin for "wandering." It's the longest cranial nerve in the body, running from the brainstem through the chest and into the abdomen, connecting to the heart, lungs, and digestive system. It's the primary channel through which the parasympathetic nervous system communicates with the body.

A 2018 study by Roderik Gerritsen and Guido Band confirmed that slow, rhythmic breathing directly stimulates the vagus nerve. Specifically, exhalation activates the vagus. Inhalation suppresses it. When breathing slows to around six breaths per minute, the ratio of exhalation to inhalation shifts, and vagal activation increases. The measurable result is higher heart rate variability, which indicates parasympathetic health and has been independently linked to better cardiac outcomes, lower inflammation, and greater emotional resilience.

Every major contemplative tradition, whether or not it understood any of this in physiological terms, has built practices that produce this effect. Buddhist meditation tracks the breath. Islamic dhikr, the practice of repetitive remembrance of God through phrases and prayer beads, creates a slow, sustained rhythm. Jewish davening, the gentle swaying and rhythmic recitation of liturgy, regulates movement and breath together. Yoga pranayama, the formal study of breath control in Hindu tradition, does this explicitly and with considerable sophistication. Christian contemplative traditions, from the Desert Fathers to the Cloud of Unknowing to the rosary, have all, in their different ways, discovered the same fact: that slowing and steadying the breath shifts the quality of the mind.

These traditions didn't develop in communication with each other. The convergence is striking. One way to read it is that thousands of years of careful human attention, directed toward the question of how to quiet the mind and open the heart, converged on the same underlying mechanism. Another way to read it is that the mechanism was always there, built into the human nervous system, and that the traditions were simply different paths to the same door.

Harvard's Discovery

In the late 1960s and early 1970s, a physician at Harvard Medical School named Herbert Benson became interested in a group of practitioners who claimed that meditation could lower their blood pressure. This was considered an unusual claim at the time. Benson was skeptical, but he measured.

He found that meditation produced a consistent and reproducible physiological state that was, in almost every measurable respect, the functional opposite of the fight-or-flight response. Heart rate slowed. Blood pressure dropped. Cortisol levels fell. Oxygen consumption decreased. The breath deepened and slowed. He called this state the relaxation response, and he spent the next several decades studying it, refining it, and confirming it across thousands of patients.

What Benson came to understand was that the relaxation response isn't a product of any particular tradition or technique. It's a biological capacity that humans possess, and which can be triggered by a remarkably simple set of conditions: a repetitive focus point (a word, a sound, a phrase, a breath), sustained for ten to twenty minutes, combined with a passive attitude toward distracting thoughts, acknowledging them and returning to the focus point without effort or frustration.

This is, structurally, what prayer is. Benson recognized that centuries of religious practice had been doing this, without the physiological vocabulary, and had delivered the benefits to billions of people. A 2015 study at Massachusetts General Hospital found that relaxation-response techniques, including meditation, yoga, and prayer, were associated with a 43 percent reduction in health care utilization for stress-related conditions. The mechanism Benson identified saves lives and reduces suffering, and it's available through the secular instructions in his books. It's also available through the rosary, through dhikr, through zazen, through davening.

This isn't a claim that prayer is merely a stress-reduction technique and nothing more. A person who prays is doing many things at once: regulating the nervous system, yes, but also narrating the self, expressing relationship with the sacred, seeking meaning, and embedding individual experience in a larger story. Those dimensions are real and valuable and not reducible to physiology.

But the physiological dimension is real too. And it's available to everyone.

Not All Prayer Is the Same

To speak of prayer as though it were a single practice is to be imprecise in a way that matters. Researchers have found that different types of prayer produce measurably different psychological outcomes, and some of those differences are important.

Psychologists have identified several distinct types of prayer that map onto different human needs.

Petitionary prayer, sometimes called supplication, is prayer that asks for something. Please help me get through this. Please heal my father. Please let the test results come back clear. This is probably the most familiar form of prayer for many people, and research suggests it's also the type most associated with anxiety. Studies have found that petitionary prayer is negatively associated with well-being. This makes intuitive sense: asking for a specific outcome directs attention toward a problem and toward uncertainty about whether the desired outcome will occur. When the prayer goes unanswered, or when the answer isn't the one hoped for, the anxiety that the prayer was meant to address may intensify.

Gratitude prayer, by contrast, consistently shows positive associations with mood, self-esteem, and reduced depression. Prayers of thanksgiving orient attention toward what has been received rather than what is lacking. This is the prayer that says: thank you for this day, for this food, for these people. The psychological research on gratitude is strong and consistent: people who regularly practice it report higher well-being, stronger relationships, and lower rates of depression. Prayer, when it takes this form, is gratitude practice with a relational dimension.

Confessional prayer operates through what researchers call the disclosure mechanism. There's a substantial body of research, much of it associated with psychologist James Pennebaker, demonstrating that putting difficult experiences into words, whether through journaling, therapy, or conversation, reduces the psychological and even physiological burden of those experiences. Confessional prayer does something structurally similar. The person tells the truth about what they've done or what they feel, to a witness they believe is both perfectly attentive and perfectly forgiving. Whether or not that witness exists in a metaphysical sense, articulating a burden out loud and releasing it to another has measurable effects. Research in the *Journal of Religion and Health* found that the relationship between confessional prayer and well-being is mediated specifically by this disclosure mechanism, and that it functions much like therapeutic self-disclosure.

Meditative and contemplative prayer is the type closest to what secular practitioners call mindfulness. It doesn't ask for anything. It doesn't confess anything. It simply attends: to the breath, to the moment, to the presence that the practitioner senses or imagines or reaches toward. This type of prayer has the strongest research support for attention regulation, emotional balance, and what psychologists call trait mindfulness, the general capacity to be present with experience rather than reactive to it. When neuroscientists study experienced meditators, the brain changes they find, including increased frontal lobe thickness and reduced activity in the default mode network, the brain's rumination circuit, are also observed in experienced contemplative pray-ers. The practices, despite their different theologies, appear to train the brain in similar ways.

The practical implication isn't that some prayer is better than others in some absolute sense, but that the type of prayer a person turns to matters. Someone in crisis who turns primarily to petitionary prayer, asking for relief without receiving it, may find that their anxiety increases rather than diminishes. The prayer traditions themselves often recognize this: many spiritual directors encourage practitioners to move from petition toward surrender, from asking for specific outcomes toward open attentiveness that neither demands nor resists. This is the kind of prayer that most closely mirrors the physiological benefits described above.

Accents of the Same Language

A pattern runs through every tradition considered in this chapter. Prayer works through mechanisms that are physiological, psychological, and social. Those mechanisms are real. They're measurable. They're not contingent on the truth of any particular theological claim.

The Catholic rosary and the Islamic dhikr are both repetitive, rhythmic, and slow. The Buddhist chant and the Jewish liturgical recitation both sustain attention and interrupt rumination. The confessional prayer and the journaling session both work through the disclosure mechanism. The gratitude prayer and the secular gratitude practice both orient attention toward abundance rather than lack. Different words, different metaphysics, different communities, but the same underlying human capacities being exercised and strengthened.

This is the "accent" relationship at the center of this book. Prayer is one of the most powerful dialects of the moral language all human cultures share, a way of working on the self through structured attention, rhythmic repetition, and honest relationship with something larger than the everyday ego. The rosary speaks it with Latin cadences, Marian imagery, a counting of mysteries. The dhikr speaks it with Arabic phrases, prayer beads, the rhythmic motion of the breath aligned with the names of God. The Zen sitting practice speaks it with a spare, non-verbal inflection. The secular mindfulness session speaks it without theological content at all.

None of these accents is wrong. Each has developed within a cultural tradition and carries the weight of that tradition's wisdom. Understanding what they're doing, beneath the doctrinal surface, deepens rather than diminishes our appreciation of them.

If you're a person of faith and you pray, the evidence suggests your prayer is doing something real in your body and your brain, something your tradition discovered and preserved over centuries. If you're a person without faith, the evidence suggests that the underlying mechanisms are available to you through secular practices that share the same structure: slow breathing, focused attention, repetition, gratitude expression. The body doesn't know or care whether the repetition is sacred or secular. It responds to the rhythm.

This isn't a reductionist claim. It's an integrative one. Saying that prayer works through the vagus nerve doesn't exhaust what prayer is, any more than saying that love involves dopamine and oxytocin exhausts what love is. The mechanisms are part of the story. They're not the whole of it.

The Research Catches Up

Religious communities have been practicing some form of slow rhythmic breathing, sustained attention, and repetitive vocalization for at least three thousand years, probably much longer. For most of that time, the practitioners had no physiological vocabulary for what they were doing. They could describe what they experienced: a sense of calm, clarity, presence, peace, closeness to the divine. They couldn't explain the mechanism.

The scientific study of meditation and prayer began seriously only in the 1970s. Jon Kabat-Zinn, a molecular biologist working at the University of Massachusetts Medical School, developed Mindfulness-Based Stress Reduction in 1979, drawing on Buddhist meditation techniques while carefully removing their religious framing. By the time clinical researchers began systematically studying these practices, they were effectively rediscovering what monasteries had preserved for centuries.

The convergence of research on secular mindfulness and religious prayer is striking. Both activate the parasympathetic nervous system. Both reduce cortisol and inflammatory markers. Both improve heart rate variability. Both decrease activity in the default mode network, the brain's autopilot circuit that generates rumination when the mind isn't occupied. Both increase trait mindfulness, the general capacity to be present with experience rather than swept away by it.

In this convergence, there's neither a victory for religion nor a victory for secular science. Both sets of practitioners were working on the same problem and arriving at similar solutions. The monastery and the mindfulness app are, at the level of mechanism, studying the same territory. The monastery has the advantage of centuries of accumulated wisdom and a community that sustains the practice over time. The mindfulness app has the advantage of accessibility and scientific validation.

For most of human history, the monastery version was the only available form of this technology. The research doesn't require us to choose between them.

What Happens Without the Words

Herbert Benson described his secular relaxation instructions with characteristic plainness. Sit comfortably. Close your eyes. Choose a word or sound, any word or sound, a name, a syllable, the word "peace," the word "one." Breathe naturally, and on each exhalation, return to your chosen word. When your mind wanders, and it will, notice it without frustration and return. Do this for ten to twenty minutes.

This is prayer stripped of everything except its physiological mechanism. No theology. No ritual context. No community. No accumulated symbolic meaning. And it still works, in the narrow sense of activating the parasympathetic nervous system, lowering cortisol, and producing the relaxation response.

There's something instructive in this. The prayer traditions add layers around this core: meaning, community, narrative, relationship, obligation, transcendence. Those layers aren't decorative extras. They're what make prayer, in its full religious form, more than a breathing exercise. They situate the practitioner in a web of relationships that extends beyond the individual, make the private struggle shared, and connect the single breath to a tradition stretching back centuries.

But the core remains, even without the layers. The body's quieting mechanism doesn't require a deity to activate it. It requires a rhythm, an attention, and a willingness to return.

Practical Reflection

The next time you find yourself anxious, whether that anxiety is about a specific problem or just the low-grade static that modern life generates, try this.

Breathe in for a count of four. Breathe out for a count of six. Repeat this for five minutes.

You don't need to call this prayer. You don't need to address it to anyone. You don't need a set of beads or a cushion or a text. You need four counts and six counts and five minutes.

What you'll notice is that the calm you feel afterward doesn't depend on resolving whatever was worrying you. The problem will still be there. But your nervous system will have shifted, measurably, toward a state in which that problem can be faced with greater steadiness. Your heart rate will have slowed. Your cortisol will have dropped. Your frontal lobe will be better resourced for the kind of sustained, non-reactive attention that problems actually require.

This is what the monk in Kyoto does every morning. This is what Rosa does with her rosary at the kitchen table before the house wakes up. This is what the congregation in Brooklyn finds, almost without noticing it, in the third verse of the psalm.

The rhythm is very old. It belongs to everyone.

Those who pray speak it in the accent of their tradition. Those who don't pray can still speak it, in whatever quiet language their own life has given them.

The body recognizes both.

Consider: What is your own relationship to rhythm and repetition as a tool for calming the mind? Do you already have a practice, however informal, that functions this way? What does this chapter suggest about why it works?

Chapter 6

Rituals and the Social Brain

There are forty-five seconds before the match begins, and something extraordinary is happening.

Thirty men from New Zealand, dressed in black, have arranged themselves in rows at the center of the field. The stadium is packed. The opposing team stands about twenty meters away, watching. The crowd has gone from noise to a particular kind of silence, the silence of something about to happen.

Then it begins.

One man calls out. The others respond. Feet stamp the turf in unison. Thighs are slapped. Chests are thrust forward. Eyes are wide and fixed. The voices rise together, roughen, build, building on each other the way a wave builds before it breaks. The chant is in te reo Māori, and many in the crowd don't understand the words. The opposing team almost certainly doesn't understand the words. But they feel it anyway. They feel it in the chest, in the spine, in some place behind the eyes that doesn't have a name.

This is the haka. It's one of the most recognizable rituals in international sport. And in those forty-five seconds, none of the thirty men are thinking about religion. None of them are thinking about theology, or doctrine, or the afterlife. They're doing something profoundly human, something that has been done in different forms for as long as humans have gathered together: they're using the synchronized movement of their bodies to transform a collection of individuals into something that feels like a single organism.

What's happening in those bodies is measurable. What's happening in the brains of the men watching is measurable. And when you measure it, what you find is that the mechanism at work in the haka is the same mechanism that powers the Sunday service, the Friday prayer, the Passover seder, and the Anzac Day dawn service.

Ritual isn't the property of religion. It's the property of the human social brain.

What Makes a Ritual a Ritual

Before going further, it's worth being precise about what we mean by the word "ritual," because it's used loosely.

A habit is a repeated behavior that serves an individual functional purpose. You brush your teeth every morning. You take the same route to work. These are habits. They're useful, they're repeated, and they're yours. But they carry no symbolic meaning beyond their function, and no one else's participation makes them more meaningful.

A ritual is different. A ritual is a structured, repeated action that carries symbolic significance, usually social significance. The meaning of a ritual isn't exhausted by its function. Often, the action isn't obviously functional at all. You could mourn a loss without a funeral. You could begin a meal without saying grace. You could start a rugby match without a haka. The ritual isn't necessary in the logistical sense. But it matters in a way that bypasses logic.

The distinction that anthropologist Dimitris Xygalatas draws, in his 2022 book *Ritual: How Seemingly Senseless Acts Make Life Worth Living*, is that rituals are defined by two features: they're rigid (the actions must be performed in a specific way) and they're causally opaque (the connection between the action and its supposed effect isn't obvious or explicable through everyday reasoning). You can't explain why exactly these movements, in exactly this order, are what matters. But they're what matters. This opacity, far from undermining the ritual's power, appears to be essential to it.

Rituals mark time as meaningful. They signal transitions. They create shared identity. They manage the emotions that are too large or too strange for ordinary language. And they do all of this through the body, through synchronized action and shared attention, through the felt experience of moving with others through something that means something.

The Chemistry of Moving Together

In 2009, Scott Wiltermuth and Chip Heath at Stanford published a study that has become something of a landmark in the science of cooperation. They designed three simple experiments in which participants either moved in synchrony with strangers, or moved similarly but not in synchrony, then participated in economic exercises that required them to decide how much to cooperate, even at personal cost.

The results were striking. Across all three experiments, people who had moved in synchrony cooperated significantly more. They gave more, sacrificed more, and were more willing to forgo personal gain for the group's benefit. On a seven-point scale measuring felt connection, synchronous participants scored 4.5 on average, compared to 2.9 for those who had moved out of sync. Walking in step, even with strangers, had created a felt sense of connection that translated into concrete behavior.

What made the finding especially interesting was that the effect didn't depend on positive emotion. Participants didn't need to enjoy the synchronous activity for the cooperation boost to appear. The physical alignment itself was sufficient.

This is why armies march. This is why congregations stand and sit and kneel in unison. This is why sports teams have warm-up drills and wedding guests have rehearsals. The collective body creates the collective mind. Synchronized bodies produce cooperative brains.

The practice is ancient and effective, and now, for the first time in human history, we can explain the mechanism.

But movement alone isn't the whole story. What happens when people sing together goes even further.

Endorphins and the Ancient Bond

Robin Dunbar is perhaps best known for "Dunbar's Number," the idea that humans can maintain only about 150 stable social relationships at any given time due to the limits of our social brain. But his work on the social function of music is equally important and less widely known.

Dunbar and his colleagues have spent years studying the neurochemical foundation of social bonding in humans and other primates. In other primates, particularly our closest relatives, the primary bonding mechanism is physical grooming. Grooming triggers the release of endorphins, the brain's natural opioid-like compounds, in both the groomer and the groomed. These endorphins produce feelings of warmth, pleasure, and attachment that cement social relationships. The problem, from an evolutionary standpoint, is that grooming can only happen between two individuals at a time. You can't groom a group.

Dunbar's argument is that humans developed communal vocalizing, singing, chanting, and coordinated rhythm, as a kind of "grooming at a distance": a way to trigger the same endorphin-based bonding that grooming provides, but simultaneously across a much larger group. When people sing together with sufficient vigor, they trigger endorphin release, and that release creates social warmth that functions like the warmth of close personal relationship.

In 2015, Dunbar's collaborator Eiluned Pearce and colleagues at the University of Oxford published a study demonstrating what they called the "ice-breaker effect." People who sang together with strangers, even for a single session, reported faster and stronger feelings of social bonding than those who engaged in other kinds of group activity. By the end of the session, the singers felt they knew and liked each other significantly more. Singing had done in an hour what other social activities might take weeks to accomplish.

This is the neurochemical explanation for something every religion has known in practice: the congregation that sings together becomes more than the sum of its individual members. The choir, the call-and-response, the communal psalm, the shared mantra aren't merely aesthetic or devotional. They're endorphin delivery systems, refined over millennia to build and maintain the social bonds that make large cooperative groups possible.

And this effect isn't limited to religious settings. The football chant that fills a stadium, the concert audience erupting into collective song when the first chord of a familiar anthem sounds, the protest crowd that finds a chant and holds it through the streets: all of them are running the same ancient program, the one built into human neurobiology before any of our current religions existed.

Two Kinds of Ritual

Harvey Whitehouse, professor of social anthropology at Oxford, has spent decades developing what has become one of the most empirically tested frameworks in the cognitive science of religion. He calls it the "modes of religiosity" theory, and its central distinction is between two fundamentally different types of ritual, each of which builds a different kind of community.

The first type Whitehouse calls the doctrinal mode. These are low-arousal, high-frequency rituals: the weekly church service, the Friday prayer, the daily liturgy, the seasonal celebrations that recur every year like clockwork. These rituals aren't intense experiences. They're routine. The point of them is the routine. Repeated regularly over years and decades, they transmit a shared body of doctrine and identity through procedural and semantic memory, the kind that stores skills and facts rather than personal experiences. They create communities that can be large and widely dispersed because the shared knowledge and practice provides a common identity that doesn't require personal connection to everyone involved. A Catholic in Sydney can walk into a church in Rio de Janeiro or Warsaw and immediately know what to do, when to stand, what words to say. The ritual itself is the connection.

The second type is what Whitehouse calls the imagistic mode. These are high-arousal, low-frequency rituals: initiation ceremonies, extreme pilgrimages, vision quests, fire-walking, tribal scarification. These aren't routine experiences. They're, often, terrifying, painful, or overwhelming. They happen rarely, sometimes only once in a lifetime. Because they're so intense, they're stored not in procedural memory but in episodic memory, the deep, vivid, emotionally saturated kind that holds the most important moments of a life.

The community built by imagistic ritual is very different from the community built by doctrinal ritual. It's smaller, because intense shared experience by its nature involves smaller groups. But it's also more cohesive, more personally committed, more what researchers call "identity-fused": the individual's sense of self becomes deeply merged with the group identity. The shared ordeal becomes a permanent feature of the self. The people who went through it with you aren't just acquaintances. They're, in some deep sense, part of you.

Religious traditions, Whitehouse argues, tend to employ both modes, with different emphases at different stages of their development. The weekly service builds the broad, stable community. The intense ritual, the confirmation, the bar mitzvah, the vision quest, the extreme pilgrimage, creates the deep personal commitment that sustains it.

But Whitehouse's framework applies equally well outside religion. Military basic training is an imagistic ritual. Sports team pre-season camps can function this way. First responders who survive disasters together describe a bond that's qualitatively different from ordinary friendship. They went through something, and that shared passage created an identity fusion that civilian relationships rarely produce.

The mechanism is the same. The ritual frame differs.

The Electricity of the Crowd

When the French sociologist Émile Durkheim published *The Elementary Forms of Religious Life* in 1912, he made a claim that was radical at the time and has only become more interesting since: God, he argued, is in some deep sense the community worshipping itself.

This isn't as dismissive of religion as it sounds. Durkheim meant something specific and empirically grounded. He observed that when people gather and participate in shared ritual, a distinctive emotional state arises that he called "collective effervescence." The assembled group generates an energy that no individual within it had brought alone. People feel something larger than themselves, something that seems to come from outside them and yet is also unmistakably present. They feel moved, elevated, part of something.

Durkheim's argument was that this experience is the experiential raw material of religion. The community then projects it onto symbols and figures, onto the totem, the deity, the sacred object, and those symbols become "sacred" because they carry the felt weight of collective energy. The sacred, in this account, isn't a metaphysical entity. It's a social fact: the felt reality of a community that's more than the sum of its members.

Modern neuroscience has given Durkheim's account more precision. Synchronized movement and shared attention produce measurable neurochemical changes. Endorphin release, as Dunbar's work shows, creates the felt warmth of social bonding. The suppression of the brain's self-boundary region, as Newberg's brain imaging shows, creates the felt dissolution of the individual into the group. The feeling of transcendence isn't illusion. It's chemistry.

And that chemistry isn't activated only in cathedrals. A 2019 study by Liebst and colleagues in *Sociological Science* documented collective effervescence in sports events, concerts, and political rallies. A stadium full of fans whose team has just scored is in the grip of collective effervescence. A mosh pit at a rock concert generates it. A protest that finds its chant and holds it generates it. Durkheim's electricity flows wherever humans gather with shared attention and synchronized expression. The specific symbols onto which it's projected vary. The underlying social physics don't.

When Pain Becomes a Bond

Among the most striking research on extreme ritual is the work of Dimitris Xygalatas, who has spent years conducting fieldwork at fire-walking ceremonies in Spain and Hindu Kavadi festivals in Mauritius.

The Kavadi festival, practiced by Tamil Hindu communities around the world, isn't a gentle occasion. Participants pierce their skin with metal skewers as an act of devotion. They carry heavy, ornate structures on their bodies over long distances. The experience is, by any ordinary measure, painful.

Xygalatas and his colleagues measured something that might seem unrelated to religious devotion: how generous the participants were afterward. They used a simple charitable giving exercise. The more intense the ordeal a participant had endured, the more money they donated. High-ordeal participants gave approximately twice as much as those who had participated only in collective prayer. The pain hadn't hardened them. It had opened them.

The effect extended outward. Observers who hadn't personally undergone the ordeal but who were closely connected to those who had, family members and close friends, showed elevated generosity too. The prosocial signal had radiated outward from the participants.

An earlier study at a fire-walking ceremony in the Spanish village of San Pedro Manrique yielded an equally remarkable result. Xygalatas and his team measured the heart rates of fire-walkers during the ceremony. They also measured the heart rates of spectators. The heart-rate patterns of fire-walkers were synchronized with the heart-rate patterns of their close relatives in the audience, even though those relatives weren't participating. The bodies of people who loved each other were tracking each other across the physical distance of the ceremony, sharing the physiological experience of the ordeal through emotional attunement.

The interpretation Xygalatas offers is that costly, high-arousal ritual functions as commitment signaling: the willingness to endure pain for the group is a credible, hard-to-fake signal of loyalty and devotion. Other members of the group can trust someone who has gone through this because the experience demonstrates a level of commitment that isn't easy to simulate. That trust, once established, generates generosity.

This isn't comfortable knowledge. The history of extreme religious ritual includes practices that were harmful and coercive, and nothing in the science of ritual suggests that all extreme practices are therefore good. What the research suggests is that the underlying mechanism, the bond created by shared costly experience, is real, powerful, and operates through the social brain in ways that are now beginning to be understood.

The Terror Beneath the Ritual

There's another layer to why ritual matters, one that runs below the neurochemical and the social and touches something more fundamental: the fact that we die.

In the 1980s, three psychologists, Sheldon Solomon, Jeff Greenberg, and Tom Pyszczynski, developed what they called Terror Management Theory. Their starting point was an insight from anthropologist Ernest Becker's 1973 book *The Denial of Death*: that humans are unique among animals in being aware of their own mortality, and that this awareness creates a specific kind of terror that must, in some way, be managed.

The researchers argued that much of human culture, including religion, can be understood as a set of strategies for managing this terror. We build cultural worldviews that extend beyond individual lives. We invest in institutions, communities, and legacies that will outlast us. We find ways to make death meaningful rather than merely random and final. Religion is, in this analysis, a supremely effective terror-management system: it offers literal immortality through afterlife beliefs, symbolic immortality through belonging to a community and tradition that continue, and a cosmic framework within which even death serves a purpose.

The experimental evidence for Terror Management Theory is extensive. Hundreds of studies across multiple countries have used "mortality salience" procedures, which typically involve asking participants to think briefly about their own death, and then measured changes in behavior and attitude. The consistent finding is that reminders of death increase people's attachment to their cultural worldview, their hostility toward those who challenge that worldview, and their support for the group symbols and rituals that embed them in something larger than themselves.

Rituals, in this framework, aren't merely social technologies for cooperation. They're also structures for managing the anxiety that underlies human social life at its deepest level. The funeral ritual doesn't just process grief. It situates death within a narrative that makes it bearable. The birth ritual doesn't just celebrate new life. It welcomes that life into a community that promises to outlast any individual within it. The seasonal ceremony confirms that the cycle continues.

This is true whether the ritual is explicitly religious or not. Anzac Day, the annual Australian and New Zealand commemoration of those who died in military service, isn't a religious ceremony, yet it carries every structural feature of religious ritual: solemnity, repetition, shared attention, the naming of the dead, the promise of remembrance. What it manages is grief, mortality, and the question of whether individual sacrifice was meaningful. Those are exactly the questions that religious ritual manages.

The ritual frame makes them bearable.

The Secular Versions

Once you understand what ritual does, you see it everywhere. You see it in places where no one would think to call it ritual.

The seventh-inning stretch at a baseball game, where tens of thousands of people stand simultaneously and sing "Take Me Out to the Ball Game," is a ritual. It marks a transition in the game, creates a collective pause, and reinforces the sense of shared identity between the crowd and the team.

The standing ovation at the end of a concert is a ritual. The audience rises together, in a collective embodied response, to affirm that something significant has happened. The applause synchronizes. Bodies align. The shared verdict creates shared meaning.

Graduation ceremonies are rituals. The academic regalia, the procession, the handshake, the turn of the tassel: none of these are strictly necessary to confer a degree. The piece of paper could be mailed. The ritual isn't about the paper. It's about marking the transition, publicly and collectively, in a way that lodges the change in the body as well as the mind.

New Year's celebrations around the world are rituals. The specific date on which they fall is arbitrary. The year doesn't physically end and begin at midnight on any particular night. But gathering with others to name and witness the transition together does something that merely watching the calendar change couldn't. It makes the transition real, shared, and meaningful.

Family dinner traditions, even very simple ones, function as rituals. Families that eat together at a consistent time, with consistent practices, whether saying grace, checking in about each other's days, or keeping a standing joke, are using the structural features of ritual to create regular moments of collective identity. The consistency, the repetition, the shared meaning embedded in familiar phrases and gestures: these are the same structural features that define religious ritual, scaled to the family unit.

Research on secular rituals confirms that they generate the same neurochemical and psychological effects as religious ones. A 2021 study in *PLoS ONE* comparing Sunday Assembly attendees (a secular, non-religious congregation format) with Christian church attendees found comparable increases in social bonding and positive affect in both groups following the collective gathering. The ritual structure, not the theological content, was the active ingredient.

The accent differs. The language is the same. Just as a computer's operating system runs the same core processes regardless of which applications sit on top, the social brain runs the same bonding and meaning-making processes regardless of which ritual tradition frames them.

What Ritual Is Doing

Stepping back, the research converges on a picture of ritual as a multipurpose tool for managing conditions that are universal to human life.

It manages uncertainty. When the world feels threatening and unpredictable, ritual provides a structure of reliable, predictable action. A 2020 study in the *Philosophical Transactions of the Royal Society* found that Mauritian women who performed religious rituals after an anxiety-inducing situation were approximately half as anxious as those who simply sat and relaxed. The precise, repetitive actions of ritual satisfy the brain's need for order by providing dependable sensory input against a background of unpredictability.

It creates transitions. Rituals mark the line between what was and what is: child and adult, single and married, living and dead, old year and new year. These transitions are psychologically real, and rituals make them socially real by enacting them publicly and collectively. They give the community the chance to acknowledge and witness a change, and they give the individual the felt sense of having crossed a threshold.

It generates belonging. Through synchronized movement, collective vocalization, shared symbolic action, and the shared experience of ordeal, ritual creates the neurochemical conditions for social bonding. It turns individuals into groups, strangers into community members, and groups into something that functions with a degree of coherence and trust that would take much longer to build through ordinary social interaction.

It manages mortality. Ritual embeds the individual in a narrative and a community that extends beyond any individual life. In doing so, it makes death less isolating, not necessarily less painful, but less meaningless.

None of these functions require supernatural belief to operate. The haka doesn't require belief in any particular theology to create the felt experience of unified purpose among the men performing it, and the felt experience of awe among those watching. The funeral ritual doesn't require belief in an afterlife to help the bereaved process grief in community. The concert audience singing in unison doesn't require doctrinal commitment to feel the endorphin warmth of shared vocalization.

Religion, across human history and across every culture yet studied, has been the primary institution for developing, transmitting, and maintaining ritual technology. This is one of its most important contributions to human social life. It deserves acknowledgment as such, regardless of theological commitments.

The Accent Speaks in Every Tongue

Every culture on earth develops rituals, just as every culture on earth develops an accent. The specific forms differ so widely that the underlying commonality can be difficult to see. The Māori haka and the Catholic mass aren't the same thing. The fire-walk in Mauritius and the graduation ceremony at a North American university aren't the same thing.

But they all use the same mechanisms: synchronized action, shared attention, embodied symbolic meaning, the marking of significance through repeated form. They all serve the same functions: bonding the group, managing uncertainty, marking transitions, creating meaning, and managing the terror of mortality. The words differ. The purpose doesn't.

Understanding this doesn't diminish religious ritual. It should increase appreciation for what the major religious traditions have developed over centuries: systems of ritual that build large-scale cooperation, manage the full range of human grief and joy, create communities of genuine mutual obligation, and do so in ways that are reliably effective across vastly different contexts.

What the science adds is the ability to say why it works. That makes it possible to extend the same benefits more broadly, to people who can't or won't access them through religious institutions, and to understand what's being lost when community rituals of any kind decline.

Practical Reflection

Think of a ritual in your own life. It doesn't have to be religious. It might be a family tradition, something you do at the same time each year, a practice that marks the beginning or end of something, a way your family or team or community comes together in a specific form.

Consider what it does. Notice whether it creates a sense of belonging that's different from ordinary social time. Notice whether it marks time in a way that makes the time feel meaningful. Notice whether it manages something, grief, anxiety, transition, celebration, in a way that ordinary experience doesn't.

You don't need to call it sacred for it to be doing sacred work. The sacred, in this framework, isn't a theological category. It's a functional one. It names the experiences and practices through which humans bond deeply, mark meaning, manage mortality, and create communities capable of genuine care.

When a stadium sings together, something real is happening. When a family lights candles at the same time each week and says the same words they've said for generations, something real is happening. When thirty men in black stamp their feet and their voices rise and the crowd holds its breath, something real is happening.

The same thing, differently accented, is happening every Friday at the mosque, every Saturday at the synagogue, every Sunday at the church.

And every time it happens, the social brain is doing what it's always done: binding people together around shared meaning, so that the work of living in community, which is the only way humans have ever survived, can go on.

Consider: Think of a ritual, secular or religious, that you have participated in that created a strong sense of belonging or meaning. What structural features of that ritual, its repetition, its synchrony, its marking of a transition, do you think were responsible for that effect?

Chapter 7

Sacred Spaces and Awe

The first thing you notice is the cold. Even in summer, the stone holds the chill of centuries. You step through the doorway and the heat of the street vanishes behind you. Then the light changes. Outside it was flat and bright, bouncing off pavement and car windows. Here it arrives in colored columns: blue from a window depicting the Virgin, amber from a scene of the disciples, deep red pooling on the floor near your feet like the shadow of a flame. Your eyes follow the columns upward, and the ceiling is so far away that it feels less like architecture and more like sky.

You're standing inside the nave of Chartres Cathedral in northern France, a building begun in the twelfth century and still standing a thousand years later with most of its original stained glass intact. Whether you were raised Catholic, Protestant, Muslim, Jewish, agnostic, or entirely without religion doesn't matter at this moment. Something has happened. The noise in your head has quieted. Your shoulders have dropped. You're looking up, which isn't how you normally walk through the world, and something about the act of looking up has loosened something inside you.

This feeling has a name. There is a neuroscience to it. It has measurable effects on your body and on how you'll behave toward other people in the hours that follow. And the remarkable thing is that the building doesn't care whether you believe in the god it was built for. The feeling arrives anyway.

That's what this chapter is about.

The Architecture of the Numinous

Every major religious tradition in the world has developed sacred architecture, and every one of those architectural traditions uses the same small set of techniques. This convergence isn't coincidence. These techniques work because of how human perception and emotion are structured, and they were discovered not by scientists but by builders and priests over thousands of years of practice.

The first technique is verticality. Cathedrals, mosques with minarets, Hindu temples with their steeply tiered towers called shikharas, Buddhist stupas, and ancient Egyptian obelisks all do the same thing: they pull the eye upward. When something is very tall and you're small relative to it, a specific set of feelings arises. Your body registers its own smallness. Your ordinary sense of self as the center of things is briefly suspended. You feel, even if only for a moment, like a small figure in a very large world.

This isn't accidental design. The builders of Chartres raised those vaults to 37 meters not because the liturgy required it but because height does something to the people inside. The same logic applies to the great mosques: the dome of the Süleymaniye in Istanbul rises 53 meters above the prayer hall floor. The gopuram gateway towers of the Brihadeeswarar Temple in Tamil Nadu soar to 66 meters. The proportions differ, the decorations are entirely distinct, the theologies are incompatible in many respects. But the experience they engineer begins with the same physiological fact: you look up, and you feel small.

The second technique is controlled light. Sacred spaces across traditions manipulate light in ways that ordinary buildings don't. Stained glass filters daylight into color, so that the mundane act of walking through a doorway transforms the quality of light around you. Gothic cathedrals fill the interior with moving, colored light that changes over the course of the day as the sun moves. The Great Mosque of Córdoba achieves a different but related effect through its forest of double arches, creating zones of light and shadow that make the vast interior feel simultaneously ordered and mysterious. Hindu temples often proceed from outer courts that are brightly lit toward inner sanctuaries that are deliberately dim, the divine presence approached through increasing darkness until the innermost chamber, the garbhagriha or "womb chamber," is almost entirely dark and illuminated only by oil lamps.

The psychological logic is the same in all of these cases: by controlling light, the sacred space signals that you've crossed a threshold. This isn't the ordinary world. Something different is possible.

The third technique is acoustic design. Religious spaces are among the longest-reverberating acoustic environments in the world. The typical reverb time in a gothic cathedral is four to eight seconds, meaning that a sound continues to echo for four to eight seconds after it stops being produced. The effect on music or chanting is transformative: notes of successive measures blend together, harmonics accumulate, and voices that are merely adequate in a dry acoustic environment seem to soar and envelop. The architecture does work that no individual singer or musician can do alone.

Researchers at the University of Salford have studied the acoustics of prehistoric caves and megalithic monuments and found that sites such as Stonehenge and Lascaux, the painted cave in France, appear to have been acoustically optimized for ritual use. The places where cave paintings were concentrated are often the places with the highest resonance. The implication is that the relationship between acoustic experience and spiritual practice may be as old as human symbolic thought itself.

The fourth technique is the managed transition. Sacred spaces across traditions make the entry deliberate. You remove your shoes before entering a mosque or a Hindu temple. You dip your fingers in holy water entering a Catholic church. You pause at a gate, the torii in Japanese Shinto, the lychgate of an English country church, the carved entrance porch of a Thai Buddhist wat. You wash your hands and face before Islamic prayer. These transitions aren't merely hygienic or logistical. They tell your body that you're moving from one kind of space to another. The act of preparation creates a psychological expectation that what follows will be different from what preceded it.

What all four of these techniques share is that they address the whole person: the eye, the ear, the skin, the body's sense of its own position in space. Religion, at the level of built environment, is an embodied technology. It works not primarily through argument or doctrine but through sensation.

Rudolf Otto and the "Wholly Other"

In 1917, a German theologian named Rudolf Otto published a book called *Das Heilige*, translated into English as *The Idea of the Holy*. Otto wasn't interested in theology in the conventional sense. He was interested in a specific quality of experience that he believed lay beneath all theology, all doctrine, all ritual. He called this experience the "numinous" (from the Latin *numen*, meaning divine will or presence).

The numinous, Otto argued, is the experience of encountering something wholly other: something that doesn't fit into any existing category of human understanding, something vast and strange and incomprehensible that nevertheless makes a powerful demand on one's attention and feeling. He described it using the phrase "mysterium tremendum et fascinans," roughly: "the mystery that is both tremendous (overpowering and awe-ful) and fascinating (captivating and attractive)."

Each part of this phrase matters. The mysterium is the quality of otherness: the feeling that you're in the presence of something that lies outside ordinary experience, something you can't reduce to familiar concepts. The tremendum is the element of power and overwhelming force: the sense of being very small before something very large, a kind of reverent fear that isn't exactly terror but shares something with it. The fascinans is the paradox: despite the overwhelming quality of the experience, you don't want to look away. You're drawn toward it. It promises something, though you can't name what.

Otto was writing as a theologian, and he believed the numinous pointed toward God. But he was careful to say that the numinous experience is prior to any theological interpretation. You feel it first. You explain it afterward, and your explanation depends on the tradition you inhabit. The person standing in Chartres Cathedral feels the numinous and says it's the presence of God. The person standing at the rim of the Grand Canyon feels the numinous and says it's nature. The person at a symphony concert feels it and says it's the sublime power of art. Otto's point was that the underlying experience is the same. Only the explanation differs.

This is, really, the distinction this book has been building toward: morality as the language, religion as the accent. The experience of the numinous is a word in that language. Every tradition has its own accent for pronouncing it, its own preferred context for invoking it, its own story about what causes it. But the experience itself belongs to the species, not to any particular faith.

Dacher Keltner and the Science of Awe

Rudolf Otto described the numinous from the inside, from the perspective of someone trying to understand a specific quality of experience. About a century later, researchers at the University of California Berkeley began studying the same experience from the outside, using the tools of experimental psychology.

Dacher Keltner, a professor of psychology and Faculty Director of the Greater Good Science Center at Berkeley, became the leading researcher in what has come to be called the science of awe. His working definition is precise: awe is "an emotional response to perceptually vast stimuli that transcend current frames of reference." It arises when you encounter something so large, strange, or powerful that your existing mental frameworks can't process it, and you're forced to expand your understanding or simply hold the experience in temporary suspension.

The key study connecting awe to moral behavior was led by Paul Piff at the University of California, Irvine, with Keltner as senior author, and published in 2015 in the *Journal of Personality and Social Psychology*. Piff, Keltner, and colleagues designed five separate experiments with a total of over 2,000 participants. The central finding was consistent across all five: people who experienced awe became measurably more generous, more ethical, and more cooperative.

One of the experiments is particularly vivid. Participants were brought to a grove of towering eucalyptus trees on the Berkeley campus and asked to look up at the trees. A control group was asked to look at a tall building. The two groups were then exposed to a minor accident (someone nearby dropped a container of pens), and researchers measured how likely participants were to help pick them up. The awe group helped significantly more. They were also more likely to endorse prosocial values and less likely to express a sense of entitlement.

The mechanism, Keltner's team found, is what they called the "small self" effect. Awe makes you feel smaller. Not humiliated or diminished, but appropriately small in the context of something much larger than yourself. That sense of appropriate smallness has a consistent downstream effect: when the self is quieted, concern for others expands. The ego that's usually busy protecting and promoting itself steps back, and something that functions like genuine generosity takes its place.

Keltner has also noted that awe activates the vagus nerve, which governs much of the parasympathetic nervous system. Even brief encounters with vast stimuli reduce inflammatory markers in the blood and promote heart health. The feeling that believers describe as the presence of God or the touch of the divine, whatever its ultimate cause, produces measurable physical benefits.

What's most striking about this research is what it implies about why religions have always worked so hard to generate awe. Every major tradition has invested enormous resources in creating the conditions for this experience: cathedrals, mosques, temples, music, incense, ritual movement, vast cosmic narratives. They weren't doing this because someone had read a psychology paper. They were doing it because they had observed, over centuries, that something happens to people in the presence of the overwhelming and the vast. People become better. They become more willing to sacrifice for others, more aware of their connection to something larger than their own interests. Awe is a social technology, and religion is, among other things, a technology for reliably producing it.

Religion didn't discover awe. It learned to guarantee it.

Julio Bermudez and the Biometric Cathedral

The idea that sacred spaces produce measurable physiological effects different from those of secular spaces received scientific confirmation from an unusual source: an architect.

Julio Bermudez is a professor at the School of Architecture at the Catholic University of America in Washington, D.C. His research question was simple but almost no one had tried to answer it rigorously: does being inside a sacred building change your brain and body in ways that a secular building doesn't?

To find out, Bermudez and his team recruited thirty devout Roman Catholic participants and had each of them visit two buildings on separate days: the Basilica of the National Shrine of the Immaculate Conception in Washington, D.C. (one of the largest Catholic churches in North America), and Union Station, also in Washington, which is architecturally grand by the standards of secular buildings. Participants wore mobile EEG headsets to record brain wave activity and biosensors measuring heart rate, blood pressure, and skin conductance. The researchers collected data at several predetermined stopping points in each building and supplemented the physiological measurements with detailed questionnaires about subjective experience.

The findings were striking. At the Basilica, participants showed increased gamma wave activity across the brain. Gamma waves are associated with high-level cognitive integration: the brain binding disparate pieces of sensory and emotional information into a unified whole. They're also associated with the meditative states that experienced meditators work hard to achieve through internal practice. At the Basilica, the space itself appeared to be inducing them.

There was also evidence of disruption to the default mode network, the brain system most active when we're mind-wandering, ruminating, and thinking about ourselves and our concerns. It's really the neural foundation of the self-absorbed chattering mind. In sacred spaces, this network showed signs of being suppressed. The architecture was doing to the brain what meditation teachers spend years trying to teach students to do for themselves: quieting the self-referential noise.

Bermudez's interpretation was that sacred architecture functions as an "external method" for inducing contemplative states. In religious traditions, the practitioner works inward through prayer, meditation, and spiritual discipline to achieve a state of focused, ego-quieted presence. What the architecture does is approach from the outside, using sensory overwhelming to create the conditions for that same state, regardless of whether the visitor has done any of the internal work.

This matters because the benefits of the contemplative state aren't available only to advanced spiritual practitioners. They're available, at least in part, to anyone who walks through certain kinds of doors.

Music and the Acoustic Sublime

One of the things most consistently reported by people in sacred spaces is that the music sounds different. Not different in the sense of different songs, but more enveloping, more transcendent, more moving than the same music would be in a regular room.

This isn't subjective impression. It's a physical cause.

A 2022 study in *Frontiers in Psychology* measured the acoustic properties of sacred architectural spaces and examined how those signatures affected the perceived transcendence of music. The researchers played both liturgical and secular music under two conditions: recorded in a standard, acoustically dry studio environment, and processed through the acoustic profile of a traditional church space with its characteristic long reverberation.

The result was clear: church acoustics increased the perceived transcendence of the music regardless of whether the music itself was liturgical or secular. A Bach chorale and a plainly secular piece both sounded more transcendent, more expansive, more spiritually moving when experienced through those acoustics than in a dry space. The architecture was amplifying a quality in the music that had nothing to do with the theology of the composer.

The long reverberation of a cathedral, typically four to eight seconds compared to less than one second in a typical living room, means that sounds accumulate. Notes sustain. Harmonics overlap. The acoustic environment wraps itself around the listener in a way that a dry space can't. When a congregation sings a hymn in a cathedral, the music is substantially augmented by the architecture: the building is, in effect, a co-composer.

This helps explain why so many religious traditions have developed musical forms adapted to sacred acoustic environments. Gregorian chant is designed for the long reverb of a stone church: the slow, sustained notes and simple melodic lines would sound thin in a dry room but are profoundly beautiful in a cathedral because the building fills out the sound. The muezzin's call to prayer, the adhan, is designed to carry in open air, but its recitation inside a mosque, with a resonant dome, takes on an entirely different quality.

Religion discovered long before the physics of acoustics was understood that certain shapes of space do certain things to sound, and that those acoustic qualities change what people feel. The sacred is partly engineered.

Awe in the Natural World: What Veterans and At-Risk Youth Taught Us

Not all awe happens in buildings. Craig Anderson, who completed his doctoral work at Berkeley with Dacher Keltner and is now a professor at HEC Paris, has spent years studying what happens when people encounter awe in the natural world.

The strongest evidence comes from a study he and Keltner conducted with two groups whose circumstances were, in different ways, psychologically severe: military veterans with combat exposure and symptoms consistent with post-traumatic stress disorder, and young people from underserved communities in the San Francisco Bay Area who had experienced high levels of community violence.

Both groups participated in white-water rafting trips on the South Fork of the American River in California. The experience was physically challenging, visually striking, and for many participants genuinely overwhelming in scale. Before and after the trips, and again one week later, participants were assessed for well-being, stress, social connectedness, and post-traumatic stress symptoms.

The results were significant for both groups. But Anderson and Keltner were particularly interested in which positive emotion was most responsible for the improvements. They measured several: joy, contentment, love, pride, and awe. Among all of them, awe alone was the unique predictor of improved well-being and reduced symptom severity one week after the experience. Not joy, not contentment, not love. Awe.

The veterans reported better sleep and improved relationships with family members. They reported a decreased sense of threat and hypervigilance. The youth reported greater community belonging and reduced emotional reactivity. All of these improvements were predicted by the degree to which participants had experienced awe during the trip.

Anderson's interpretation, consistent with Keltner's "small self" research, is that awe recalibrates the nervous system's sense of proportion. In post-traumatic stress, the nervous system has been tuned to treat ordinary environments as dangerous and ordinary social interactions as threats. Awe interrupts this tuning by confronting the nervous system with something genuinely, clearly vast. When the self temporarily steps back, the self's suffering also recedes into perspective, and the nervous system has an opportunity to reset.

This research matters for our larger argument because it demonstrates that the therapeutic and prosocial effects of the numinous don't require a religious framework. These veterans weren't attending a religious service. They weren't invoking the name of God. They were on a river in California, surrounded by mountains and rapids. The awe they experienced was entirely secular in its content. Its effects, however, were the same effects that religious traditions have claimed for centuries of sacred experience: restoration, belonging, connection, healing.

The Same Feeling, Different Names

Consider the range of spaces and experiences that reliably produce awe, the numinous, the small self, the mysterium tremendum. The list is longer than it might first appear.

A cathedral: the vaulted ceiling, the colored light, the echoing silence. A mosque with a great dome, the geometry perfect, the calligraphy running around the walls in a language you may or may not be able to read. A Hindu temple, dense with sculpture, the air thick with incense and the sound of bells. A Buddhist shrine, spare and still, the statue of the seated figure radiating a quality of calm that seems to push back against the noise in your own head.

Now the secular list: the Grand Canyon at sunrise, when the shadows shift across a mile of layered rock and the scale of geological time becomes viscerally real. A symphony orchestra at full power, the sound filling a concert hall so completely that you feel it in your chest. A stadium during a championship, fifty thousand people erupting simultaneously in a sound that seems to have a life beyond any of its component voices. A planetarium, the ceiling opening onto the Milky Way, the narrator's voice making the distances real in a way that the words "billion light-years" never quite do on their own. The Rothko Chapel in Houston, where fourteen paintings of deep, dark purple and black hang in a space designed to make them the only thing your attention can settle on, and where an inexplicable emotion arises that visitors struggle to name.

The physiological and psychological responses across all of these are, as far as researchers can measure, the same. Goosebumps (technically "piloerection"), which researchers have found to be a reliable physical marker of awe. A slowing of the breath. A sense of smallness experienced not as shame but as a form of relief. A desire to connect, to share the experience with whoever is nearby, to say simply: do you feel this too?

What differs is the story each tradition or context places on top of the experience. The cathedral says this feeling is the presence of God. The moral implications are particular to the faith that built this space. The concert hall says you're feeling the power of human creativity and the strange magic of organized sound. The Grand Canyon says you're feeling the weight of geological time and your own smallness within it. The stadium says you're feeling the belonging of tribal identity and the joy of collective achievement.

In the accent-and-language metaphor that has run through this book, awe is a word in the universal moral language. It's one of the most important words, because it consistently produces the same moral effect: it makes us less selfish. But each tradition pronounces it differently, and the pronunciation shapes what the listener takes away. The cathedral's pronunciation is particularly powerful because it connects the experience of smallness directly to a moral framework, a specific set of obligations and commitments, a community of people who have made the same experience the center of their lives. This may be why religiously-framed awe so reliably generates prosocial behavior beyond even the baseline effects that secular awe produces.

But this isn't an argument that only the religious version counts. It's an argument that the experience itself is the thing, that the experience is available in many forms, and that any context that reliably generates awe is doing something that matters for human moral life.

What the Brain Does in a Sacred Space

The evidence from Bermudez's biometric research, Keltner's awe studies, the neuroscience of meditation, and the psychology of music and acoustic experience converges on a picture of what's actually happening in the brain and body during a deep experience in a sacred or awe-inducing space.

The parietal cortex, specifically the region that constructs our sense of where our body ends and the world begins, shows decreased activity. Newberg found this same parietal quieting in Franciscan nuns during deep prayer and in Buddhist monks during meditation. The experience of dissolving into something larger, of boundaries becoming permeable, has a specific neural correlate.

The default mode network shows reduced activity. The frontal lobes show increased activity. Gamma waves are elevated. Inflammatory markers in the blood decrease. Vagal tone increases.

Taken together, this profile describes a state of calm, focused attention with reduced self-preoccupation and increased integration of experience. It's a genuinely beneficial state, associated with reduced stress, reduced inflammation, improved emotional regulation, and the prosocial behaviors that come with a quieted ego.

Religion has been producing this state through architecture, music, ritual, and community for as long as we have evidence of human symbolic behavior. The sacred grove, the painted cave, the standing stones, the cathedral, the mosque are all, at one level, technologies for producing a beneficial state in the people who use them. The fact that science can now describe the state in neural and hormonal terms doesn't make it less real, any more than describing the chemistry of a kiss makes it less meaningful.

The feeling is real. The body's response is real. The prosocial effects are real. What varies is the story that different traditions tell about what produced the feeling. That story matters enormously to people inside each tradition, and this book has no interest in dismissing it. But the story isn't the only thing going on.

Seeking Awe as a Deliberate Practice

There's a practical question lurking in all of this research, and it's worth naming directly.

If awe produces measurable benefits, including increased generosity, reduced selfishness, improved health, reduced symptoms of traumatic stress, and a recalibration of the nervous system toward calm, then how often you experience awe isn't merely a philosophical or spiritual question. It has consequences for who you are as a person and for how you treat others.

Keltner's research identifies eight reliable sources of awe across cultures: the natural world, moral beauty (witnessing acts of courage or compassion), collective effervescence, music, visual design, spiritual and religious experience, the facts of life and death, and "big ideas," the feeling produced by encountering a thought or discovery that at its core changes how you see the world.

You don't need a cathedral. You don't need to believe in anything. You need to put yourself, with some regularity, in the presence of things that are genuinely larger than you are.

This isn't always easy in the structure of ordinary modern life. The environments in which most people spend most of their time, offices, shopping centers, television screens, the interior of cars, have been designed for efficiency and consumption rather than for the production of awe. They're acoustically flat, vertically uninspiring, informationally dense in ways that keep the default mode network very busy. You can spend an entire day in such environments and never once have the experience of looking up.

Religious communities have always known that this kind of environment produces a kind of spiritual and moral poverty, and that regular exposure to awe-inducing spaces is necessary for human flourishing. The sabbath, the Friday prayer, the Sunday service: these aren't simply theological obligations. They're scheduled encounters with the vast, regular recalibrations of the self's sense of proportion.

For those outside religious communities, the equivalent practice requires more intentionality: going outdoors into natural spaces with genuine scale, attending live music or theater, spending time in great buildings, looking at the night sky with attention, reading ideas that genuinely challenge your existing frameworks.

When was the last time you felt genuine awe? What triggered it? Did the feeling need a religious explanation to be meaningful? Almost certainly not. The feeling arrived, or it didn't, and if it did, you know it: something shifted. The noise in your head quieted. You were briefly, genuinely present to something larger than your own concerns.

Consider what it would mean to seek that experience deliberately, as a practice. Not because a theology demands it. Because the science suggests it's good for you, and because it consistently makes people behave better toward each other. That's reason enough.

A Note for Believers and Non-Believers Both

This chapter has tried to explain the experience of the sacred in terms that don't require any particular theological commitment. Some believers may find this unsatisfying. The experience in the cathedral, they might say, isn't merely a neural state. It's an encounter with God. And they're right that the science doesn't, and can't, prove otherwise. The science can describe what's happening in the body and the brain. It can't resolve the question of what is in the end causing it.

For those without religious faith, the research offers permission to take these experiences seriously without needing to package them in a theological framework. The feeling of the numinous isn't a delusion or a symptom of irrationality. It's a real experience with real effects, and it can be sought and cultivated for entirely secular reasons.

For everyone, the capacity for awe is one of the most important moral resources we have. It's the mechanism by which the self is reliably humbled and expanded, the closest thing that science has found to a reliable path from selfishness to generosity.

The cathedral built it into stone. The mosque built it into geometry. The temple built it into sculpture. The concert hall built it into acoustics. The mountain simply is it.

All of them, in the end, are pointing at the same experience. The story they tell about what produced it may differ. The feeling itself doesn't.

Chapter 8

Community: The Real Engine of Belonging

The calls started arriving on a Tuesday morning, within hours of the news spreading through the congregation. By Wednesday there was a sign-up sheet on the church's website. By Thursday there were casseroles on the doorstep, labeled in neat handwriting with reheating instructions. On Friday a neighbor from the church appeared with three hours of childcare, unasked and insistent. On Sunday two deacons drove the family to the service and sat with them in the pew.

The family's circumstances were as bad as circumstances can be: a sudden death, a spouse gone without warning, children confused and frightened, a house that felt wrong in every room. The grief was enormous and would take a long time to work through. But the family wasn't alone in it. The congregation arrived, not in a single overwhelming wave but in a steady, organized, practical stream. There was coordination happening somewhere, someone was keeping a list and making calls, but from inside the grief it simply felt like being held.

Now consider a different story, three states away. A woman is diagnosed with a serious illness and, the week after her diagnosis, finds an anonymous note in her apartment building's mailbox from a neighbor she barely knows: "I heard the news from Maria. I have Tuesdays free. Please let me help with groceries or anything you need. You don't have to manage this alone." Within days, a small group from the building has organized themselves: a rotating schedule of meals, a shared document for managing appointments, a group chat for practical coordination. No church, no theology, no institutional framework. Just neighbors who had built, slowly and without fanfare, the kind of trust that makes this kind of response possible.

These two stories are structurally identical. The mechanisms are the same: regular contact had built trust, trust had built a sense of mutual obligation, and mutual obligation produced action in a crisis. What differs is the infrastructure that made the regular contact possible. In one case it was a congregation with a building, a calendar, a weekly rhythm, and a shared set of commitments that gave members a reason to show up. In the other case it was a dense urban building where people had chosen, over time, to know each other.

This chapter is about what those two stories share, and what it means that the religious version has historically been far more common and far more scalable. It's also about what we lose, at a societal level, when we allow either kind of community to atrophy, and about what the science tells us would be required to build it back.

Robert Putnam and the Architecture of Civic Life

Robert Putnam is a political scientist at Harvard who has spent much of his career studying "social capital": the networks of trust, reciprocity, and mutual obligation that make communities function. His 2000 book *Bowling Alone* documented the long decline of civic participation in America across the second half of the twentieth century. His 2010 book *American Grace*, co-written with David Campbell, turned its focus to religion's role in what remains of American civic life.

The central finding of *American Grace* deserves to be quoted directly: roughly half of all social capital in America is religious. Putnam found that if you add up all the civic organizations in the country, the Rotary Clubs, the sports leagues, the garden clubs, the parent-teacher organizations, and place them in one pile, and then add up all the religious organizations in another, "those two piles are about equally high." Religion isn't a supplement to American civic life. It's approximately half of it.

Putnam's data also showed that religiously engaged Americans are markedly more likely than their secular counterparts to volunteer, give money to charity, donate blood, help a neighbor, and participate in local civic organizations. Religious Americans are up to twice as civically active as secular Americans on most measures.

The reflex reaction to these findings, among both secular and religious readers, is to explain them theologically: religious people are more charitable because their faith teaches them to be. But Putnam looked carefully at the data and found something more specific and more interesting.

The civic benefits of religious participation aren't primarily a product of belief. They're a product of belonging. The mechanism, Putnam found, is the social network formed within congregations. People who attend religious services regularly but have no close friends within their congregation don't show the same civic benefits as people who attend and have built real relationships there. The friendship is the active ingredient. The theology is the container that holds the friendship in place.

This finding has a somewhat humbling quality. For the theologian, it may seem to reduce something sacred to something sociological. But it can be read the other way: the power of friendship and mutual obligation isn't a lessening of the religious tradition. It's an argument that the tradition got something at its core right. Humans need each other, and the institutional form that has most reliably given people a reason to show up for each other, across generations and life transitions, has been the religious congregation. The theology may or may not be the point. The showing up is.

The Critical Question: What Is Actually Driving the Benefit?

In 2010, Chaeyoon Lim, then at the University of Wisconsin-Madison, and Robert Putnam published a paper in the American Sociological Review that went further than anything before in identifying the specific mechanism by which religion improves life satisfaction.

Lim and Putnam worked with the Faith Matters Survey, a large dataset of about 3,000 Americans, and set out to answer a straightforward question: among the many things that religious participation involves (prayer, belief in God, theological commitment, doctrinal knowledge, ritual observance, and social relationships), which ones actually predict life satisfaction?

The answer was unambiguous. It's the friendships. Specifically, it's having close friends within one's congregation.

People who attended religious services regularly and had a substantial number of close friends in their congregation were dramatically more likely to report being "extremely satisfied" with their lives. People who attended the same services with equal frequency but hadn't formed close friendships there didn't show the same effect. Private religious practice, prayer at home, reading scripture, personal devotional activity, showed virtually no life satisfaction benefit independent of the social component.

The theological beliefs of participants mattered very little once social relationships were accounted for. Whether someone prayed frequently or rarely, described themselves as very or moderately religious, or held orthodox or heterodox views: none of these were strong predictors of life satisfaction once the friendship variable was controlled for. What predicted life satisfaction was the answer to a simpler question: do you have close friends at your place of worship?

Lim and Putnam called this one of the most important findings of the study, because it specifies the mechanism in a way that has practical implications. You can't make people believe differently. You can design communities in ways that make friendship formation more likely. If friendship is what produces the benefit, then improving human well-being through community becomes a question of institutional design as much as theology.

For religious communities, this research argues for taking the relational aspects of congregational life as seriously as the theological ones. A congregation that has excellent preaching but leaves people feeling like strangers to one another is, by this measure, failing at something important. For secular communities, the same logic applies: if you want to produce the benefits of religious community without the religion, you need to produce the close friendships, and that requires the same things: regular meeting, shared purpose, mutual accountability, and enough time spent together that people become genuinely known to each other.

Tyler VanderWeele and the Epidemiology of Belonging

A body of evidence in public health epidemiology raises the stakes considerably. The question isn't just whether religious community makes people happier. The question is whether it keeps them alive.

Tyler VanderWeele, a professor of epidemiology at the Harvard T.H. Chan School of Public Health and Director of Harvard's Human Flourishing Program, has spent much of the last decade working with large-scale longitudinal datasets to understand the relationship between religious participation and health outcomes. His findings are striking.

His flagship study was published in JAMA Internal Medicine in 2016. It followed 74,534 women enrolled in the Nurses' Health Study over sixteen years. The question was simple: does attending religious services predict survival?

The answer was yes, substantially. Women who attended religious services more than once per week had a 33 percent lower risk of dying during the follow-up period compared to women who never attended. One-third lower mortality, over sixteen years, for the highest-attendance group. The effect remained significant even after controlling for a wide range of confounding factors including health status at baseline, education, income, depression, and prior social engagement.

A 2020 study, following three large cohorts of both men and women across the full range of adulthood, found a 26 percent lower all-cause mortality for weekly attenders compared to those who never attended. The same study found 34 percent lower heavy drinking, 29 percent lower smoking, and significant reductions in depression, anxiety, hopelessness, and loneliness. The benefits showed up consistently across different demographic groups and study populations. These sub-statistics are drawn from that 2020 VanderWeele publication. Readers seeking to verify individual figures should consult that source directly, as specific estimates can vary depending on which cohort and outcome are being examined.

A third finding warrants particular attention: VanderWeele's work on what epidemiologists call "deaths of despair": suicide, drug overdose, and alcohol poisoning. Using data from the Nurses' Health Study and the Health Professionals Follow-Up Study, a combined sample of over 100,000 people, he and his colleagues found that regular religious service attenders were significantly less likely to die from any of these causes.

The phrase "deaths of despair" was coined by economists Anne Case and Angus Deaton to describe a pattern they identified in mortality data: a rising wave of preventable deaths in middle-aged Americans driven not by physical disease but by social and psychological suffering. Opioid overdoses, alcohol-related liver disease, suicide: all have risen sharply in recent decades, particularly in communities where traditional social structures, including employment, civic organizations, and religious community, have declined. VanderWeele's finding that religious attendance is protective against deaths of despair isn't merely a statistical observation. It describes a real human process: community and shared meaning make people less likely to be consumed by the kinds of despair that lead to self-destruction.

The mechanisms VanderWeele identifies are social and behavioral rather than supernatural. Social support explains about 23 percent of the mortality reduction. Reduced depression, reduced smoking, and optimism explain additional portions. No single mechanism accounts for the full effect, and multiple pathways operate simultaneously. All of them are comprehensible in entirely secular terms.

VanderWeele notes that the strongest predictors of health are the communal aspects of religious participation: attending services and the social integration that follows. Private religious practice doesn't show the same mortality associations. What protects people is showing up, and the relationships that form because they do.

High-Trust Networks and the Community-as-Infrastructure

The social capital generated by religious congregations has a particular quality worth examining: it's unusually high in trust.

Trust isn't a vague feeling. It's a specific confidence that the other person will behave predictably and won't exploit your vulnerability. In ordinary social settings, trust builds slowly, through repeated interactions, demonstrated reliability, the gradual accumulation of evidence that someone is who they say they're. In a congregation, a set of mechanisms accelerates this process in ways that secular communities struggle to replicate.

The first mechanism is the shared moral framework. Members share explicit commitments about how to treat others, publicly professed, regularly reinforced through services and teaching, and accountable to God as well as to the community. This creates a basis for trusting a stranger that goes beyond statistical expectation: when you share a moral framework with someone, you can predict their behavior before you know them personally.

The second mechanism is the regularity of contact. A congregation that meets weekly means its members see each other roughly fifty times a year, often for extended periods. Most adult friendships are maintained through far less frequent contact, which means relationships in congregations build and sustain themselves more easily than those in most secular contexts.

The third mechanism is mutual obligation that extends to the practical. Congregations aren't merely social clubs. In their historical form, they're mutual aid societies. They organize support for members in crisis, care for the sick and elderly, and maintain networks of help that function regardless of what the state provides. Faith communities are among the largest non-governmental providers of social services in the United States: food banks, homeless shelters, addiction recovery programs, disaster relief, mental health support.

A 2024 review in the public health literature examined 32 partnerships between faith communities and mental health services. The conclusion was that faith communities serve as "de facto providers of mental health care" and "gatekeepers to the formal mental health care system," possessing "greater familiarity and understanding of an individual's life history and context" than professional services are typically able to develop. The person in the pew knows that the congregant in the next row was laid off last year, went through a divorce two years ago, struggles with anxiety, has a daughter who is ill. A therapist who sees someone once a week doesn't necessarily have access to this context.

This is the congregation as high-trust network. It functions not because everyone in it is unusually virtuous, but because the institutional structure creates conditions in which trust, obligation, and practical support are organized and sustained.

Sunday Assembly: The Secular Congregation Experiment

If the benefits of religious community flow through the social structure rather than the theology, then it should be possible to build secular communities that produce comparable benefits. This is precisely what the Sunday Assembly set out to test.

The Sunday Assembly was founded in 2013 in London by two comedians, Sanderson Jones and Pippa Evans, who had both grown up in religious households and found themselves missing something after leaving the faith. What they missed, they concluded, wasn't the theology. It was the gathering: the weekly rhythm of showing up with the same people, singing together, hearing something worth thinking about, connecting over coffee afterward. They decided to replicate the structure without the theology.

A Sunday Assembly service looks, structurally, much like a church service. There's collective singing (secular songs, usually popular music). There's a talk from a speaker on some aspect of living well. There's a moment of guided reflection. There's a social gathering before and after. The motto of the Assembly is "Live Better, Help Often, Wonder More." There's no liturgy, no creed, no theological doctrine of any kind.

The research on the Sunday Assembly is limited but suggestive. A longitudinal study by Price and Launay tracked 92 Sunday Assembly members over time and found that attending services improved composite well-being measures. The most important factor wasn't the formal service itself but the informal socializing before and after. The friendships, again, were the active ingredient.

A 2021 study published in PLOS ONE by Charles and colleagues compared Sunday Assembly attendees directly with Christian church attendees, measuring social bonding and affect before and after services. Both groups showed comparable increases in social bonding from before to after the ritual gathering. The Sunday Assembly group went from a mean social bonding score of 4.27 before the service to 4.96 after. The change in the church group wasn't significantly different in magnitude. Both groups also showed increased positive affect and decreased negative affect. The researchers concluded that "secular rituals might play a similar role to religious ones in building feelings of social connection and boosting positive affect."

This is an important finding. It suggests that the community mechanism, the thing that accounts for religion's documented health and well-being benefits, can in principle be replicated outside a religious framework. But there's a crucial qualifier: it works only when the secular community provides the same structural elements. Regular meeting. Collective ritual. Shared purpose. Genuine friendship formation over time. The Sunday Assembly succeeds not because it's religious but because it's rigorously communal, and those aren't the same thing.

The qualifier matters because it identifies what's hard about the secular alternative. You can't replicate the benefits of a congregation by simply telling people to spend more time with their neighbors. The congregation's power comes from its institutional structure: the fixed weekly meeting time, the reason for people to show up, the rituals that mark the gathering as distinct from ordinary socializing, and the moral framework that gives the community a shared sense of purpose and accountability. Building these things without the theological scaffolding that has historically supported them requires deliberate effort and institutional design. Most secular communities aren't designed with this kind of intentionality. As a result, they tend to produce weaker versions of the same benefits, or they dissolve before the deep friendships have had time to form.

The Loneliness Epidemic

The conversation about what religious community does for human beings has acquired particular urgency because the alternative, a society without strong community structures, is becoming measurable in its effects.

In 2023, Vivek Murthy, then the Surgeon General of the United States, issued a formal advisory on what he called "our epidemic of loneliness and isolation." The findings were alarming. Approximately half of American adults report experiencing loneliness, as measured by the UCLA Loneliness Scale, which captures a broad range of social disconnection. A separate Gallup survey found that one in three adults reports feeling lonely, using a single direct question about the experience. One in four lacks adequate social and emotional support. From 2003 to 2020, the time Americans spent alone increased, while the time they spent in face-to-face social engagement decreased.

The health consequences of loneliness aren't metaphorical. Loneliness increases the risk of premature death by an amount roughly equivalent to smoking fifteen cigarettes a day. Social isolation is associated with a 50 percent increased risk of dementia, a 29 percent increased risk of heart disease, and a 32 percent increased risk of stroke. The economic costs are also substantial: stress-related absenteeism attributed to loneliness costs American employers an estimated 154 billion dollars annually.

In 2025, the World Health Organization published findings from its Commission on Social Connection, which found that one in six people globally is affected by loneliness, contributing to an estimated 871,000 deaths per year, nearly 100 deaths every hour, worldwide. The commission found that social connection reduces inflammation, lowers the risk of serious health conditions, supports mental health, and helps prevent early death.

These are the costs of the absence of what religious communities have historically provided. The research doesn't suggest that the solution is universal religious conversion. But the decline of religious community participation in Western societies, without an adequate secular replacement, is contributing to the loneliness crisis in a way that shouldn't be ignored.

Putnam's research showed that religious community generates roughly half of all social capital in America. As that resource has declined, with rising numbers of Americans describing themselves as religiously unaffiliated (now roughly a third of American adults and rising), the loneliness numbers have moved in the corresponding direction. This isn't a coincidence to be dismissed. It's the structural consequence of removing, at scale, the most important institution for regular community building that most people have had access to, without replacing it with anything equally reliable or equally capable of generating the depth of social connection necessary for human health and flourishing.

This observation isn't an argument for religion. It's an argument for the function that religion has served, and for the urgency of building secular alternatives that serve it equally well. The fact that we haven't yet done so at comparable scale is one of the more significant unresolved challenges of secular modernity.

What Makes a Community a Community

The research points toward a set of structural features necessary for community to produce the benefits described. It's worth naming them explicitly, because they clarify what the secular world would need to build.

The first is regularity. The benefits of community compound over time, as repeated contact builds trust and repeated acts of mutual support build obligation. A community that meets occasionally isn't the same as one that meets weekly. The weekly rhythm of religious gathering isn't incidental to its effectiveness. It's part of the mechanism.

The second is shared purpose. Communities organized around a clear purpose that members genuinely care about, a mission larger than individual socialization, generate stronger bonds than purely social organizations. The religious congregation's purpose, to worship, to practice, to support each other in living according to shared values, gives every gathering a reason beyond the merely pleasant. It also generates the moral vocabulary that makes mutual accountability possible.

The third is ritual. Shared rituals, whether religious or secular, mark the gathering as distinct from ordinary social interaction. They create a threshold between everyday life and communal life. They engage the body as well as the mind, and as the research on synchronized movement, collective singing, and shared practice shows, the bodily engagement isn't incidental. Ritual produces feelings of belonging and social bonding more reliably than conversation alone.

The fourth is genuine friendship formation. The benefits don't come from attending a community. They come from knowing and being known within it. This requires the community to be small enough for people to be recognizable to each other, or to have smaller structures within it, small groups, fellowships, study circles, where genuine friendship can form. The mega-church with thousands of seats but no structure for real relationships may generate the experience of belonging without the substance of it.

The fifth, perhaps the most difficult to engineer in secular contexts, is duration. Religious communities endure across decades and generations. They're present at births and deaths, at marriages and divorces, at professional failures and health crises. They're there not because a member has asked for help but because the community has a standing commitment to be present. This durational quality is what transforms a social club into a genuine mutual aid society. It's also what's most difficult to replicate in cultures organized around mobility, individual choice, and the constant renegotiation of commitments.

Community as a Word in the Moral Language

The metaphor of morality as language and religion as accent runs through this book. If awe, as the previous chapter argued, is a word in the universal moral language, then community is perhaps the most important word in the entire vocabulary.

Every major religious tradition has a specific word or concept for the gathered community of the faithful, and each carries weight that reflects how central the concept is to the tradition. The parish, the congregation, the ekklesia (Greek for "church," literally an assembly of those called out). The sangha, the Buddhist community of monks, nuns, and lay practitioners. The ummah, the global community of Muslims. The minyan, the quorum of ten Jewish adults required for communal prayer. The satsang, the community of truth-seekers in Hindu and Sikh traditions.

These words aren't just labels for groups of people who happen to share the same building on Sundays. They're theological and ethical concepts. They describe what people owe to each other, how they should regard each other, what responsibilities and privileges membership confers. The community isn't a means to other ends. In most traditions, it's itself constitutive of the religious life. You can't be fully religious alone. You need the others.

The secular world hasn't yet found equally powerful words or concepts for this dimension of human experience. The closest equivalents, "my community," "my network," "my people," tend to be thinner and more contingent than their religious counterparts. They describe whom you happen to be connected to rather than whom you're obligated to. The difference matters enormously in a crisis, when practical support depends not on who you know but on who is obligated to show up.

The universal moral language includes this concept: the need for humans to live in structures of mutual obligation, regular contact, and shared commitment that go beyond the transactional. Every tradition pronounces it in its own accent: the parish, the sangha, the ummah, the minyan, the neighborhood mutual aid network, the running club that becomes a family. The accent varies. The underlying need doesn't. Humans can't flourish alone, and the research has been unambiguous on this point for decades.

What the Ledger Also Shows

The full accounting of what secular and religious societies have each achieved and forfeited belongs to the next chapter.

A Practical Reflection

It's worth pausing here for a moment of personal inventory, not as an exercise in self-criticism but as a genuine assessment of your own situation.

Think about the people in your life who constitute your community: not your acquaintances or professional contacts, but the people who know your circumstances, who have seen you in difficulty, who have some sense of who you actually are beneath the version of yourself that you present to the world. Who would bring you a meal in a crisis? Who would show up at your door, unasked, in the week after a serious diagnosis or a death?

For many people in contemporary Western societies, this list is smaller than they'd like it to be. This isn't a personal failing. It's a structural one. The environments in which most people live their adult lives weren't designed to produce these relationships. The office, the apartment building, the neighborhood of people who commute elsewhere during the day, the suburb organized around private property and private life: none of these are structurally optimized for the kind of mutual knowledge and regular contact that produce the depth of community the research describes.

If your list is small, that's not a theological problem. You don't need to find a god to find a community. But it may be a structural problem: insufficient regular, shared, purposeful gathering with the same group of people over time. The research is clear about what changes it: showing up, regularly, with the same people, around something you share a commitment to, for long enough that real friendship forms.

That might look like a religious congregation. For many people it does, and the evidence suggests the religious congregation does this best when it takes the relational dimension as seriously as the theological one. But it might also look like a Sunday Assembly or a humanist community. A mutual aid network in a neighborhood, organized with genuine discipline and continuity. A volunteer fire department. A community garden with real commitment. A co-housing development whose members have deliberately built the structures of shared life. A running club that has evolved into something more than exercise.

What these all share with each other, and with religious congregations at their best, is the willingness to treat community as a serious project rather than a pleasant accident. The communities that produce the benefits described in this chapter don't happen spontaneously. They're built, maintained, and protected by people who understand that the alternative is loneliness, and that loneliness is, as the research shows, genuinely dangerous.

The question to sit with isn't theological. It's structural. What regular, shared, purposeful gathering exists in your life, or could exist, that would produce the kinds of relationships that would still be there in a crisis? What would it take to build it, if it's not already there?

That's not a question about God. It's a question about how you want to live, and about what you want available to you when the world becomes what it sometimes becomes. The answer isn't simply a matter of personal preference. It's, as decades of careful research makes clear, a matter of health, longevity, and the quality of the moral life.

The congregation discovered this first. The epidemiologists confirmed it later. Both are pointing at the same truth: you need people who will bring you a casserole. The task of building a life in which such people exist, whatever institutional form that takes, is one of the most important projects available to any human being.

PART III

MORALITY WITHOUT ABSOLUTES

Chapter 9

Moral Lives Beyond Faith

Ingrid is a retired nurse who lives in a small flat in Aarhus, Denmark's second city, a few streets back from the harbour. She is seventy-one. She raised two children, worked for thirty-eight years in the municipal hospital system, and now spends her mornings walking along the canal with a neighbour's dog, a black Labrador named Søren. On Sundays she reads, meets a friend for coffee, and sometimes visits her grandchildren. She doesn't go to church. She hasn't been to a service since her own confirmation at fourteen, which she remembers mostly for the white dress and the cake afterward.

When Phil Zuckerman, an American sociologist, sat across from her in her kitchen during his fourteen months of fieldwork in Scandinavia, he asked her what she believed about God. She paused, stirred her coffee, and said something he heard, in various forms, from dozens of other Danes and Swedes: she didn't think about it much. She supposed there might be something, but she didn't know what, and it didn't especially matter. What mattered, she said, was treating people decently. Helping when you could. Not making a fuss about it.

Zuckerman asked her where that moral sense came from, if not from religion. Ingrid looked mildly puzzled by the question, as though he had asked her where she learned to breathe. "From my parents," she said. "From school. From working with sick people for so many years. You learn what matters."

Ingrid isn't unusual. She is, by the data Zuckerman collected, typical. Denmark is one of the least religious nations on Earth. On any given Sunday morning, the old Lutheran stone churches hold only a scattering of worshippers. Fewer than a quarter of self-identified Danish Christians believe in a personal God. Fewer than one in ten believe in hell. The theological content of Christianity, for most Danes, has become a cultural inheritance, a set of traditions and aesthetic associations, rather than a living commitment.

And yet by almost every measure social scientists use to assess how well a society is treating its people, Denmark ranks near the top of the world. Its violent crime rate is roughly one-fifth of the American rate. Its income gap between rich and poor is among the smallest of any wealthy nation. Its citizens report some of the highest levels of life satisfaction ever recorded. Its public institutions are trusted. Its children are, on most indicators, thriving.

Scandinavians didn't become moral when they found God. They remained moral when they quietly left.

How is this possible? If religion is the foundation of morality, if the fear of divine judgment or the love of God is what keeps human beings from cruelty and selfishness, then Aarhus should be troubled. It isn't. Ingrid should be adrift. She isn't. The question her life quietly asks is one of the most important questions in the science of human behaviour: where does morality come from when it doesn't come from religion?

This question isn't rhetorical, and it's not asked in a spirit of hostility toward faith. It's asked because the honest examination of evidence requires it. The chapters ahead will look carefully at what happens when religion harms, and at the ways religious communities have been indispensable partners in some of humanity's greatest moral achievements. None of that's lessened by also asking, with equal seriousness, whether morality can thrive in the absence of religious foundations. The evidence, as we'll see, suggests that it can.

The Sociologist Who Stayed Fourteen Months

Phil Zuckerman is a professor of secular studies at Pitzer College in California, where he founded the first dedicated secular studies department in the United States. In the mid-2000s, he went to Scandinavia to find out whether the least religious societies on Earth were also the least moral. He stayed for fourteen months, conducting nearly 150 interviews with ordinary Danes and Swedes, people like Ingrid, asking them about meaning, morality, death, community, and what they believed. What he found was published in 2008 as *Society Without God: What the Least Religious Nations Can Tell Us About Contentment*.

The picture that emerged wasn't one of nihilism or selfish individualism. The people Zuckerman spoke with described a moral code grounded in empathy and the Golden Rule, in concern for neighbours and strangers, in respect for others' dignity. Very few grounded any of this in God. Most didn't think about God much at all. Christianity, for most of them, had become a set of holidays and hymns, a way of marking births and deaths, rather than a living theological commitment.

Yet these weren't people without moral compasses. Zuckerman described them as living what he called "a secular Lutheran morality," a deeply rooted set of values about kindness, hard work, social responsibility, and fairness, carried by culture rather than by doctrine. The moral content had survived the departure of its religious container. The values had been absorbed so thoroughly into the civic culture that their religious origins had become invisible, like the Latin roots in English words that no one thinks of as Latin anymore.

His 2014 follow-up, *Living the Secular Life: New Answers to Old Questions*, examined secular Americans and found a similar pattern. Nonreligious Americans, he argued, operate from an empathy-based conscience rather than a divine-command framework. Their moral lives are built on three pillars: a confidence that each person can work out what is right through reason and reflection, a practical commitment to outcomes over rules, and an abiding allegiance to the

Golden Rule.

Zuckerman found something particularly striking in the children of secular households. Contrary to the assumption that religious upbringing is necessary for moral development, children raised without religion showed strong moral development and a clear sense of right and wrong. Their moral education happened through relationship, conversation, and experience rather than through catechism or religious instruction. They weren't, as critics sometimes assumed, moral blank slates. They were moral agents drawing on a different, but no less substantial, set of resources.

What Zuckerman's research offers is simpler and more valuable than provocation: proof of concept. The Scandinavian societies demonstrate that religion isn't the only path to a functioning moral community. They're not the final word on anything, and their specific conditions (small populations, high social equality, centuries of civic culture) can't simply be transplanted elsewhere. But they exist, and they matter. The question is no longer whether secular moral communities are possible. It's how they work, what sustains them, and what they might lack.

The Correlation Data and What They Do (and Do Not) Prove

A few years before Zuckerman published his Scandinavian research, an independent researcher named Gregory Paul published a study in the *Journal of Religion and Society* that attempted something bolder: a quantitative comparison of religion and social health across the prosperous democracies of the developed world.

Paul's 2005 paper compared seventeen wealthy democracies, including the United States, Japan, and Western European nations. He measured religiosity through indicators like belief in God, frequency of prayer, and church attendance, and societal health through indicators like homicide rates, teen pregnancy, and income inequality. His finding was striking: in almost every category, the most religious of the wealthy democracies, prominently the United States, performed worst. The most secular, predominantly Scandinavian and Western European nations, performed best.

Paul extended this work in a 2009 paper, adding more indicators and a larger dataset. The correlations between high religiosity and measures of social dysfunction were in some cases remarkably strong. The correlation between religiosity levels and gonorrhea infection rates, for example, was positive and very high (around 0.94). Homicide rates correlated positively with religiosity at around 0.61. Under-five mortality correlated positively with religiosity at around 0.84. Paul argued that religiosity functions primarily as a coping mechanism for socioeconomic insecurity, that people turn to religion when their material circumstances are precarious, and that improving those circumstances tends to reduce religiosity while also reducing dysfunction.

Paul's research methodology has been heavily criticized in peer-reviewed responses for selection bias and ecological fallacy, though his broad directional finding, that the most religious wealthy democracies don't outperform the most secular ones on social health indicators, has been supported by subsequent analyses. The ecological fallacy concern is important: national-level correlations don't tell us about individual behaviour. A country can be both highly religious and highly unequal without those two facts being causally connected in any simple way.

There's also a critical caveat that any honest treatment of this research must present clearly: correlation isn't causation. Independent analyses have found that variables like income inequality, education levels, and racial composition explain more of the variance in social outcomes than religiosity does on its own. The United States is an extreme outlier in both its religiosity and its levels of income inequality. Paul's data don't prove that religion causes social dysfunction, nor that abandoning religion would produce Scandinavian outcomes. The data more plausibly show that prosperous, equal, well-governed societies tend to become less religious over time, not that becoming less religious causes prosperity. The causal arrow, insofar as there's one, likely runs the other way.

This interpretation reinforces Zuckerman's argument. What matters most is whether a society's basic material and psychological needs, security, healthcare, education, fair economic participation, are reliably met. When they are, religion tends to recede as a primary organizing force while moral culture persists. The moral content was never uniquely religious in the first place. It was human, and the religious institution had been the container that organized and transmitted it.

For this book's argument, the more modest reading is all that's needed: these data don't support the claim that religion is a prerequisite for social health. The relationship between religious practice and societal outcomes is complex and shaped by many other factors. That's simply a true thing to know.

The Philosophical Alternatives

If religion isn't the only path to morality, what are the others? Philosophy has been developing answers for a very long time. The most substantial ones aren't mere academic abstractions. They're frameworks that real people use, often without knowing the names attached to them.

Virtue ethics, developed most fully by Aristotle in his *Nicomachean Ethics* around 350 BCE, begins with a deceptively simple question: what does it mean to live well? Aristotle's answer was that human flourishing, *eudaimonia*, best rendered as "the good life fully lived," comes from developing and exercising the virtues: justice, courage, temperance, generosity, and practical wisdom.

These virtues aren't commandments handed down from above. They're skills, developed through practice and habit, the way a musician develops the ability to play. A person becomes courageous by doing courageous things repeatedly, even when frightened, until the disposition becomes stable. Just as no one becomes a carpenter by reading about carpentry, no one becomes virtuous by memorizing rules. Virtue is a practice, and it requires a community in which to practice it.

This last point is often overlooked. Aristotle wasn't describing a solitary moral project. He believed that virtue could only be developed and sustained within a *polis*, a community of people engaged in shared life. The virtuous person needs friends, not merely for pleasure or advantage, but because moral development happens in relationship. You learn what courage looks like by watching someone act courageously. You learn what generosity requires by being the recipient of it and by practicing it yourself in situations where it costs something. The community isn't incidental to virtue ethics. It's the soil in which virtue grows.

Aristotle's ethics require no deity. They derive entirely from what it means to be a human being living among other human beings. This is why they've enjoyed a major revival in contemporary moral philosophy, led by thinkers like Alasdair MacIntyre, Philippa Foot, and Martha Nussbaum. MacIntyre's *After Virtue* (1981) argued that modern moral philosophy had lost its way by abandoning the Aristotelian framework, trying to derive moral rules from abstract reason alone while ignoring the practices and communities that make moral formation possible. Nussbaum's "capabilities approach" extended Aristotle's insights into political philosophy, arguing that a just society enables its citizens to develop and exercise their fundamental human capabilities, including practical reason, affiliation, and concern for other species. These secular projects match what psychological research shows about how moral character actually develops: not through rule-following but through habit, practice, and the influence of a moral community.

Care ethics, developed in the 1980s by psychologist Carol Gilligan and philosopher Nel Noddings, begins from a different starting point: not from abstract principles but from human relationships. Gilligan's landmark 1982 book *In a Different Voice* argued that standard accounts of moral development, which focused on abstract reasoning about rules and rights, had systematically ignored a different kind of moral thinking, one focused on relationships, responsibility, and the work of caring for others.

She was responding to Lawrence Kohlberg's influential theory of moral development, which placed abstract rule-based reasoning at the apex of moral maturity. Gilligan argued that this framework was built primarily on male subjects and male experience, and that it systematically undervalued a relational, contextual, and responsive kind of moral thinking she observed, especially but not exclusively, in women. Where Kohlberg's framework asked "What is the right rule?", care ethics asks "What does this relationship require of me?"

Noddings extended this in *Caring: A Feminine Approach to Ethics and Moral Education* (1984), arguing that the experience of being cared for and caring for others isn't the soft background to real ethics but its central content. The caring relationship, she argued, is the fundamental ethical unit: one person attending to another, receiving the other's reality into their own experience, and responding in a way that maintains and deepens the relationship. This isn't sentimentality. It's a rigorous description of what moral engagement actually looks like in practice, whether in a hospital ward, a classroom, or a family.

The implications are substantial. Care ethics challenges the idea that morality is primarily about applying abstract rules to particular situations. Morality, it suggests, begins in attentiveness: the capacity to see another person clearly and respond to what they actually need. This insight has been taken up in nursing ethics, education theory, disability studies, and political philosophy, where thinkers like Joan Tronto have argued that care isn't a private virtue but a public necessity, and that a just society must ensure that the work of caring is fairly distributed and properly valued. Care ethics is grounded in the universal human experience of dependence and relationship. Every person alive was once entirely dependent on someone else's care, and most of us will be again.

Secular humanism synthesizes the insights of the Enlightenment into an explicit moral framework: human dignity, reason, compassion, and equality are the foundations of ethics. As researchers have described, secular humanism isn't simply the absence of religion but a positive set of commitments to human welfare, to reason as the best tool for understanding the world, and to the project of creating more just and flourishing societies.

The intellectual roots run deep, from the Greek Stoics through the Renaissance humanists to the Enlightenment thinkers: Locke's arguments for natural rights, Kant's insistence that every person must be treated as an end and never merely as a means, and Mill's utilitarian calculation that the right action produces the greatest well-being for the greatest number. What unites these thinkers, despite their considerable disagreements, is the conviction that human beings possess the rational and moral resources to determine how they ought to live, without needing instruction from a supernatural authority.

Modern secular humanism has developed its own institutions, communities, and traditions of moral formation. Organizations like the American Humanist Association, the British Humanist Association, and Humanists International provide naming ceremonies, weddings, funerals, and community gatherings that serve many of the social functions traditionally performed by religious congregations. Humanist chaplains serve in hospitals, prisons, and universities. Secular humanism is, in this sense, doing many of the same things that religious communities do, building shared identity, transmitting values, organizing service, but on explicitly non-theistic foundations. Whether it does them as effectively is a question the later chapters of this book will examine with care, because the honest answer isn't a simple yes.

Effective altruism, associated most prominently with the philosopher Peter Singer at Princeton University, takes a more demanding approach. In his famous 1972 essay \"Famine, Affluence, and Morality,\" Singer argued that if we can prevent something bad from happening without sacrificing anything of comparable moral importance, we're obligated to do it. His "drowning child" thought experiment makes the case simply: if you walked past a child drowning in a shallow pond, you'd wade in and save the child without hesitation, even if it ruined your expensive clothes. Singer asks why the fact that a dying child is thousands of miles away rather than a few feet away should change your moral obligation. It shouldn't.

The argument is deliberately uncomfortable. Singer isn't describing charity as a nice thing to do. He's describing it as a moral obligation as binding as the duty not to let a child drown in front of you. His logical implication, which he has never flinched from, is that the affluent citizens of wealthy nations are in a state of ongoing moral failure whenever they spend money on luxuries while people die of preventable causes. The argument is remarkably difficult to refute, and it's motivated real changes in behaviour.

His later work on effective altruism applies this reasoning to charitable giving: don't just give, give to the causes that do the most measurable good per dollar. Organizations like GiveWell and the Against Malaria Foundation show the approach, using rigorous evidence to identify the interventions that save the most lives per unit of money spent. The effective altruism movement has generated a significant community of people, many of them young professionals in technology and finance, who commit to donating substantial proportions of their income (often ten percent or more, echoing the ancient practice of tithing) to effective charitable causes, not because God requires it, but because reason applied to the facts of global suffering demands it.

The movement has also faced serious criticism. Some philosophers argue that its emphasis on quantifiable outcomes undervalues goods that can't be measured, like justice, dignity, and cultural preservation. The spectacular collapse of the cryptocurrency exchange run by Sam Bankman-Fried, a prominent effective altruism adherent, raised hard questions about whether ends-justify-means reasoning can become a licence for recklessness. These criticisms matter. But the core insight, that moral seriousness requires attending to consequences and not merely to intentions, remains powerful, and it requires no religious foundation whatsoever.

And then there's existentialism, particularly the version developed by the French philosopher Jean-Paul Sartre in his 1945 lecture published as \"Existentialism Is a Humanism.\" Sartre's famous claim was that "existence precedes essence": human beings don't come into the world with a pre-given purpose or nature. Meaning is something we create through our choices, relationships, and commitments. Rather than receiving a moral code from above, we're, as Sartre put it, condemned to be free.

This isn't comfortable news. It places the full weight of moral responsibility on human shoulders, with no cosmic safety net. If there's no God to define what is good, then the human being must define it, and must accept full responsibility for the definition. Sartre was unsparing about what this means: every choice a person makes is, implicitly, a statement about how all people should live. When you choose to act honestly, you're endorsing honesty as a human value. When you choose cowardice, you're endorsing that too. There's no hiding behind divine commands or inherited rules. The responsibility is total.

But Sartre insisted this is also, in the deepest sense, liberating. We're not constrained by an assigned role but are genuinely the authors of our own lives. The existentialist tradition, extended by thinkers like Simone de Beauvoir (whose *The Ethics of Ambiguity* of 1947 developed the ethical implications Sartre often left abstract) and Albert Camus (whose concept of "the absurd" addressed how to live meaningfully in a universe that offers no inherent meaning), offers something that more systematic moral theories sometimes lack: an honest confrontation with the anxiety and difficulty of moral life. Existentialism doesn't promise that doing the right thing will be easy, or that the right thing will always be clear, or that moral struggle will be rewarded. It promises only that the struggle is real, that it matters, and that the person who engages in it honestly is living a genuinely human life. For many people who have left religious frameworks behind, this unflinching honesty isn't a deficiency. It's precisely what they were looking for.

These aren't fringe positions held by rebels or contrarians. They're some of the most influential moral frameworks in human intellectual history, and they share a common starting point: human beings, their experiences, their relationships, their capacities for reason and empathy, are sufficient grounds for ethics. No additional supernatural architecture is required.

Secular Moral Exemplars in Practice

Philosophy is one thing. What does secular moral life look like when it reaches the heights of genuine self-sacrifice and committed service?

Médecins Sans Frontières (Doctors Without Borders) was founded in 1971 by French physicians who had worked in the Nigerian civil war and were determined to provide emergency medical care regardless of political boundaries. The organization is explicitly secular, grounded in Enlightenment philosophy and a simple conviction: human life has value regardless of the political or national identity of the person in question. Its "ethic of refusal," the refusal to accept the world as it's when lives can be saved, and its practice of "témoignage" (bearing witness to what its workers observe), represent an extraordinary moral commitment that's entirely secular in its motivation.

The people who work for Doctors Without Borders, often in dangerous conditions for relatively modest pay, aren't demonstrating that secular motivation is superior to religious motivation. They're demonstrating, with their lives, that it's sufficient. The moral language they speak doesn't require a religious accent. It's spoken clearly and at great personal cost in a dialect of Enlightenment humanist values.

Intellectual honesty also requires acknowledging the other side of the ledger. Secular societies have achieved things that religious societies historically resisted: the emancipation of women, the recognition of LGBTQ equality, scientific freedom from doctrinal authority, and democratic government as a principle rather than an exception. The question isn't which world is better, the religious or the secular, but what each has built, what each has lost, and what we can learn from both.

Viktor Frankl, who survived Auschwitz and wrote about the experience in *Man's Search for Meaning* (1946), was a religious thinker in important ways, but his central insight belongs equally to secular and religious readers. Frankl observed that the prisoners who survived most often were those who maintained a sense of meaning and purpose, who had something to live for: a person, a task, a commitment. The capacity for meaning-making, he argued, is the fundamental human capacity, prior to religion and secular philosophy alike. The question isn't whether meaning comes from God or from human freedom. The question is whether the framework a person lives within allows them to find and sustain genuine meaning through the full range of human experience, including suffering.

This is the standard by which secular moral frameworks deserve to be evaluated: not whether they invoke God, but whether they give human beings adequate resources for living well, facing loss with resilience, sustaining moral commitment over a lifetime, and belonging to something larger than themselves. The frameworks described above, virtue ethics, care ethics, secular humanism, effective altruism, and existentialism, each provide some of these resources. None of them, taken alone, provides all of them. The same is true of any single religious tradition.

The Charitable Giving Question

An honest treatment of secular morality must grapple with data that complicate the picture. Religious people, at least in the United States, give more money to charity and volunteer more of their time than secular people do.

Arthur Brooks, then a professor at Syracuse University, analyzed data from roughly thirty thousand respondents in the Social Capital Community Benchmark Survey and found that religious Americans were about twenty-five percentage points more likely to donate to charity than secular Americans (ninety-one percent versus sixty-six percent), and about twenty-three percentage points more likely to volunteer their time. The dollar amounts were striking: religious respondents gave an average of around $2,200 per year; secular respondents averaged around $640. More recent data from the Lilly School of Philanthropy found similar patterns. Monthly church attenders gave nearly $3,000 per year on average; non-attenders averaged around $700.

These data are real, and they deserve to be taken seriously. Religious communities are extraordinarily effective at organizing moral behaviour. They provide regular gatherings, clear identity, shared purpose, and social accountability. When the collection plate comes around, the whole community is watching. When the church runs a food drive, the infrastructure for participation is already in place. The organizational power of religious institutions isn't incidental to their moral impact. It's central to it. Pew Research Center data from 2024 found that religiously affiliated Americans who attend services at least monthly volunteer at a rate of forty-one percent, compared to seventeen percent for both non-attending religious people and those with no religious affiliation.

But several nuances are worth noting. First, a substantial portion of religious giving goes back into religious institutions themselves. When researchers focus specifically on giving to secular causes, the gap narrows. Second, the most relevant comparison isn't between actively religious people and casually secular ones, but between actively religious people and actively secular ones, those who participate in civic organizations and voluntary associations. When that comparison is made, the gap narrows further still. Pew's 2024 data also show that atheists and agnostics, as a distinct group, turn out to vote at rates rivalling religiously affiliated adults, suggesting that civic engagement is alive in the secular community.

Third, and perhaps most importantly, the pattern shifts dramatically in countries with strong social safety nets. In Scandinavia, the gaps in healthcare, housing, and poverty relief are closed by public institutions, so the need for private charity is simply lower. When that's the baseline, the gap in private charitable giving means something different.

The conclusion these data point to isn't that secular people are as morally active as religious people in the American context. The data don't clearly support that claim. The more defensible conclusion is that religious communities have developed a remarkably effective social technology for organizing moral behaviour, and that secular alternatives need to take that organizational reality seriously. Building community, building institutions, creating rituals and recurring obligations: these aren't peripheral to moral life. They're its infrastructure. The charitable giving gap is less an argument for the necessity of religious belief than an argument for the necessity of religious community. And community, as later chapters will argue, can be built on foundations other than theology.

The Same Language, a Different Accent

Throughout this book, we've used a central metaphor: morality is a language shared by all human societies. The deep grammar, care for children, reciprocity, protection of the vulnerable, fairness in distribution, is universal, written into our evolutionary history and our neural architecture. The accents vary. Different cultures, traditions, and belief systems have developed different ways of pronouncing the same fundamental moral content, shaped by history, geography, theology, and collective experience.

Secular ethics isn't the absence of an accent. It's an accent in its own right, and a rich one. When a secular humanist says that human dignity is the foundation of ethics, they're speaking the same moral language as a Christian who says every person is made in the image of God. When an effective altruist commits to giving away a significant portion of their income to reduce suffering, they're making the same basic moral claim as the religious tradition that commands tithing and care for the poor. When a follower of care ethics insists that relationships and responsibilities to particular others are the heart of moral life, they're saying something deeply consonant with traditions that ground morality in covenantal bonds and loving obligation.

These secular accents aren't lesser versions of the moral language. They deserve the same respect, and the same scrutiny, as religious moral systems. A secular framework can be intellectually lazy, self-serving, or tribal just as easily as a religious one. The history of secular ideologies in the twentieth century, which produced some of the most organized killing in human history, should put to rest any comfortable assumption that removing God from the equation automatically elevates moral quality. The question is whether a moral framework is honest, whether it has the intellectual courage to confront its own failures, whether it keeps human welfare genuinely at its centre, and whether it builds the kind of community that makes moral behaviour sustainable over a lifetime.

What Zuckerman's Scandinavians demonstrate, and what philosophers from Aristotle to Singer have argued, is that secular moral life isn't a pale substitute for religious moral life. It's a full human achievement in its own right, built from the same raw materials, the same evolved capacities for empathy, fairness, and social reasoning, that religious traditions have long worked with. The difference isn't in the material but in the architecture.

A Reflection for the Reader

This chapter ends with an invitation rather than a conclusion. Whatever your relationship to religion, whether you're a committed believer, a casual participant, or someone who has never been in, take a moment to think about the actual foundation of your moral life.

What three principles most reliably guide how you treat other people? Not what you think you should say, but what actually governs your behaviour when a situation is hard and the right answer isn't obvious.

Where did those principles come from? A tradition? A parent? A philosophical argument you once encountered? A painful experience that taught you something you couldn't unlearn? A relationship that changed how you saw the world? The answer matters, because understanding where a moral principle comes from tells you something about its stability, and about what would need to change for it to hold in conditions different from the ones in which it was formed.

And here's the harder question: would those principles survive the removal of whatever label is attached to them? If the religious justification were taken away, would the principle still hold for you? If the secular framework were stripped out, would the commitment remain? If the answer is yes, you're describing something real, something that lives in you rather than in a label. If the answer isn't quite, that's worth knowing too. A moral principle that depends entirely on its doctrinal wrapper may be more fragile than it appears.

The moral language belongs to all of us. The accent we speak it in is our own to choose, and to keep choosing, every day.

Chapter 10

The Ordinary Sacred: How Science and Survival Shaped What We Call Virtue

The previous chapter looked at people who live outside religious frameworks and find that the moral language speaks itself clearly enough without theological scaffolding. This chapter looks at a harder question: what about the practices that look most unambiguously religious? What about the customs and gestures that even secular people perform, often without knowing why, and that many believers understand as the direct expression of faith? It turns out that the history of those practices is equally surprising.

Watch a parent teach a child to say "thank you" and you're watching one of the oldest pedagogical scenes in the human story. The child receives a gift, a toy, a cookie, a kind word from a neighbor, and the parent leans down and says, quietly but firmly: "What do we say?" The child murmurs the words. The parent nods. Lesson absorbed. Next time it will come faster, and then faster still, until the phrase flows without thinking, a reflex as natural as breathing.

The parent in this scene almost certainly believes they're teaching basic morality. They're passing on something they received from their own parents, who received it from theirs: the idea that gratitude is a virtue, that acknowledging what others do for you is right, that forgetting to give thanks is a small moral failure. Many parents who do this are religious, and they understand the practice in religious terms. We thank God for our blessings, and we thank people in the same spirit. But the word they're teaching, "thank," has nothing to do with prayer or divinity. Its roots go somewhere altogether more practical and more human.

The English word "thank" derives from the Proto-Germanic *thankoz*, meaning "thought" or "a thinking of, a remembering." That word traces back to the Proto-Indo-European root *tong-*, meaning simply "to think, to feel." As Etymonline documents, in 8th-century usage the word *thanc* didn't mean gratitude at all. It meant "thought" or "reflection." To thank someone wasn't to invoke the gods on their behalf. It was to say: *I will keep what you did in my mind. I will remember it.* Gratitude, in its deepest etymology, was a memory device. A social contract written in neurons.

This is one of the smallest and most instructive details this book has to offer. The moral vocabulary we use every day, the words and gestures and habits we assume are the products of religious cultivation, often turns out, on close inspection, to have roots that are older than religion, more practical than theology, and more universal than any single faith. Religion didn't invent these practices. Science, survival, and social coordination did. Religion, in many cases and in many cultures, was one of the vehicles that carried them forward, amplified them, gave them sacred authority. That's a real contribution, and it shouldn't be dismissed. But it's a different claim from the one usually made.

This chapter is about that difference. It's a tour through the ordinary sacred: the everyday practices and moral reflexes that feel religious but began as something else. Some are linguistic, the very words we use to express virtue. Some are physical, gestures and customs that predate the civilizations that later claimed them. Some are philosophical, ideas so universal that no single tradition could have invented them. All of them illuminate the same truth: that the moral life is older than the gods who were later asked to sanction it.

Part One: The Language of Virtue

"Thank You": From Memory to Morality

The word "thank" isn't alone in its secular origins. Consider what happens when you move across languages. In French, *merci*, thank you, derives directly from the Latin *merces*, meaning wages, fee, or reward, and from the ecclesiastical sense of "mercy" as the power one has over a debtor. To say *merci* in medieval France was, at its root, to acknowledge that you had placed yourself in another person's power, that you were in their debt. It was commercial and social, not divine.

In Portuguese, *obrigado* means "obligated," I am bound to you. In Italian, *grazie* shares its root with "grace" and "gratitude," all tracing back to the Latin *gratus*, meaning pleasing, agreeable, favorable. The Greek *efcharistó* is older still, and *eucharist*, the central rite of Christian communion, draws on the same word. What we call the Eucharist, the act of sacred thanksgiving, is etymologically the same gesture as saying thank you at the dinner table.

The deeper point is one the anthropologist David Graeber made in his landmark work *Debt: The First 5,000 Years*: Graeber argued that the compulsive, reflexive use of formulas like "please" and "thank you" in all routine transactions, not the underlying impulse of verbal gratitude itself, but its near-automatic deployment in every exchange, first spread through middle-class commercial culture during the 16th and 17th centuries, among those who staffed the bureaus, shops, and offices of an expanding market economy. The language of gratitude spread not through churches but through counting houses. It was the vocabulary of ledgers and contracts, of exchange and obligation, translated into daily social life.

This doesn't mean that gratitude itself is new, or that religions were wrong to sanctify it. Every major tradition has found in gratitude a spiritual principle worth elevating. What it means is that the practice preceded the theology. People learned to thank each other because they were embedded in webs of exchange and mutual dependence, because social memory, remembering who helped you, who fed you, who carried water when you couldn't, was adaptive. Religion, when it arrived, gave this habit a new frame and a larger audience. But the habit was already there.

Even across cultures where the specific linguistic formula is absent, the underlying practice isn't. Anthropologist Dan Sperber, who conducted fieldwork among the Dorze people of Ethiopia, found that within households and tightly knit groups, everyday cooperative acts weren't linguistically marked by thanks. It was understood that such acts were simply part of communal life. Thanking was reserved for the extraordinary, for acts that stepped outside the normal economy of reciprocity. What looked like an absence of gratitude was actually a finely calibrated social system: ordinary help was woven into the fabric of mutual dependence and didn't require verbal marking. Only the exceptional required a word.

The lesson here isn't that gratitude is somehow less than we thought. It's that gratitude is more ancient than its verbal formulas, and those formulas, when they did emerge, were shaped far more by commerce and social pragmatics than by divine command.

"Bless You" -- From Galen to Reflex

When someone near you sneezes, you say "bless you," or, if you're German, you say *Gesundheit*, which means simply "health." You probably don't think about what you're saying. It's become a pure reflex, a social tic, the verbal equivalent of a held-open door.

But the phrase has a history, and that history isn't primarily Christian. It's primarily medical.

The ancient Greco-Roman medical tradition connected sneezing to the brain and to the life force, but the popular response to sneezing long predated any medical codification of those ideas. In Homer's *Odyssey*, when Telemachus sneezes, his mother Penelope takes it as a favorable omen, a sign that Odysseus will return and kill the suitors. When Xenophon's mercenaries, stranded in a hostile foreign land, heard a soldier sneeze during one of their commanders' speeches, the whole army broke out in spontaneous worship. A sneeze meant the gods were listening. Or, in purely medical terms, that the body was speaking. When the physician Galen, writing in the second century

CE, finally set down a systematic account, sneezing as the head's most direct operation, allowing excess steam and mucus to escape, he wasn't introducing a new idea into popular culture. He was giving learned authority to a belief that had already been embedded in Greek and Roman life for centuries.

Across the ancient Mediterranean, responses to sneezing were common long before Christianity existed to bless anyone. Romans said *Salve*, health to you. Greeks invoked Zeus. Hindus said *Live*, to which the sneezer replied *With you*. The Jewish tradition connected sneezing to moments of temporary life-and-death transition. All of these responses drew on the same deep well: the ancient understanding that a sneeze was a bodily event of medical and perhaps supernatural significance.

The Christian phrase "God bless you" did intensify during particular historical crises. One popular account, of uncertain historical basis, places its formal adoption during the pontificate of Gregory the Great, when a plague swept through Rome and sneezing was feared as an early symptom of death. But as even the most conservative historians acknowledge, the practice of responding to sneezes with a verbal blessing is ancient, pagan, and medical in its origins. The Internet Sacred Text Archive's collection of popular superstitions cites Aristotle as noting that "people consider a sneeze as divine," and adds that the practice was "accounted very ancient even in the time of Aristotle." Christianity inherited the custom and gave it new words. It didn't invent it.

The German *Gesundheit*, still used widely today, including in secular North America, is probably the more honest reflex. It strips away the theology and returns to the bare original meaning: I hope you are well. I have noticed your body. I am with you.

Part Two: The Body and Its Wisdom

The Handshake -- Peace Before Piety

The most common formal greeting in the Western world has no religious origin at all. It's a military one.

One of the earliest known depictions of a handshake is a 9th-century BCE Assyrian stone relief now housed in the Iraq Museum in Baghdad. It shows King Shalmaneser III of the Neo-Assyrian Empire clasping hands with a Babylonian king. The context is diplomatic: two rulers confirming an alliance. The gesture signals something concrete and physical. I'm not holding a weapon. My hand is open. I come in peace.

The theory that the up-and-down motion of handshaking was designed to dislodge hidden knives from sleeves may be apocryphal, and the underlying principle, that extending the open right hand was a gesture of deliberate vulnerability, a way of displaying that the sword hand was empty, is a widely cited and plausible hypothesis, though its specific origins remain unverified prior to the Assyrian diplomatic record. The general logic isn't hard to follow: in societies where men routinely carried weapons and where strangers were presumed dangerous until proven otherwise, an open hand was a gesture made visible. To offer your sword hand was to say: I have made a choice. I choose not to fight you.

What transformed this diplomatic gesture into a universal daily greeting is a fascinating piece of social history. As the Cambridge University Press study on the spread of the handshake documents, two specific social networks drove the handshake's popularization in Britain between 1700 and 1850. One was the merchant class, who shook hands to confirm deals, not as a legal instrument but as a public pledge of good faith, a social commitment made visible. The other was the Quakers.

The Religious Society of Friends, founded in the aftermath of the English Civil War, were conscious egalitarians. They refused to bow or curtsey to their social superiors, refused to remove their hats as a sign of deference, refused all the hierarchical theatre that ordered 17th-century English social life. In place of all that ceremony, they shook hands with everyone, high and low alike. As the historian

David Hackett Fischer recorded in *Albion's Seed* and noted in the *Friends Journal*, by 1700 the universal handshake had become a central Quaker practice: "a decency which Friends extended to everyone, even their social superiors." When Quakers emigrated to Pennsylvania and other American colonies, they carried this custom with them. Over time, the Quaker greeting, egalitarian, direct, warm without being intrusive, outcompeted the more elaborate hierarchical customs imported by Anglican Virginians. The handshake became the American greeting.

What the Quakers did was use a very old gesture for a very new purpose. They didn't invent the handshake. It predates them by thousands of years. But they democratized it, extracting it from the realm of diplomatic necessity and royal treaty-making and placing it within the reach of every person on every street corner. This was a religious innovation, yes, but the innovation was social and political, not doctrinal. The handshake's power came not from any theology but from its elegant practicality: it was a way to meet a stranger and say, immediately and physically, *I regard you as an equal.*

<hr>

Food Taboos -- Parasites Before Prophets

When the Hebrew Bible declares the pig to be unclean, "from their flesh, you shall not eat, and their carcasses you shall not touch" (Leviticus 11:7-8), it presents this prohibition as divine command. And for the billions of people who have observed it, and who observe it today, it carries that sacred authority. But the archaeological and historical record tells a more complicated and more interesting story.

The pig had been raised and eaten across the ancient Near East for thousands of years before the prohibition was written. Pigs appear to have been domesticated independently in several locations in the ancient Near East, with the earliest clear evidence in the region between modern Turkey and Syria around 8000 to 8500 BCE. In the southern Levant, the region most directly relevant to Israelite dietary practice, the earliest signs of domestication appear at Tel Motza, near

Jerusalem, around 7000 BCE. By the Bronze Age (3500-1200 BCE), pigs were eaten enthusiastically in the region's earliest cities. As archaeologist Max Price, author of *Evolution of a Taboo: Pigs and People in the Ancient Near East*, notes: pigs disappeared from the archaeological record of Israelite settlements not because priests commanded it, but because the mobile, pastoral lifestyle of highland shepherds and goat-herders simply didn't include pig farming. Pigs don't travel well, don't produce wool or milk as secondary products, and compete directly with humans for water and grain in arid landscapes.

Pig consumption had already declined dramatically, to less than one bone in twenty at Israelite Highland sites by 1600 BCE, before the biblical prohibition was codified. "There's no sign of a sudden taboo, disease, or environmental change," Price told Archaeology Magazine in 2025. "What is clear is that sheep, goats, and cattle took over." The biblical writers, he argues, formalized and sanctified an existing pattern, one shaped by ecology, pastoralism, and practical economics.

The anthropologist Marvin Harris made a similar argument decades earlier: pigs compete with humans for calories in dry climates, are difficult to preserve without refrigeration, and provide little beyond their meat, unlike the multipurpose ruminants that formed the backbone of ancient Near Eastern economies. Whether Harris's specific cost-benefit analysis fully accounts for the taboo or not, Price finds it incomplete, the deeper point holds: the pattern of behavior preceded the theological explanation for it. Priests didn't forbid what was common practice. They codified what was already disappearing.

The *Journal of Ethnobiology and Ethnomedicine* reached a broader version of this conclusion in a 2009 study of food taboos across cultures: "An ecological or medical background is apparent for many, including some that are seen as religious or spiritual in origin." The study found that food taboos routinely serve practical functions, resource conservation, health protection, disease prevention, ecological management, and that the religious framing often came after the practice was established. What God commands, it turns out, people had often already started doing for entirely earthly reasons.

This pattern isn't a debunking of religious dietary law. It's a recognition that the laws emerged from a world of genuine practical wisdom, and that the religious codification preserved that wisdom and extended its reach. The priestly insight, if we want to call it that, was recognizing what was already working and surrounding it with sacred authority so it wouldn't be forgotten.

The Sabbath -- Neurology Before Theology

In 2025, a study published in *BMC Public Health* found that Jewish religious participants who observed the Sabbath had, on average, earlier chronotypes, longer sleep durations on rest days, and lower social jetlag than their secular peers. The researchers concluded: "The weekly sleep-wake pattern established through Sabbath observance may serve as a valuable model for promoting circadian stability, a well-documented protective factor for both physical and mental health."

This is modern neuroscience arriving, via a circuitous route, at something that ancient cultures intuited. The brain needs a weekly reset. The body needs a rhythm. Rest isn't a luxury. It's a physiological requirement.

The Sabbath appears in the Torah as divine commandment, grounded in cosmological narrative: God rested on the seventh day, and so shall you. This framing gave the practice enormous cultural staying power. If the Creator of the universe considered rest worthy of an entire day, who were humans to argue? But the practice of periodic collective rest appears to predate its monotheistic framing. The Babylonians observed rest days tied to lunar cycles. Ancient Mesopotamian calendars marked days of ill omen on which certain activities were suspended. The idea that regular temporal rhythm, work, then rest, then work again, was necessary for human wellbeing is as old as agriculture itself.

The modern evidence for this is striking. The National Geographic Blue Zones research, led by Dan Buettner, identified five regions of the world where people live measurably longer and healthier lives. One of those regions is Loma Linda, California, home to a large community of Seventh-day Adventists. The study's conclusion was, as one of the lead researchers summarized: Adventists who follow their church's key lifestyle recommendations live approximately ten years longer than comparable Californians. The benefit is associated with a cluster of practices including plant-based diet, regular physical activity, non-smoking, and community bonds, alongside the weekly Sabbath rest.

And yet the benefit isn't confined to believers. Secular frameworks worldwide have arrived at identical conclusions under different names. "24 hours unplugged" is a practice adopted by executives and therapists and productivity researchers. "Intentional timeout" appears in mindfulness literature. The concept of a "digital Sabbath" has spread through secular culture with no religious framing at all. What ancient priests encoded as divine law, contemporary neuroscientists are recommending as clinical advice. The biology hasn't changed. Only the vocabulary has.

The Sabbath is one of the clearest cases in this book's argument: a practice grounded in physiological reality, discovered and refined over millennia of human experience, that religion elevated to the sacred and thereby preserved. It wasn't invented by priests. But it survived, in part, because priests made it non-negotiable.

Part Three: The Architecture of Moral Philosophy

The Golden Rule -- Evolution Before Ethics

"Do not do to others what you would not wish done to yourself." Confucius said it around 500 BCE. The Egyptian *Instructions of Ankhsheshonq*, a Late Period wisdom text composed around the 4th to

3rd centuries BCE, stated: "Do to the doer to cause that he do thus to you." The Buddha taught it in the 6th century BCE. Zoroaster taught it. The Rabbi Hillel, asked to summarize the entire Torah while standing on one foot, said: "What is hateful to you, do not do to your neighbor. That is the whole Torah; the rest is commentary." Jesus expressed it as the positive command to love your neighbor as yourself. Islam's hadith tradition recorded it as: "Do unto all men as you would wish to have done unto you."

The Golden Rule is the most universal ethical principle in human history. Its appearance across civilizations that had no contact with each other, across millennia of independent moral development, is one of the most significant facts about human ethics. And the explanation for that universality isn't that God whispered the same message to prophets across time and space. It's that the Golden Rule is what a cooperative social species, shaped by millions of years of evolution, arrives at independently.

The evolutionary psychologist's account is straightforward. Reciprocal altruism, the strategy of treating others well in anticipation of being treated well in return, is adaptive. In small groups where individuals interact repeatedly, reputations matter, trust accumulates, and cooperative behavior has measurable survival advantages. Robert Trivers formalized this in 1971, and Robert Axelrod demonstrated it empirically a decade later in his famous computer tournament on the evolution of cooperation. Axelrod invited game theorists, mathematicians, and social scientists to submit strategies for a repeated prisoner's dilemma, a game in which cooperation or betrayal produce different payoffs. The winning strategy, submitted by political scientist Anatol Rapoport in both tournaments, was called Tit for Tat. It was disarmingly simple: cooperate on the first move, and then mirror whatever the other player did last. Never be the first to defect. Forgive quickly. Be clear.

The lesson Axelrod drew from this was clear: in a world of repeated interactions among individuals with memory, cooperation based on reciprocity isn't just possible but optimal. Cooperative strategies outperform selfish ones, not because they're morally superior but because they generate more total value. "The key to doing well," he wrote, "lies not in overcoming others, but in eliciting their cooperation."

This isn't a cynical account of the Golden Rule. It's an explanatory one. The rule emerged because it works, because organisms that treat others as they'd be treated themselves, in the context of repeated social interaction, do better over time than organisms that don't. This was true long before any prophet articulated it. It was true, in a rough functional sense, for social primates before language existed to formulate it. The prophets who gave it words, the traditions that gave it sacred authority, weren't creating the rule. They were recognizing it, and then embedding it in cultural structures powerful enough to make people follow it even when it was inconvenient to do so.

That last part isn't nothing. One of the genuine contributions of religious ethics is the extension of moral concern beyond the immediately visible. It's one thing to treat your neighbors well because you'll see them again tomorrow. It's another to treat strangers well on the other side of a mountain range, or to extend moral consideration to future generations you'll never meet. The religious framing of the Golden Rule expanded its reach in ways that pure evolutionary self-interest couldn't. But the kernel itself, the recognition that reciprocity is the foundation of social life, is older than religion. It's written into the structure of what we are.

Hospitality to Strangers -- Diplomacy Before Deity

In Homer's world, strangers were under the protection of Zeus Xenios, Zeus of the guests. To harm a traveler was to risk divine punishment. The sacred obligation of hospitality (*xenia*) was among the most solemn duties in the Homeric moral order. And yet the practical reasons for the custom weren't hard to see even in Homer's own narratives. In a world without central institutions, no police, no courts, no international law, the only thing protecting a traveler was the network of reciprocal hospitality obligations. If you hosted strangers generously, your reputation spread, and when your own sons were far from home in foreign lands, strangers would host them in return.

The anthropologist Andrew Shryock at the University of Michigan, who has spent decades studying hospitality in the Middle East and across cultures, puts it directly: hospitality "developed into and alongside religion," each reinforcing and extending the other. But the practical foundations came first. As his research in Jordan found, the man who was *karim*, generous, noble, hospitable, earned political credit, built alliances, and secured his family's safety in a world where formal institutions couldn't be relied upon. Generosity to strangers wasn't simply altruism. It was enlightened mutual security.

Edward Westermarck, in his sweeping early 20th-century survey of traditional societies, documented hospitality practices across dozens of cultures, across Africa, Asia, the Pacific, and the Americas, in which strangers were given extraordinary privileges: food, shelter, protection. The practice was nearly universal in societies without strong central authority, and the mechanism was always recognizably the same: you can't know when you'll be the stranger in need of shelter yourself. A world that honors the duty to guests is a world safer to travel through.

What religion did with hospitality is what religion does with many pre-existing practices: it gave it a transcendent frame. In Islam, the guest is sent by God. To refuse hospitality is to refuse God's messenger. In Judaism, the commandment to love the stranger, "for you were strangers in Egypt," roots the obligation in shared historical suffering. In Christianity, the parable of the Good Samaritan extends the definition of "neighbor" to include even those from hostile groups. These are powerful moral elaborations. But the underlying impulse, *the stranger at your door is a human being who needs help, and your community's reputation depends on how you treat them*, requires no theological scaffolding to make sense.

Burial of the Dead -- Grief Before God

The impulse to care for the dead is one of the oldest and most universal behaviors in the human record. And it almost certainly predates religion as we understand it.

Archaeological evidence of deliberate burial goes back to Neanderthals, a species that diverged from our own lineage roughly 400,000 to 700,000 years ago. At Shanidar Cave in the Erbil Governorate of what is now Iraqi Kurdistan, the archaeologist Ralph Solecki excavated remains of ten Neanderthals in the 1950s and 1960s, dating to between 65,000 and 35,000 years ago. The question of whether Neanderthals specifically buried the dead with flowers remains contested. More recent analysis suggests the pollen found near one individual may have been deposited by burrowing rodents. But the broader evidence for deliberate, repeated interment isn't contested. Multiple articulated Neanderthal skeletons have been found at multiple sites across Europe and the Near East, positioned carefully, in contexts that many archaeologists interpret as evidence of deliberate interment. New Scientist notes that modern humans were burying their dead at least 100,000 years ago, and Neanderthals appear to have been doing something similar at roughly the same time.

What's not in doubt is that the impulse to bury the dead, to mark their passing with ritual and care, is older than any surviving religion. It's older, almost certainly, than the kind of abstract theological reasoning that gives rise to beliefs about the afterlife and divine judgment. The simplest explanation is also the strongest: grief is biological. Attachment is biological. Social species that care for their injured (the same Shanidar cave preserved the remains of a Neanderthal who had survived a crippling arm injury for months, evidence of sustained communal care) are also species that respond to death with something recognizable as mourning. Burial is grief made concrete. It's the social processing of loss given physical form.

Religion, when it arrived, didn't create this impulse. It interpreted it. It gave the dead somewhere to go, gave mourners a set of words and gestures and timelines, gave grief a narrative structure that made it bearable. This is one of the genuine gifts of religious practice: the transformation of raw biological mourning into meaningful ritual. But the raw mourning came first. The biological bond between the living and the dead isn't a theological achievement. It's an evolutionary one.

Confession and the Talking Cure -- The Burden Named

One of the most psychologically sophisticated practices in religious life is confession. Across traditions, Catholic auricular confession, Jewish *teshuvah*, the Islamic practice of *tawbah*, there's a recognition that naming what you have done wrong, aloud, to another person, in a structured context, produces relief. The burden is shared. The hidden thing loses its power.

Modern psychotherapy has arrived at the same conclusion via entirely different reasoning. Sigmund Freud consciously distanced psychoanalysis from the Catholic confessional. He positioned it as a scientific rather than religious practice and was dismissive of the parallel when contemporaries raised it. Carl Jung took a different view, drawing more openly on religious frameworks and acknowledging confessional practices as genuine forerunners of psychological transformation. Together they offered secular people a path to the same catharsis without the theological superstructure, though they understood what they were doing very differently. Freud's concept of bringing unconscious material to consciousness, of naming what had been suppressed, is structurally identical to confession: the act of articulation transforms the relationship between the person and the thing they carry. What was hidden and shameful becomes visible and therefore manageable.

The psychologist James Pennebaker spent decades studying the effects of disclosure, and his findings illuminate what confession has always been doing. Naming what you have been carrying, he showed, gives you power over it. The named thing is no longer a shapeless internal pressure but a defined object you can examine. Sharing a burden with a trusted listener provides both interpretation (you're helped to understand what you're carrying) and release (you're no longer carrying it alone). The confessor, whether priest or therapist, plays the same structural role: a witness with the authority to hear, the patience to not flinch, and the wisdom to respond without judgment.

What's striking isn't that therapy and confession are similar. It's that they're similar because they're drawing on the same psychological reality. The human nervous system isn't designed to carry secrets in isolation. The act of voicing what we have done, what we fear, what we have been carrying in silence, has measurable effects on cortisol levels, rumination, and social cognition. These aren't effects that religion discovered. They're effects that religion found ways to reliably produce, through practices that turned out, without anyone knowing quite why, to work. The therapy room and the confessional are different architectural expressions of the same biological necessity.

Monogamy -- Property Before Sacrament

In the Catholic tradition, marriage is a sacrament, a channel of divine grace, indissoluble by human authority, reflecting the eternal covenant between Christ and the Church. In much of Protestant Christianity, it's a sacred covenant, blessed by God, meant to reflect divine fidelity. In popular culture across the Western world, monogamy is treated as the natural and moral form of human partnership, with departures from it understood as moral failures.

The genetic and archaeological evidence offers a different and less comfortable story.

Paleoanthropological and genetic data suggest that reproductive monogamy, the pattern in which most men and women pair-bond and have children with a single partner at a time, wasn't typical of human reproductive patterns through most of our species' history. Molecular genetic analysis, comparing Y-chromosome diversity against autosomal DNA to track historical reproductive patterns, has found that sexual polygyny was typical of human reproductive patterns until the shift to sedentary farming communities approximately 10,000 to 5,000 years ago in Europe and Asia. What drove the shift wasn't a change in theology. It was a change in property.

When human groups became sedentary farmers, land became something that could be owned, cultivated, accumulated, and passed on. For a man who had spent decades clearing forest, building irrigation channels, and developing a productive farm, the question of who would inherit his labor wasn't abstract. Paternity certainty, knowing that the children who would receive your land were biologically yours, became economically urgent in a way it hadn't been when everything was mobile and shared. Monogamy, and the social and legal structures that enforced women's sexual exclusivity, emerged as a property-protection strategy.

The Catholic Church developed its sacramental theology of marriage in the 12th century, when canon lawyers and theologians articulated matrimony as one of the seven sacraments. The formal requirement of a church ceremony for a valid marriage came later still, legislated at the Council of Trent in 1563. Both developments built on centuries of earlier Church involvement in regulating marriage, but they were distinct contributions separated by four hundred years. This was enormously consequential, giving monogamy divine sanction and institutional backing across European civilization. But the practice preceded the theology by thousands of years, and it preceded the theology by economic necessity, not moral insight.

None of this means that monogamy is wrong, or that religious elaborations of it are worthless. The theological treatment of marriage, the idea that fidelity has spiritual significance, that commitment is itself a form of love, that the long work of building a life together is an act of grace, adds genuine depth and meaning to a practice that would otherwise be merely contractual. Religion, again, is doing what it does best: taking a human practice with practical origins and surrounding it with meaning, obligation, and beauty. The critique here isn't of the practice but of the claim that the practice was divinely invented. It wasn't. It was economically invented, and religion inherited it.

Conclusion: The Same Language, Different Accents

Return, for a moment, to the parent and the child. The child is being taught to say "thank you." The parent is, in a very real sense, doing something sacred: transmitting the moral inheritance of the human species, the accumulated wisdom of ten thousand years of social life compressed into a two-word phrase.

What the parent may not know, what no one who teaches this to a child tends to know, is how long that phrase has been in use, and how many different people, in how many different times and places, arrived at the same wisdom by different routes. The word itself is a memory device, a cognitive bookmark: *I won't forget what you did for me.* That's not a religious insight. It's a survival strategy, evolved in a species that depends, more than any other, on mutual aid and remembered reciprocity.

The same pattern holds for every practice examined in this chapter. The handshake, a gesture of military peace, democratized by religious egalitarians, spread by commerce. "Bless you," a medical observation about the significance of the brain's most dramatic involuntary action, given theological clothing by medieval Christianity. The pork taboo, an ecological adaptation to the demands of pastoral life in an arid climate, codified by priests who recognized a practical wisdom already at work. The Sabbath, a neurological necessity that ancient cultures discovered through experience, validated by modern sleep science, and preserved by the institutional power of religious law. The Golden Rule, evolution's own discovery, articulated by prophets, tested and confirmed by game theorists. Hospitality to strangers, practical diplomacy given divine authority. Burial of the dead, grief made ritual, before the gods were invited to attend. Confession, the talking cure, discovered and re-discovered across millennia. Monogamy, property logic, elevated to sacrament.

In each case, the structure is the same. A practice emerges from necessity, biological, ecological, social, economic. It works, or it serves, or it survives because it solves a problem that needed solving. Over time, culture surrounds it with meaning. Religion, in many cases but not all, gives it transcendent authority, extends its reach, makes it obligatory for people who might otherwise have found reasons to opt out. The practice is preserved across generations not just because it's useful but because it's sacred.

This is religion's genuine contribution to the moral life: it's one of history's most powerful preservation technologies. It takes practices that work and makes them non-negotiable. It takes the Golden Rule and says: this isn't merely good strategy, it's divine command. It takes the Sabbath and says: this isn't merely healthy, it's holy. It takes the care of the dead and says: this isn't merely grief, it's love reaching past the boundary of mortality.

These are real achievements. They're not lessened by knowing where the practices came from. If anything, they're clarified. When we know that the Sabbath isn't only a religious obligation but a neurological one, we can appreciate it more fully, as a practice that serves the body, the mind, the community, and, for those who see the world that way, the soul. When we know that the Golden Rule isn't only a divine command but an evolutionarily stable strategy, we can defend it on more grounds, to more people, with more evidence.

The accents of faith are real. They give moral language music and authority and resonance. But the language itself, the grammar of reciprocity, rest, gratitude, care, and honesty, was spoken long before the gods were given their names. It was spoken by people in need of each other, in a world that wouldn't let them live alone.

That's not a reason to discard religion. It's a reason to understand it more honestly: as one of several vehicles that carried the accumulated moral wisdom of the species forward through time, giving it new names, new music, new urgency, but not, in the end, creating it. The roots were already there, grown deep in the soil of what it means to be human.

And those roots, it turns out, are strong enough to stand on their own.

Chapter 11

The Hidden Laboratory: When Religious Rules Were Survival Science

The Refrigerator That Didn't Exist

Here's a problem most modern people don't think about. It's August in the ancient Levant. The temperature outside is 105 degrees. You've just slaughtered a goat. You have no refrigerator, no freezer, no vacuum seal bags, no preservatives, no ice. You have about six hours before the meat becomes a breeding ground for salmonella, E. coli, and campylobacter. You have a family to feed and no margin for error, because in the ancient world, a bad case of food poisoning could kill a child or an elder.

Now imagine you're not a food scientist. You're a shepherd. You don't know what bacteria are. You've never heard of microbiology. But you've noticed, over generations, that certain practices keep your family alive and certain practices don't. The families that drain the blood from meat and salt it heavily lose fewer children. The families that avoid shellfish in the summer months get sick less often. The families that keep their milk vessels away from their meat vessels seem to do better. Nobody knows why. But the pattern is real, and it's consistent, and it matters.

This is where a remarkable number of religious dietary laws began. Not in divine revelation, although that's how they were later understood and transmitted. They began in the accumulated survival wisdom of people who couldn't afford to be wrong about food.

The previous chapter examined practices like the Golden Rule, the Sabbath, and burial of the dead, showing how these began as practical human solutions before religion gave them sacred authority. This chapter goes deeper into one specific domain where the pattern is especially striking: the rules that religions developed around what to eat, how to eat, when to eat, how to wash, and what to do with the body. In each case, the tradition that billions of people follow as divine command turns out to have roots in something older and more practical. Something that looks, in retrospect, a lot like science.

The Kosher Code: A Food Safety System Before the Name Existed

The laws of kashrut, the Jewish dietary code, are among the most detailed and demanding food regulations in human history. They specify which animals can be eaten and which can't. They require that blood be completely drained from meat before consumption. They mandate the total separation of meat and dairy products, down to separate cookware, separate sinks, separate refrigerators in strictly observant households. They require that animals be slaughtered by a trained specialist, the shochet, using a single uninterrupted cut across the throat with a perfectly sharp blade, severing the carotid arteries and causing rapid loss of consciousness, typically within seconds.

For observant Jews, these rules are divine commandments, rooted in the Torah and elaborated over centuries of rabbinic interpretation. The Torah states three times, "Don't cook a kid in its mother's milk" (Exodus 23:19, Exodus 34:26, Deuteronomy 14:21). The rabbis expanded this into a comprehensive system of separation between meat and dairy that governs every aspect of the kosher kitchen.

But look at what the system actually does.

Draining blood from meat isn't just ritual. Blood is one of the fastest vectors for bacterial growth in slaughtered animals. Removing it extends the usable life of the meat and reduces the risk of contamination. The salting process used in koshering, covering the meat in coarse salt and letting it sit, draws out residual blood and moisture. This is, functionally, the same preservation technique that every pre-modern culture figured out independently. Salt kills bacteria. Dry meat lasts longer than wet meat. The kosher process achieves both.

The separation of meat and dairy has a practical dimension that's easy to miss from a modern kitchen. In a world without refrigeration, dairy products spoil at different rates and through different microbial pathways than meat. Mixing the two creates cross-contamination risks that neither product carries alone. The waiting period between eating meat and dairy, three to six hours depending on tradition, isn't arbitrary either. The classical rabbinic explanations are practical in their own way: Rashi taught that fatty residue from meat lingers in the mouth and throat, and Maimonides noted that meat lodged between the teeth retains its legal status for approximately six hours. The six-hour figure derives from the typical interval between the two daily meals in the Talmudic period. These aren't mystical justifications. They're observations about how food actually behaves in the human mouth.

The prohibited animals tell a similar story. Shellfish, explicitly forbidden in Leviticus 11, are among the highest-risk foods in warm climates. They spoil faster than fin fish, accumulate toxins from algal blooms, and were a common source of paralytic shellfish poisoning in the ancient Mediterranean. Pork, the most famous prohibition, poses its own well-documented risks. As discussed in the previous chapter, pig consumption at Israelite highland sites had already declined dramatically well before the biblical prohibition was codified. Pigs don't travel well with nomadic herders, don't produce wool or milk, compete directly with humans for grain and water, and are difficult to preserve in arid heat. The biblical writers didn't invent the avoidance. They formalized it.

None of this means the kosher laws are "just" food safety. The system became, over centuries, something far richer than hygiene. It became identity. It became community. It became a daily discipline that turned every meal into an act of intention. And it's worth noting that the ecological explanation isn't the only scholarly framework. The anthropologist Mary Douglas argued in her influential 1966 book *Purity and Danger* that the Levitical prohibitions aren't about practicality at all. They're about symbolic classification: the pig is forbidden because it's taxonomically anomalous, having cloven hooves but not chewing cud, violating the categories that order the biblical world. Douglas's argument remains widely cited and has never been fully resolved against the functionalist reading. The honest answer is probably that both forces were at work, practical advantage and symbolic boundary-making, reinforcing each other across centuries.

But the foundation, the rules themselves, started with something profoundly practical: don't eat what kills you.

And the Passover cleaning tradition belongs in this picture too. The thorough removal of all chametz, all leavened and fermented food products, from the home before the holiday is the original spring cleaning. It was presented as a religious obligation tied to the Exodus narrative. But in practice, it meant that Jewish households systematically purged old, potentially spoiled food from their kitchens at the same time every year, coinciding with the season when stored food was most likely to have gone bad.

Fish on Friday: The Economy of Sacrifice

Here's something that confused me for years as a kid in Catholic school. On Fridays during Lent, you couldn't eat meat. This was presented as sacrifice and penance, honoring the day Christ died. But you could eat fish. And somehow a plate of beer-battered cod with tartar sauce counted as sacrifice. It didn't add up, even to a ten-year-old.

The history clears it up.

The Catholic tradition of abstaining from meat on Fridays traces back to at least the first century of Christianity. The theological reasoning is straightforward: Christ sacrificed his flesh on a Friday, so the faithful abstain from flesh meat in remembrance. The Latin word for meat, caro, which gives us words like carnivore, was understood to mean the flesh of warm-blooded land animals. Fish, being cold-blooded and aquatic, fell outside the category. As Britannica notes, "scholars note that the code's original Latin uses the term carnis, which is interpreted as meat from warm-blooded animals."

That's the theology. But the practice emerged in a world where the distinction between meat and fish wasn't just spiritual. It was economic.

In the medieval world, meat from cattle, pigs, and poultry was expensive and associated with feasting. Fish was cheap and abundant, especially dried, salted cod and herring, which could be preserved and transported inland. As the Archdiocese of Saint Paul and Minneapolis explains, "in former times flesh meat was more expensive, eaten only occasionally, and associated with feasting and rejoicing; whereas fish were cheaper, eaten more often, and not associated with celebrations." Giving up meat on Friday wasn't giving up food. It was giving up the expensive food.

There's a preservation angle too. In the pre-refrigeration world, the spring season, which is exactly when Lent falls, was the most dangerous time to eat preserved meat. The salted and smoked meats that families had put up in autumn were reaching the end of their safe shelf life by March. Meanwhile, spring was also birthing season for livestock. Slaughtering animals in spring meant fewer calves, lambs, and piglets for the coming year. The Friday abstinence, and the broader Lenten fast, functioned as an ecological circuit breaker.

It protected both the food supply and the herds during the most vulnerable season.

The economics got political, too. When Henry VIII broke with Rome in the 1530s to divorce Catherine of Aragon, eating fish on Friday became a loyalty test. Catholics ate fish. Anglicans, who derided it as "popish flesh," didn't. The change devastated the English fishing industry so badly that Henry's son Edward VI reinstated meatless days explicitly "for the benefit of the commonwealth, where many be fishers, and use the trade of living," as noted by Vital Choice. Religious law was doubling as economic policy.

And the tradition's economic footprint continues. In 1962, a McDonald's franchisee named Lou Groen was struggling with sales every Friday in his heavily Catholic neighborhood in Cincinnati. His solution was the Filet-O-Fish, which still accounts for roughly a quarter of McDonald's annual Lent sales. A first-century penitential practice, filtered through medieval economics and Reformation politics, is still shaping fast food menus in the twenty-first century.

Washing Before God: Islam's Five-Times-Daily Hygiene Protocol

Five times a day, before each of the required prayers, observant Muslims perform wudu, ritual ablution. The process is specific and sequential. Wash the hands three times. Rinse the mouth three times. Clean the nostrils with water three times. Wash the face. Wash the arms to the elbows. Wipe the head with wet hands. Wash the feet to the ankles. If wudu is broken by any of several specified events, including using the bathroom, passing gas, or falling asleep, it must be performed again before the next prayer.

For Muslims, this is about spiritual purity. The concept of taharah, ritual cleanliness, is a precondition for standing before God. The Prophet Muhammad is reported to have said, "Cleanliness is half of faith."

For epidemiologists, it's something else entirely. It's a hand-hygiene protocol performed five times daily, more than a thousand years before Ignaz Semmelweis figured out that doctors should wash their hands between the morgue and the maternity ward.

Studies of wudu's physical effects have found that the practice measurably reduces nasal bacterial load, with each of the five daily washings cutting it further. Regular ablution provides real protection against bacterial infection, particularly in the nasal passages, which are a primary entry point for respiratory pathogens.

During the COVID-19 pandemic, Indonesian Islamic scholars pointed out that the wudu practice naturally aligned with World Health Organization handwashing recommendations, including the extension of hand washing to the wrists and forearms, a technique surgeons use but that the general public rarely follows. The article in Open Forum Infectious Diseases concluded that "Islamic teachings on cleanliness, such as regular handwashing and purification before prayers (wudu), naturally align with public health" practices.

The historical irony is sharp. When Semmelweis proposed in the 1840s that physicians should wash their hands between treating patients, he was ridiculed by the medical establishment and eventually committed to an asylum, where he died. Meanwhile, Jewish and Islamic communities had been prescribing ritual handwashing for thousands of years. As a paper from Touro College noted, the Jewish tradition of handwashing "can be traced back to the Biblical era, to children of Israel wandering in the desert in the 14th Century Before the Common Era." When Semmelweis reduced maternal death rates in his clinic from around ten percent to under two percent, he wasn't discovering something new. He was rediscovering something that religious practice had been quietly doing for three millennia.

The Sacred Cow: When Theology Is Economics

The Hindu veneration of the cow is probably the most misunderstood religious practice in the Western world. To outsiders, it looks irrational: people starving while cattle wander freely. The easy explanation is that Hinduism imposes an absurd taboo that prioritizes religious sentiment over practical survival. The anthropologist Marvin Harris, in his famous essay "India's Sacred Cow," argued the opposite. The cow isn't sacred despite economics. It's sacred because of economics.

Harris laid out the accounting. A living cow in India provides milk, yogurt, and ghee for cooking. Its male offspring provide oxen, which are the primary source of draft power for plowing fields. Cow dung, collected and dried, provides fuel equivalent to an estimated 43 million tons of coal per year. That same dung serves as fertilizer for fields and as a building material and floor covering with demonstrated antimicrobial properties. When a cow eventually dies of natural causes, its leather is used by lower-caste communities for a range of essential goods.

Kill the cow, and you get a few days of protein. Keep the cow alive, and you get years of fuel, fertilizer, draft power, dairy, and economic stability. For a subsistence farming family, losing a cow doesn't just mean losing an animal. It means losing the means of production. No oxen to plow, no dung for fuel, no milk for the family, no way to farm the land. The family that eats its cow in a famine might survive the week but loses its ability to survive the year.

Harris argued that the religious prohibition against beef consumption "arose to prevent the population from consuming the animal on which Indian agriculture depends." The prohibition didn't start in the Vedas. In fact, early Vedic texts contain references to ritual cattle slaughter. The shift toward the cow's sacred status happened gradually, consolidated by the Brahman priesthood by roughly 200 CE, as India's population grew and the economic role of cattle became more critical. The priests codified what practical necessity had already made obvious.

I think Harris's analysis has been fairly criticized for being reductive. He treated religion as an afterthought to economics, and critics like those writing in JSTOR have pointed out that he understated the genuine theological and spiritual dimensions of cow veneration. But the core observation holds: the practice made overwhelming practical sense, and the religious framing preserved and strengthened it across centuries. The sacred and the practical weren't opposed. They were reinforcing each other.

Cut and Heal: Circumcision Across Millennia

Here's one of the stranger convergences in this book. A surgical procedure practiced for thousands of years as a religious obligation turns out, when subjected to modern clinical trials, to have measurable health benefits that nobody involved in the original practice could have known about.

Religious circumcision is practiced in Judaism, where it occurs on the eighth day of life as a sign of the covenant between God and Abraham, and in Islam, where it's considered sunnah, following the practice of the Prophet. It's also practiced in various traditional cultures across Africa and the Pacific. In each tradition, the framing is theological or cultural, not medical. The ethics of neonatal circumcision is a genuine and ongoing debate. The point here is narrower.

The medical evidence, accumulated over the past two decades, is striking.

Three large randomized controlled trials conducted in Africa found that male circumcision reduces the risk of acquiring HIV by 51 to 60 percent, as reported in JAMA in 2011. Long-term follow-up showed the protective effect increased over time. Two of the trials also demonstrated that circumcision reduces the risk of genital herpes by 28 to 34 percent and the risk of oncogenic human papillomavirus by 32 to 35 percent. Benefits extended to female partners: a 28 percent reduction in high-risk HPV, 40 percent reduction in bacterial vaginosis, and 48 percent reduction in trichomoniasis.

Based on this evidence, the World Health Organization and UNAIDS adopted a policy advocating male circumcision in regions with high HIV prevalence. The United States Centers for Disease Control and Prevention projected that neonatal circumcision would be cost-saving over a lifetime due to reduced HIV infections and treatment costs.

Nobody is claiming that Abraham knew about HIV. The point is subtler. In societies where sexually transmitted infections posed significant threats, and where medical treatment was nonexistent, circumcision provided a meaningful reduction in disease risk. Communities that practiced it may have experienced lower rates of certain infections without knowing why. The practice survived, was transmitted across generations, and was eventually encoded in religious law because it was associated, at a population level, with better health outcomes. The theological explanation was layered on top.

This follows the exact pattern we've seen throughout this book. A practice that works gets preserved. Religion provides the preservation technology, the narrative, the ritual, the commandment, that makes the practice non-negotiable across generations. The original practical reason may be forgotten or never consciously understood. What remains is the rule, dressed in sacred language.

Fasting: From Penance to Autophagy

Every major religion prescribes some form of fasting. Muslims fast from dawn to sunset for the entire month of Ramadan. Jews fast on Yom Kippur and several other days throughout the year. Christians fast during Lent. Hindus observe various fasting days tied to specific deities and lunar cycles. Buddhists practice moderated eating, with many monastic traditions restricting food intake to the morning hours.

The religious explanations vary. Self-discipline. Solidarity with the poor. Purification of the body and spirit. Submission to divine will. Gratitude for what one has.

The biology is increasingly clear.

A 2024 study published in *Scientific Reports* found that the Ramadan fasting model, approximately sixteen hours of daily fasting for thirty consecutive days, modulated biomarkers associated with longevity, reduced inflammation, and improved metabolic health markers in both human and animal models. Specifically, the study found "significant overexpression of regulatory proteins involved in immune system function, cytoskeleton remodeling, DNA repair, lipid and glucose metabolism, circadian clock regulation, and cognitive function."

A separate study in Molecular Biology Research Communications found that Ramadan fasting significantly upregulated the expression of Beclin-1, a key marker of autophagy, the process by which cells break down and recycle damaged components. Autophagy, which literally means "self-eating," is now understood to be a crucial mechanism for cellular maintenance. When it's working well, it clears out damaged proteins, defective organelles, and cellular debris. When it's not, those damaged components accumulate and contribute to cancer, neurodegenerative disease, cardiovascular disease, and aging.

The researchers concluded that "people observing Ramadan may benefit from the autophagy pathway to compensate reduction in energy and vital metabolites in the face of food restriction." Fasting during Ramadan, they found, "doesn't have any adverse effects on biochemical, hematological, and inflammatory parameters" and may actively promote cellular repair.

This isn't a coincidence. Intermittent fasting, the health practice that's become enormously popular in the past decade, is really a secular rebranding of what religious communities have been doing for thousands of years. The 16:8 protocol, sixteen hours of fasting and eight hours of eating, is a close approximation of the Ramadan pattern. The health benefits are the same because the biology is the same.

The religious traditions didn't know about autophagy or Beclin-1 gene expression. They knew something simpler: that periodic abstention from food made people feel better, think more clearly, and appear to live longer. They encoded this observation in sacred law, gave it spiritual meaning, and transmitted it across generations with a consistency that no secular health recommendation has ever matched. The World Health Organization can recommend intermittent fasting all it wants. Islam has been enforcing it for fourteen centuries.

The Pattern

Step back and look at what we've covered.

Kosher laws turned out to be a comprehensive food safety system. Blood drainage, salt curing, separation of meat and dairy, avoidance of the highest-risk animals in hot climates. The tradition called it divine command.

The Catholic fish tradition turned out to be ecological and economic common sense. Protect herds during birthing season, stretch the food supply through spring, eat the cheapest and most preservable protein. The tradition called it penitential discipline.

Islamic wudu turned out to be a five-times-daily hygiene protocol that measurably reduces bacterial loads on the hands, face, and nasal passages. The tradition called it spiritual purification.

Hindu cow veneration turned out to be an economic strategy that protects the most valuable multi-purpose asset in subsistence agriculture. The tradition called it sacred prohibition.

Circumcision turned out to be associated with measurable reductions in sexually transmitted infections, including a 51 to 60 percent reduction in HIV risk. The tradition called it a covenantal sign.

Religious fasting turned out to activate cellular autophagy, reduce inflammation, and modulate longevity biomarkers. The tradition called it spiritual discipline.

In every case, the structure is the same. A practice that works, that solves a real survival problem, gets discovered through generations of trial and error. Nobody has the science to explain why it works. But it does work, and the communities that follow it do better than the communities that don't. Religion provides the enforcement mechanism: the practice becomes commandment, becomes sacred, becomes identity. It's transmitted with an authority and consistency that no mere recommendation could achieve. "You should probably wash your hands" is advice. "Purify yourself before standing before God" is obligation.

This is one of religion's genuine and underappreciated achievements. It wasn't just a source of moral guidance or cosmic meaning. It was, for most of human history, the primary technology for preserving and transmitting practical survival knowledge across generations. The priests and prophets and imams didn't know they were encoding public health recommendations. They were encoding what worked. And because they wrapped it in sacred authority, it stuck.

What This Doesn't Mean

I want to be careful here, because this argument gets misread in two directions.

The first misreading is: "Religious rules are just primitive science, and now that we have real science we don't need them." This is wrong. The rules became something far more than their practical origins. Keeping kosher isn't just about food safety. It's about identity, community, discipline, intentionality, connection to ancestors and to God. The Friday fish tradition isn't about protein economics. It's about penance, remembrance, and the rhythm of a moral life. Wudu isn't just handwashing. It's a five-times-daily practice of presence and preparation. Reducing these traditions to their practical origins is like saying music is "just" organized vibrations of air molecules. It's technically true and completely misses the point.

The second misreading is: "If the rules have practical origins, then the religions were wrong about their meaning." Also wrong. Religions weren't lying when they said these practices were sacred. They were doing something more interesting: they were recognizing, intuitively, that certain practices made life better. They didn't have the vocabulary to explain it scientifically. So they surrounded those practices with the strongest preservation technology available to them. Sacred authority.

The honest conclusion is more interesting than either dismissal or defense. It's that human beings, long before they had the tools of science, were already doing science. They were observing, testing, preserving what worked, and discarding what didn't. They were running the longest clinical trial in history. Thousands of years. Billions of participants. And religion was the body that set the rules and made sure people followed them.

And the results, written in the dietary laws and hygiene codes and fasting practices of the world's great traditions, turn out to be surprisingly good.

Chapter 12

Religion as Optional Means, Not Ultimate End

In 1901, William James traveled to Edinburgh to deliver the Gifford Lectures, a prestigious series on natural theology running since 1888. James was fifty-nine years old, recovering from serious heart disease, and well aware that the lectures might be among his last significant intellectual contributions. He was also, by the standards of his era, an unusual choice for a series on religion. He was a scientist and a philosopher, trained in medicine, the founder of American psychology, and the developer of pragmatism: a philosophical method that evaluated ideas not by their abstract coherence but by their practical consequences. He believed in the reality of religious experience. He was also skeptical of religious institutions and uncommitted to any particular theology.

What James produced from those Edinburgh lectures, published in 1902 as *The Varieties of Religious Experience: A Study in Human Nature*, was a radical reframing of the entire question of religion's value. James set aside whether religious doctrines are literally true. He set aside debates about the existence of God. He turned instead to the one question his pragmatist method demanded: what does religious experience actually do to people? What are its fruits?

He found, in the enormous range of first-person accounts he assembled, that genuine religious experience could produce profound transformations. A sense of peace in the face of suffering, liberation from obsessive self-concern, deepened compassion, heightened moral resolve, and what he called a "new zest for life." These were real effects, measurable in changed behavior and reported experience. They were, James argued, the proper measure of religion's worth. Not its metaphysics, not its institutional history, not its doctrinal correctness, but its fruits. "By their fruits ye shall know them," he quoted from the Gospel of Matthew, and turned the phrase into a scientific hypothesis.

This is the key that unlocks this book's final chapter. James wasn't trying to debunk religion, and he wasn't trying to defend any particular version of it. He was proposing an evaluative framework fully compatible with science, psychology, and the evidence assembled across these pages. Judge religious and spiritual practices by what they produce in human lives. The standard is the same for all traditions, and for secular alternatives: do they produce people who are kinder, more just, more compassionate, and more deeply connected to others?

The Central Claim, Stated Plainly

The argument has been built from many directions. The practical question remains: what does it mean to live by it?

The ultimate end of moral life is human flourishing: lives lived with kindness, justice, compassion, honesty, and genuine connection to other people. This end isn't controversial. Virtually every moral tradition, religious or secular, identifies it as the goal, even when their descriptions differ.

Religion is one means toward that end. So is secular philosophy, a secular humanist community, a committed therapeutic relationship, a stable family, a rigorous liberal education, a life of service, a deep friendship. None of these has exclusive access to the end. None automatically produces it by virtue of its existence. They're tools, and tools are evaluated by how well they do their job.

The question "is religion good or bad?" is the wrong question. It's like asking whether surgery is good or bad. Surgery can save a life or end one, depending on the skill of the surgeon, the condition being treated, and the quality of follow-up care. The right questions are: what specific religious practices, in what specific contexts, produce what specific effects in people's lives? And what do those effects look like when measured against the standard of human flourishing?

These are empirical questions. They're increasingly answerable with evidence. The research literature of the past three decades points toward conclusions that are neither "religion is the answer" nor "religion is the problem," but something more useful: some religious practices reliably help, others reliably harm, and the difference can be observed, studied, and described.

Let me be direct about what the evidence shows. Religious belief, as a propositional claim about God's existence, isn't a necessary condition for moral behavior, for belonging to a moral community, or for living a life of exemplary service. The evidence is unambiguous on this point, and it doesn't diminish religion to say so. It clarifies what religion is actually doing.

Think of it through a metaphor that has run through this book from the beginning. Morality functions like a human language: deep, universal in its basic structure, yet expressed through vastly different accents, dialects, and idioms. Religion is one of those accents, and a particularly rich and durable one. It functions best understood as something like the operating system on which the moral software runs: it structures, organizes, and amplifies moral capacities already present in the species, and different operating systems can run the same essential programs through quite different means.

The Spiritual but Not Religious Phenomenon

One of the most significant developments in the religious landscape of wealthy Western nations over the past generation is the rapid growth of a population that identifies as "spiritual but not religious." These are people who have left or never joined institutional religious communities but who retain a sense that spiritual experience, transcendence, and meaning-making are important parts of human life. They're not, by and large, simply atheists under another name.

As of 2024, Pew Research Center data shows that twenty-eight percent of American adults are now religiously unaffiliated, known colloquially as "nones." This is now the largest single religious category in the United States, surpassing Catholics (twenty-three percent) and evangelical Protestants (twenty-four percent). As recently as 2007, nones represented only sixteen percent of the adult population.

The more illuminating figure is a different one. Pew's parallel research finds that forty-one percent of American adults say they've grown more spiritual over the course of their lives, while only twenty-four percent say they've grown more religious. More people report an increase in their sense of connection to something larger than themselves than report greater involvement with organized religion. Spirituality and institutional religion are separating in the American experience.

What drives this? The sociological literature points to several factors: loss of trust in religious institutions following repeated scandals, a cultural emphasis on individual autonomy that makes institutional belonging feel constraining, the decline of inherited religious identity, and a genuine hunger for meaning and transcendence that institutional religion isn't successfully meeting for many people.

Most "nones," as Pew's data makes clear, aren't secular materialists. They believe in God or a higher power. They pray. They have spiritual experiences. They're just doing it outside the walls of organized religion, mixing elements from different traditions and following their own internal compass rather than an institutional one.

General Social Survey data analyzed through 2022 shows that the "very spiritual" category has grown from twenty-two percent of Americans in 1998 to twenty-six percent in 2022, while the "not at all spiritual" category has also grown, from twelve to fifteen percent. The middle is thinning. Spiritual life in America is bifurcating: some people are engaging more deeply with transcendence while others are abandoning the category altogether. What's declining is the middle ground of habitual, culturally inherited religious practice that asks little of participants and offers little in return.

This isn't, on the whole, a flight from meaning. It looks more like a search for meaning conducted outside traditional institutional structures.

The Promise and the Peril of Hybrid Paths

Many people today don't identify with any single tradition but construct a spiritual and moral life from elements drawn across traditions. Yoga from Hinduism. Meditation from Buddhism. An ethical framework of care and service from Christianity or Judaism. A commitment to reason and evidence from secular humanism. A contemplative practice from Sufism or Zen. These hybrid paths reflect genuine creativity, but they also raise a question the evidence presses us to take seriously: can they provide what religion provides, at its best, without its institutional structure?

The research on secular mindfulness offers a useful test case. Beginning in 1979, Jon Kabat-Zinn developed Mindfulness-Based Stress Reduction, stripping mindfulness of its Buddhist doctrinal context and adapting it for clinical and secular use. Over the following four decades, the program generated hundreds of randomized controlled trials demonstrating its effectiveness for reducing stress, anxiety, depression, and chronic pain.

A 2022 study examining how the framing of mindfulness practice affected its outcomes found something counterintuitive: when mindfulness was presented as a "scientifically proven tool" rather than a "sacred Buddhist practice," the secular framing was significantly more effective at increasing participants' happiness. The practice matters more than the theological packaging, at least for participants not embedded in a living Buddhist community. The technique can be extracted from the tradition and function effectively on its own terms.

This is good news for hybrid paths. But there's a qualification. A 2013 study by King and colleagues found that people identifying as "spiritual but not religious" showed higher rates of anxiety, depression, and neurotic disorder than both consistently religious people and consistently secular ones. A 2022 longitudinal study found similar patterns in young people: consistently identifying as "spiritual but not religious" was associated with worse physical and mental health outcomes compared to consistently religious identification.

The King and colleagues study was cross-sectional, so the direction of causality can't be determined. People experiencing anxiety and depression may be drawn to individual spirituality precisely because of their distress, rather than the identification causing distress.

The hypothesis that emerges isn't that spirituality is harmful. It's that the community and ritual structure of organized religion provide specific psychological and social benefits that informal spiritual practice doesn't automatically replicate. People who practice mindfulness alone in their apartments don't receive the benefits of belonging to a community that knows them, holds them accountable, marks the transitions of their lives with shared ritual, and provides concrete support during crisis. The practice is real. The community is also real. They're not interchangeable.

This is one of the most practically important insights in the research literature on religion and human flourishing: the benefits of religious practice aren't all located in the content of the belief. Many are located in the social structure that surrounds the belief. For someone building a moral and spiritual life outside traditional religion, this means the practice alone isn't enough. The community must be deliberately constructed as well.

The Hive Switch and the Emotions of Transcendence

Jonathan Haidt, in *The Righteous Mind* (2012), introduces a concept he calls the "hive switch." He observes that human beings have a dual psychological nature: for most of our lives, we function as what he calls "ninety percent chimp," pursuing our own interests, managing our own status, navigating our own concerns. But under certain conditions, something shifts. People lose themselves in something larger. Individual concerns fall away. The group becomes the unit of experience. Haidt calls this the "ten percent bee," drawing on the self-transcendent, collectively functioning nature of social insects.

The hive switch can be triggered by religious worship: communal prayer, shared music, ritual movement, a sense of divine presence that dissolves individual boundaries. But it can also be triggered by great music heard in a crowd, military service and the bonds formed under shared hardship, collective political action, awe-inspiring encounters with nature, or what psychologists studying self-transcendent emotions call moments of "peak experience." The emotional architecture that religion activates reliably through ritual and community isn't religion's exclusive property. It's a feature of human psychology.

Haidt identified a related moral emotion in an earlier paper: "elevation." Elevation is the warm, uplifting feeling that arises when we witness extraordinary moral beauty: a person risking their safety to help a stranger, someone showing exceptional compassion in the face of hostility. Haidt found that elevation produces physical sensations (often described as warmth in the chest), a desire to become a better person, and increased prosocial motivation. People who experience elevation are more likely to volunteer, to help others, and to act on their moral commitments. Elevation is a secular moral emotion that does much of the same work that religious awe and conversion experiences do for believers.

These findings matter for this book's argument because they suggest something specific about what any viable alternative to religious moral formation needs to include. It's not enough to have correct moral beliefs or to follow rational ethical principles. Human moral life is deeply emotional and social. It's energized by transcendent experiences, by moments of awe and beauty, by the warmth of genuine community, by the felt sense of belonging to something larger than the self. Any framework for moral living, religious or secular, that neglects these dimensions will have less traction in human lives than one that engages them.

Growth Through Suffering

One of the strongest bodies of research on meaning-making comes not from the study of religious practice but from the study of trauma. Richard Tedeschi and Lawrence Calhoun at the University of North Carolina Charlotte spent decades studying people who had survived major life crises, including serious illness, bereavement, accidents, and violence, and who reported coming through those experiences changed for the better in ways they couldn't have anticipated.

They coined the term "posttraumatic growth" to describe this phenomenon, distinguishing it carefully from mere resilience, the capacity to return to baseline after adversity. Posttraumatic growth is something more: a genuine positive transformation that exceeds the person's pre-trauma level of functioning. It shows up in five domains: deeper relationships, new possibilities for one's life, greater personal strength, heightened appreciation for life, and what Tedeschi and Calhoun called "spiritual development," a term they used broadly to include both religious and secular deepening of the existential dimension of life.

The mechanism they identified is cognitive and narrative. Major trauma shatters what psychologists call "assumptive worlds," the background beliefs most people carry about how life works: that the world is broadly fair, that people get what they deserve, that the future is predictable. When those beliefs are shattered, the person must rebuild their understanding of reality. The rebuilding process requires sustained reflection, emotional processing, social support from what Tedeschi and Calhoun call "expert companions," and the gradual construction of a new narrative. The person who completes it has a richer, more textured understanding of life and a deeper relationship with their own humanity.

Religion provides a ready-made framework for this process. Most major traditions have developed detailed theologies of suffering, narratives of meaning-making in the face of loss, rituals for marking grief and transition, and communities of people who have survived their own crises and can offer companionship to those currently in the midst of one. For people embedded in a living religious tradition, these resources are immediately available when suffering arrives.

Secular people can access the same growth, and the research confirms they do. But they typically need to construct their own meaning-making framework more deliberately, through therapy, honest conversation with trusted others, reading that opens up philosophical or literary approaches to suffering, and the slow, difficult work of narrative reconstruction.

The difference isn't in the capacity for growth, which appears to be universal, but in the scaffolding available to support the process. Religious communities have been building and maintaining that scaffolding for millennia. Secular communities are, in many cases, still learning how to build it.

What to Keep, What to Release, What to Build

If the pragmatic framework inherited from William James is the right one, the practical question becomes: what specifically passes the test? What practices, structures, and habits reliably produce more flourishing human lives, and what reliably produces less?

This isn't an abstract question. Every person negotiating their relationship to religion, or building a moral life outside it, faces it concretely. A few answers emerge clearly from the evidence.

Begin with what to preserve. Communal gathering, regular and reliable, is among the most robustly beneficial of all human practices. The social capital built through regular contact with the same group of people, the sense of mutual obligation, the informal support networks that form through sustained relationship, are powerful determinants of mental health, longevity, and resilience. Whether that gathering happens in a church, a mosque, a synagogue, a secular humanist community, a neighborhood dinner club, or a mutual aid network matters less than whether it happens consistently and with genuine commitment to one another.

Ritual matters too. Humans mark the transitions of their lives with ceremony not because it's irrational but because it serves a real psychological function. Births, deaths, marriages, transitions into adulthood, endings and new beginnings: these moments need marking. They need shared language and shared witness. Religious traditions have developed rich ritual repertoires for exactly this purpose. Secular life, in its emphasis on individual autonomy and its suspicion of the ceremonial, has sometimes let this go. It can be recovered without requiring theological commitment.

Contemplative practice, whether called prayer or meditation or simply quiet reflection, reliably reduces anxiety, improves emotional regulation, increases empathy, and deepens self-knowledge. The form matters less than the regularity and the intention. Even five or ten minutes of daily silence, taken seriously as a practice of attention, produces measurable benefits over time.

Gratitude practice is one of the most consistently supported interventions in positive psychology. Regular attention to what is good in one's life, what one has received, who has helped, what deserves appreciation, produces genuine increases in wellbeing and motivates prosocial behavior. Every major religious tradition includes practices for this, from Jewish blessings over daily activities to Buddhist reflections on interdependence to Christian Eucharistic thanksgiving. It can also be practiced entirely outside any religious framework.

Moral storytelling, telling and hearing stories about how people faced difficult situations with courage and compassion, transmits moral wisdom in a way that abstract instruction rarely does. Every tradition knows this. Secular communities can do it too, but they need to make the deliberate choice.

Service to others: the research consistently shows that people who orient their lives toward the welfare of others, through volunteering, caregiving, community involvement, or careers in service, report higher wellbeing, greater resilience, and deeper meaning than people oriented primarily toward self-interest. Religion has been extraordinarily effective at channeling people into service. Secular communities can do the same, but the infrastructure must be intentionally built.

There are also things worth releasing. Fear as the primary moral motivator doesn't produce the flourishing it promises. Compliance built on the fear of divine punishment or social shaming may suppress certain behaviors, but it doesn't build character. It builds anxiety, rigidity, and a moral life that depends on external enforcement rather than internal conviction. Research on moral development consistently shows that internalized values, chosen freely and owned personally, produce more consistent and generous moral behavior than externally imposed rules.

Intolerance of doubt is similarly corrosive to genuine faith and genuine moral development. The traditions that have produced the most morally serious people have, almost without exception, been traditions that could hold questions: Job's confrontation with God, the Psalms of lament, the Zen koan that can't be answered by the ordinary mind, the Talmudic tradition of preserving minority opinions alongside majority rulings. The deepest spiritual and moral formation happens in the presence of genuine questions, not in their suppression.

Shame as a chronic moral tool is different from appropriate guilt. Guilt says "I did something wrong and I can repair it." Shame says "I am something wrong." The research on shame, associated particularly with the work of Brené Brown, shows that chronic shame doesn't motivate moral improvement. It motivates concealment, disconnection, and self-destruction. Any community that relies on shame as its primary method of moral formation is using a broken tool.

Dogmatism, whether religious or secular, is the conviction that one's own tradition has the complete and final answer to moral questions, and that encounters with other traditions are threats rather than opportunities. The history of every tradition includes moments when dogmatism enabled cruelty. It includes, equally, moments when the tradition's prophetic voices, calling the community back to its own highest ideals, broke through the dogmatism to produce change.

Finally, there are things to build. One of the most honest observations about the current moment in the developed world is that many people, having drifted away from or deliberately left traditional religious communities, find themselves without the infrastructure those communities provided. They haven't lost their moral instincts or their hunger for meaning. They've lost the social technology that organized those instincts and that hunger into something sustainable over time. If you've left religion, or were never part of it, the evidence suggests you may need to deliberately construct several things that religious communities provide automatically. A regular gathering of people who know you and whom you know. Practices that mark time and transition. Rituals for loss and gratitude. Ways of holding yourself accountable to moral commitments over the long arc of a life. And some form of service that connects you to others whose lives are different from yours. None of these build themselves. They require intention, effort, and commitment. That's not a weakness of secular life. It's a reality that secular communities have sometimes been slow to acknowledge.

Learning to Hear Other Accents

Gordon Allport, the Harvard psychologist who developed the foundational research on prejudice in his 1954 book *The Nature of Prejudice*, identified what he called "contact theory": prejudice between groups is reliably reduced when members of those groups interact under certain conditions. Those conditions include equal status between the groups in the contact situation, common goals that require cooperation, genuine interdependence, and the support of recognized authorities. When those conditions are met, sustained contact between groups consistently reduces prejudice, fear, and hostility.

Interfaith dialogue, when done well, meets these conditions. A 2022 systematic review in the Journal of Sociology and Inter-Religious Research found that interfaith dialogue reduces intolerance, builds bridges, and challenges extremism most effectively when it proceeds through three stages: initial contact, joint activities and shared learning, and the formation of genuine personal friendships across tradition boundaries. The goal isn't to merge all traditions into one. The goal is to develop the capacity to recognize that different accents of the same moral language are legitimate, that the person speaking from a different tradition is trying to answer the same questions, and that we might have something to learn from one another.

People who engage seriously with traditions other than their own consistently develop more nuanced moral thinking, lower levels of prejudice toward religious outgroups, and a deeper appreciation for the complexity of the questions that religious and secular traditions alike are trying to address. This doesn't require abandoning your own tradition. It requires approaching other traditions with genuine curiosity rather than defensive suspicion.

The Dialogue Institute describes interfaith dialogue as playing a "fundamental role in reducing tensions and conflicts, countering extremism, and opening society towards tolerance." When religious leaders from different traditions speak together against extremism and violence, they send a powerful counter-signal to those who would use religion as a justification for harm. They're saying, in effect: this isn't what our tradition is for.

The vision that animates this book's conclusion isn't complicated: a world in which a Catholic and a Muslim and a Buddhist and a secular humanist and an agnostic can sit at the same table and recognize, across their differences, that they're all working on the same problem. How should I treat other people? What makes a life worth living? How do I face suffering and death without being destroyed by them? What do I owe to my community, and what does my community owe to me?

The answers will differ. They differ within traditions as much as between them. But the questions unite us. They're the questions that make us human.

The Value of Understanding

Daniel Dennett argued in *Breaking the Spell* that studying religion scientifically would diminish its hold on us. He was half right. The scientific study of religion does demystify certain mechanisms. But it doesn't diminish what those mechanisms accomplish. Understanding that the rosary synchronizes cardiovascular rhythms doesn't make the rosary less valuable to the person who prays it. If anything, it adds a second layer of appreciation: the recognition that a practice refined over centuries by millions of people has been doing, with extraordinary precision, something that modern cardiology is only now learning to describe. Knowing how a tool works doesn't make it less useful. It makes it more fully understood, and understanding is the precondition for wise use.

The Language Underneath

We've traveled a long way in this book. We began with the evolutionary and neurological foundations of moral life, with the evidence that human beings come into the world equipped with the basic capacities for empathy, fairness, reciprocity, and care. We examined how religion emerged, across cultures and across millennia, as the most comprehensive and powerful system human societies have developed for organizing those capacities, channeling them into durable institutions, and transmitting them across generations.

We examined the ways that different religious and secular traditions have shaped moral behavior, sometimes expanding the circle of moral concern and sometimes contracting it. We looked honestly at religion's capacity for both extraordinary good and extraordinary harm, and found that the capacity for each is rooted not in religion itself but in the human psychology that religion amplifies and channels.

Throughout, we've returned to a single image. Morality is the language. Religion is one of the accents in which that language is spoken. The accent is real. It shapes how the language sounds, what emotional resonances it carries, what cultural memories it evokes, what community it summons. But the accent isn't the language. The moral content, the care for children, the demand for fairness, the importance of honesty, the weight of suffering that calls for response, runs deeper than any accent. It belongs to the species, not to any tradition.

This means several things. No tradition holds exclusive title to the moral language. Believers and non-believers are engaged in the same fundamental project, even when they describe it in entirely different terms. The encounter between different traditions, if honest and patient, is always an encounter between people trying to answer the same questions. The person who prays and the person who meditates and the person who simply lives with deliberate care for those around them are all, in the deepest sense, doing the same thing.

This book isn't anti-faith. It's tried, from the first page to this one, to be a serious and respectful engagement with what religion actually is, what the evidence shows about what it does to human beings and communities, and what that means for how we should think about the role of faith in moral life. The answer isn't that faith is dispensable. The answer is that faith is one path among paths, one accent among accents, that it has remarkable capacities and also real dangers, and that it deserves to be understood on those terms rather than either defended uncritically or dismissed impatiently.

The invitation, at the end, isn't to reach a conclusion. It's to carry a question forward.

A Final Reflection

Not a summary, but an invitation.

Somewhere in your life, there's a person who speaks a different moral accent than yours. Perhaps they believe what you don't believe. Perhaps they practice what you've left behind, or they've left behind what you still practice. Perhaps they approach the questions of meaning, suffering, and obligation from a framework that feels foreign to you. Perhaps they're raising children with different values, or mourning in a different way, or building a community you don't quite understand.

What would it mean to take that person seriously as a fellow practitioner of the moral language? Not to adopt their accent. Not to pretend the differences are unimportant. But to recognize, in the specificity of their practice and the depth of their commitment, the same fundamental effort that animates your own: the effort to live with some integrity, to treat others with some decency, to face the uncertainties of a human life without becoming cruel or indifferent.

The question to carry from this book is a simple one. It requires no theology and no philosophy. It requires only honesty and the willingness to act on what you find.

What is the next right thing I can do for someone who speaks a different accent than mine?

That question, asked seriously and answered honestly, is where the moral language lives.

PART IV

THE SECULAR CONGREGATION

Chapter 13

The New Congregations

On a Saturday afternoon at Anfield, fifty-four thousand people rise to their feet. The opening bars of "You'll Never Walk Alone" swell from the Kop end and roll through the stadium like a wave of sound that has no discernible origin. It simply exists, simultaneously everywhere. Arms stretch wide. Scarves lift overhead, held taut between two fists, swaying in unison. The voices aren't good, aren't tuneful, aren't remotely concerned with pitch. They're something better than good. They're together.

A visitor from another century (a sociologist, say, one who had spent years studying Aboriginal ceremonies in central Australia) would recognize what is happening immediately. Émile Durkheim called it *collective effervescence*: those moments when individuals dissolve into something larger, when the boundaries between self and group grow thin, and a shared emotional intensity reaffirms the bonds of the collective. Durkheim saw it in religious ritual. Liverpool supporters experience it every other Saturday.

This chapter is about what happens when communities that aren't religious begin to serve functions that were once the near-exclusive province of religious congregations. Some of these communities provide moral formation. Some provide belonging without any moral content at all. Many fall somewhere along that spectrum, offering pieces of what a church or synagogue or mosque once bundled together in a single weekly gathering. The question running through all of them isn't whether they work (they demonstrably do, in specific and measurable ways) but whether any of them can do the full work of a congregation across the arc of a whole life.

If morality is the language, as this book has argued, and religion is the accent, then these secular communities are developing accents of their own. Some are rich and expressive. Others are rudimentary, limited to a few phrases. The challenge isn't just finding community (human beings are resourceful enough to do that almost anywhere) but finding community that speaks in a moral register, that shapes who you are and not merely where you spend your time.

The Stadium as Temple

The research on sports fandom keeps confirming what observation has always suggested. Michael Serazio's ethnographic study of Philadelphia Phillies supporters found that fans reaffirm their relationships through the team in precisely the way Durkheim suggested Aboriginal tribes worshipped their society through the totem. The team logo, Serazio argued, functions as a sacred symbol that "can cut across difference, integrate subpopulations, and materially index belonging". The jersey is a vestment. The stadium is a cathedral. Match day is the sabbath.

The most striking evidence is neurological. A 2017 brain imaging study of Portuguese football fans found that viewing their team's winning moments activated the ventral tegmental area, the substantia nigra, the amygdala, and the medial prefrontal cortex, the same reward and emotional-cognition regions activated by romantic love. Team devotion isn't metaphorically like love. At the level of brain chemistry, it's love: a strong motivational state that biases empathy and helping attitudes toward fellow group members.

The Belonging That Fandom Builds

Daniel Wann, the leading empirical researcher on sports fan psychology at Murray State University, has spent decades documenting the psychological benefits of team identification. His studies of older adults found that the more strongly a person identified with their local team, the lower their loneliness scores, with team identification accounting for significant unique variance in both collective self-esteem and social connectedness. As Wann put it in a 2025 interview with the American Psychological Association, "If you reside in a local community and you follow the local team, it's hard to feel lonely. It's hard to feel isolated."

A separate study of 478 American fans and 490 English Premier League supporters confirmed that social identification boosts fans' social well-being through three mechanisms: purpose and meaning, progroup norms, and in-group trust. The researchers found that teams need not win for fans to benefit, since supporting a team with a poor record can sometimes provide even greater psychological benefits, because the community, not the victory, is doing the psychological work.

And then there are the rituals. Consider the haka, the traditional Māori dance performed by the New Zealand All Blacks before every test match for more than 120 years. It's a practice rooted in Indigenous spirituality. Haka signify conquests of life over death and are performed to generate collective inspiration before a challenge. The Ka Mate haka, composed by the Ngati Toa chief Te Rauparaha around 1820, opens with the words *Ka mate, ka mate, ka ora, ka ora,* meaning "I die, I die, I live, I live." When the All Blacks perform it, the stadium goes silent. Every player stamps, chants, and widens his eyes in synchronized fury. It's not entertainment. It's a ritual that unites the players and focuses them on their shared purpose, connecting them to every team that has performed it before. In the fullest Durkheimian sense, it's a ceremony.

Or consider the synchronized chanting of football ultras. A two-year ethnographic study published in *Nature: Humanities and Social Sciences Communications* found that ultra supporters' rituals (choreographed chants, tifo creation, synchronized movements sustained for ninety minutes) blur self-other distinctions and produce deep psychological bonding. Away expeditions, where fans travel long distances at considerable personal expense, were significantly stronger predictors of identity fusion than home games. The costlier the commitment, the deeper the bond. Religious scholars will recognize this pattern immediately.

The Mixed Moral Record

Honesty requires acknowledging that sports fandom's relationship with morality is genuinely complicated. The belonging is real and powerful. The moral formation is inconsistent.

On the prosocial side, research shows that team victories increase charitable donations. Wins induce positive emotions that spill over into prosocial giving, including both monetary and returnable cup donations from home fans. Fandom can channel collective identity toward generosity.

On the antisocial side, a study of Swedish soccer supporters found that team identification predicted violent intentions, with the combination of high identification and low honesty-humility producing the greatest violence risk. Research consistently documents a "bracketed morality" in sports contexts, a perception that antisocial behaviors otherwise condemned are somehow licensed within the tribal boundaries of fandom.

The honest assessment: sports fandom generates powerful belonging but not straightforwardly moral formation. It speaks the language of community fluently, but its moral accent varies wildly depending on the specific fan culture and what norms that culture rewards. A Liverpool supporter who has sung "You'll Never Walk Alone" for forty years has participated in something genuinely sacred. Whether that sacred experience has made them a better person depends on factors the stadium can't control.

The Gym as Church

In 2015, two researchers at Harvard Divinity School set out to understand where young Americans were finding community outside religious institutions. Casper ter Kuile and Angie Thurston surveyed more than a hundred organizations and published their findings in a report called *How We Gather*. Their conclusion startled the theological establishment: CrossFit gyms, SoulCycle studios, and similar fitness communities were functioning as de facto congregations, complete with community, personal transformation, accountability, and even ritual grieving for deceased members whose names were inscribed on memorial workouts.

Ter Kuile was direct: "These things are actually religious. You should treat these institutions as religious options that people find." His co-author Thurston described communities "helping people aspire toward goals, transform themselves, and work toward change while holding each other accountable to make things better." The Pew Research Center had found that more than a third of millennials were religiously unaffiliated (double the rate of Baby Boomers), and of those unaffiliated, only 10 percent were looking for a religious community. The rest were finding belonging elsewhere, whether they recognized it as belonging or not.

The empirical research bears this out. The first study to directly measure community belonging in CrossFit, published in the *Journal of Health Psychology* in 2018, found that CrossFit members reported significantly higher social capital and community belongingness than traditional gym members, with large effect sizes on all measures. A 2024 qualitative study in the *Journal of Sport and Social Issues* described CrossFit as a "peg community", where individuals temporarily align their self-developmental strivings with others in a space where "the norms of the outside world do not necessarily apply." Members described bonds that were real and meaningful but also, crucially, ones they could leave behind when the community no longer served their needs.

This is an important limitation. A community you can walk away from without breaking a promise is a different creature from one that holds you through difficulty. The "leave your ego at the door" ethic found across multiple CrossFit studies creates genuine humility within the box. But a peg community, by definition, is transient. It forms around shared aspiration and dissolves when that aspiration fades.

parkrun: The Closest Thing to a Secular Congregation

If CrossFit is the high-intensity startup church, parkrun is the quiet parish that may outlast them all.

For readers unfamiliar with it: parkrun is a free, weekly, timed 5-kilometer run or walk held every Saturday morning in approximately 2,200 locations across more than 23 countries, with between 360,000 and 390,000 finishers participating every weekend. It costs nothing. There's no membership fee, no equipment requirement, no minimum fitness level. You register once with a barcode, show up at 9 a.m. on Saturday, and walk or run alongside anyone else who turned up. Then you go home, or stay for coffee, or volunteer to help run the event the following week.

The structural parallels to a congregation are striking. It happens at the same time, in the same place, every week: the Saturday morning sabbath. It's open to everyone regardless of ability or background. Every event requires dozens of volunteers, and approximately 51,000 people volunteer globally each weekend. There are no spectators at parkrun. Everyone is either a participant or a volunteer. Often they're both.

The health evidence is substantial. A 2025 study by Sheffield Hallam University surveying nearly 80,000 participants found that 74 percent reported improved life satisfaction from running or walking and 73 percent reported improved life satisfaction through volunteering. Mental health improvements drove life satisfaction more than physical health improvements, meaning that parkrun's social context, not merely the exercise, was generating the benefit. For those who rated their health as "very bad" at registration, the estimated improvement was 1.6 points on the Office for National Statistics life satisfaction scale. A transformative change.

The most revealing finding comes from a 2023 study of parkrun participants living with mental health conditions. Researchers compared those who both ran and volunteered against those who only ran. The results were dramatic: 56 percent of runner-volunteers felt part of a community, compared to just 29 percent of runners alone; 60 percent of runner-volunteers had met new people, compared to only 24 percent of runners alone. The service dimension, not just the physical activity, was what generated the genuine sense of congregation.

This finding has real implications. It suggests that the secret ingredient in community formation isn't shared experience alone but shared service. Showing up and participating is good. Showing up and giving is what makes it a congregation.

It's worth noting that the popular narrative of oxytocin as a straightforward "moral molecule" has been substantially complicated by subsequent research. Work by Carolyn De Dreu and others has shown that oxytocin promotes in-group altruism while simultaneously increasing out-group derogation. Oxytocin is a bonding hormone, not a universal compassion hormone, and its effects mirror the in-group bias documented throughout this book. The communities described in this chapter generate powerful bonds, but those bonds, like all human bonds, carry the shadow of exclusion.

parkrun doesn't have an explicit moral code, a sacred text, or a Higher Power. But it has regularity, inclusivity, embodied gathering, and a culture of service. It's probably the best current secular congregation model in existence, and it arose not from any attempt to replace religion but from a simple invitation to run together on Saturday mornings.

The Rooms: Alcoholics Anonymous and the Architecture of Moral Community

The communities discussed so far provide powerful belonging. Some provide elements of moral formation. But one secular community provides virtually the complete architecture of a religious congregation with such structural precision that scholars, courts, and its own critics have spent decades debating whether it's, in fact, a religion.

Alcoholics Anonymous was founded in 1935 when two men, a New York stockbroker named Bill Wilson and an Akron surgeon named Bob Smith, discovered that talking honestly with each other about their drinking was more effective than anything medicine or willpower had managed alone. From that single conversation, a fellowship grew that today operates in approximately 180 nations with an estimated two million members and more than 123,000 groups worldwide.

The entry point is desperation. Nobody joins Alcoholics Anonymous out of curiosity about community building. They join because alcohol has brought them to their knees. This community was formed in crisis, and that fact is essential to understanding both its extraordinary power and its unusual structure.

The Twelve Steps as Moral Framework

The Twelve Steps of Alcoholics Anonymous are, on their face, a program for recovering from addiction. But read them carefully and something else emerges. Step Four asks members to make "a searching and fearless moral inventory" of themselves. Step Five requires admitting "to God, to ourselves, and to another human being the exact nature of our wrongs." Steps Eight and Nine involve making a list of all persons harmed and making direct amends to those people wherever possible. Step Ten demands continuing personal inventory and prompt admission of wrongdoing. Step Twelve calls members to carry the message to other alcoholics and to "practice these principles in all our affairs."

This isn't merely a recovery program. It's a comprehensive moral framework: honest self-examination, confession, restitution, ongoing accountability, and service to others. As one literature review noted, more of the Twelve Steps deal with improving relationships than with abstinence. The Steps address how you treat other people, how you reckon with the harm you've caused, and how you orient your life toward something beyond your own needs. These are the central questions of moral philosophy, dressed in the language of recovery.

The Ritual Structure

Walk into any Alcoholics Anonymous meeting anywhere in the world and you'll encounter a ritual structure as consistent as a Catholic Mass. The meeting opens with a reading, often the Serenity Prayer ("God, grant me the serenity to accept the things I cannot change, courage to change the things I can, and wisdom to know the difference"), attributed to the theologian Reinhold Niebuhr (though the attribution has been disputed) and adopted by the fellowship in its early years. Passages from the Big Book are read aloud. Members share their stories following established conventions: "My name is _____ and I am an alcoholic." The meeting closes with another prayer or declaration. Sobriety milestones are marked with chips or coins, physical tokens of transformation that function precisely like sacraments.

There are speaker meetings, where one person tells their story at length. There are discussion meetings, where a topic is raised and members share in turn. There are step meetings, devoted to working through a single Step. The formats vary, but the liturgical rhythm is remarkably stable across continents. A member can walk into a meeting in Sydney, São Paulo, or Stockholm and recognize the order of service within minutes.

Sponsors: The Accountability Relationship

The most structurally significant feature of Alcoholics Anonymous may be the sponsor relationship. A sponsor is a more experienced member who guides a newcomer through the Twelve Steps, providing one-on-one accountability, honest feedback, and a human connection that's simultaneously practical and deeply personal. Research has found that 82 percent of all members report having a sponsor, with 74 percent acquiring one in their first 90 days. The perceived cohesiveness of the group is the strongest predictor of whether a newcomer will acquire a sponsor.

The sponsor relationship has no secular parallel outside mentorship. It isn't friendship, though friendship often develops. It isn't therapy, though it can be therapeutic. It's closer to what a spiritual director provides in religious traditions: a person who knows your worst truths and walks beside you anyway. Recovery-specific support from Alcoholics Anonymous members is uniquely powerful: one longitudinal study found that past 30-day sobriety rates were 42 percent for those with no support, 58 percent for those with non-Alcoholics Anonymous support, and 77 percent for those with Alcoholics Anonymous-based support. The community itself, not just the program, is the mechanism.

The Sacred Ambiguity

Here we arrive at the tension that makes Alcoholics Anonymous so fascinating for any study of secular community. The program explicitly invokes a "Higher Power" and references God in six of its Twelve Steps. Yet it insists, with equal emphasis, that each member may define that Higher Power however they choose: as God, as the group itself, as the universe, as the process of recovery, or as anything else that isn't the self. The program formally identifies as spiritual but not religious.

Courts haven't always agreed. Multiple American courts have ruled that mandating attendance at Alcoholics Anonymous meetings violates the separation of church and state, recognizing that the program's practices (prayers, confessions, sacred texts, moral codes, and calls for spiritual awakening) constitute religious activity in all but name.

This ambiguity isn't a flaw. It may be the feature that explains the program's endurance. The 2020 Cochrane systematic review analyzed 27 studies containing 10,565 participants and found that Alcoholics Anonymous performed at least as well as established treatments like cognitive behavioral therapy on all outcomes, and often outperformed them specifically on abstinence, while also demonstrating higher healthcare cost savings. Something in this structure works, and the best evidence suggests that what works isn't the theology but the community, the accountability, the ritual, and the moral framework that together produce what researchers call a variety of positive qualitative and quantitative changes in social support networks.

Alcoholics Anonymous is, probably, the most structurally religious secular community in existence. It has a sacred text, a moral code, rituals of confession and restitution, a mentorship structure, regular gathering, and a call to serve others. It blurs the line between sacred and secular so thoroughly that the line itself begins to seem less useful than we thought. In the language of this book, Alcoholics Anonymous speaks with an accent so close to the religious originals that even native speakers struggle to tell the difference.

The Village: Parent Communities and the Bonds of Shared Biology

There's a kind of community that forms not around shared interest or shared crisis but around a shared biological reality: you have a small child, and so do I, and neither of us is sleeping.

New parent groups, whether organized by hospitals, maternal health services, community centers, or sheer proximity, represent one of the most widespread forms of secular congregation in the developed world. They arise organically whenever people are thrust into the same overwhelming transition at roughly the same time. A case study published in *The Journal of Perinatal Education* found that attendance at a new parent group created opportunities for mothers to "talk to other mothers and meet people who were going through the same thing and gain reassurance," providing "a fixed opportunity and something to look forward to each week". Participation directly increased mothers' feelings of confidence, competence, and self-efficacy in their new role.

The community that forms around children expands as those children grow. School communities, kids' sports leagues, music programs, and scout troops create dense networks of parents who know each other's children, share logistical burdens, and accumulate social capital, the norms, trust, and reciprocity that make collective life possible. Research from Brigham Young University has shown that family social capital, the bonds parents build both within the home and through community connections, is remarkably durable, with effects persisting through college enrollment and completion years after the initial bonds were formed.

As one researcher put it, "Social capital is an academic measurement of your village. Building those relationships surrounds your child with people who may reinforce positive norms and potentially give them resources you couldn't."

When the Village Is Tested

The real measure of any community is what happens when things go wrong. Here, parent communities reveal both their extraordinary power and their characteristic fragility.

When a new mother develops postpartum depression, a condition affecting 10 to 15 percent of women globally, the difference between isolation and community can be clinically significant. Social support interventions reduce depressive symptoms, decrease loneliness, and increase perceived social support among at-risk mothers. As Postpartum Support International notes, "Connecting with others who are also navigating new parenthood reminds you that you're not the only one figuring it out. Sharing stories, struggles, and small victories can validate your emotions and reduce feelings of overwhelm or inadequacy."

When a child is seriously ill, the parent community rallies, organizing meal trains, covering school pickups, sitting in hospital waiting rooms. When a marriage fractures, the parents who have been standing beside you at Saturday soccer for three years become your first line of support. These aren't trivial bonds. They can be life-sustaining.

But parent communities have a structural vulnerability that churches don't: they're organized around a stage of life, not a permanent commitment. The group that formed around infant swimming lessons may dissolve when the children start school. The tight-knit circle of primary school parents may scatter when families choose different secondary schools. The sports league parents who shared every weekend for five years may lose touch entirely when the children age out of the sport. The community was real, the bonds were genuine, and then the organizing principle evaporated.

Some parent communities transcend this pattern. They're the ones where people showed up not only when they needed something but when they had something to give. They're the ones where the habit of gathering persisted even after the logistical reason for gathering faded, where the parents kept meeting long after the children left home. The difference, in every case, is the same difference that distinguishes a crisis network from a congregation: whether you show up only when you're desperate, or whether you show up every week, in good times and bad, simply because that's what you do.

The Secular Challenge: From Survival to Thriving

Across all of these communities, a pattern emerges. Human beings are remarkably good at finding each other when they need to. The biological drive toward belonging is so powerful that community will sprout in almost any soil: a shared team, a shared workout, a shared addiction, a shared child. The research confirms this at every turn. Team identification reduces loneliness. CrossFit builds social capital. parkrun improves life satisfaction. Alcoholics Anonymous produces measurable changes in social support networks. Parent groups buffer against depression and isolation.

But there's a crucial distinction between a community you lean on in crisis and a community that sustains you across a whole life. To merely survive, you use community when desperate: when the diagnosis comes, when the marriage ends, when the addiction takes hold. To thrive, you participate in community through good times and bad, through the ordinary weeks when nothing is wrong and the extraordinary ones when everything is. This is precisely what religious congregations have done, almost automatically, for centuries. You show up on Sunday (or Saturday, or Friday) not because you're in crisis but because it's the day you show up. The ritual carries you when motivation fails. The community holds you when you have nothing particular to give and nothing urgent to receive.

Robert Putnam's research has shown that more than 50 percent of American social capital is generated by faith communities, but he argues that the mechanism isn't belief itself. It's the repeated, face-to-face gathering that generates norms of reciprocity. This implies that secular institutions could replicate this effect if they achieved similar density and frequency of social encounter. The problem is that secular communities, lacking the theological foundation of obligation and sacred time, must rely on something else to keep people coming back when they no longer feel like it.

Alcoholics Anonymous solves this through the urgency of survival: you keep coming because the alternative is a return to the bottle. parkrun solves it through simplicity and habit. It's free, it's Saturday, it's the same place, and it asks nothing of you except that you show up. Sports fandom solves it through emotional investment. The season never ends, the next match is always coming, and the community is always there when you return to the stands. Parent communities solve it, when they do, through the slow accumulation of shared history: the parents who weathered the early years together develop bonds that outlast the organizing occasion.

None of these communities is a perfect substitute for a religious congregation. Each provides some elements of the bundle (belonging, ritual, moral formation, service, accountability, regularity) while lacking others. The stadium provides collective effervescence without moral direction. The CrossFit box provides accountability without permanence. parkrun provides regularity and service without explicit moral formation. Alcoholics Anonymous provides nearly everything a congregation offers, but only to those who have passed through a specific form of suffering. Parent communities provide deep bonds anchored in a shared reality, but often dissolve when that reality changes.

The secular challenge, then, isn't whether human beings can build community without God. They obviously can and do, every day, in millions of forms. The challenge is whether they can build the *habit* of community, the weekly, unsummoned, sustained participation that transforms a crisis network into a congregation and a congregation into a way of life. The new accents of secular community are being spoken in stadiums and gymnasiums, in meeting rooms and at school gates, in parks at 9 a.m. on Saturday mornings. Some are still halting, still searching for the right words. Others, such as parkrun's quiet commitment and Alcoholics Anonymous's hard-won wisdom, are beginning to sound like something you could pass down to your children.

The question isn't whether these accents will survive. It's whether they will deepen.

Sources and Further Reading

Sources for this chapter: Michael Serazio, "The Elementary Forms of Sports Fandom", Communication & Sport, 2013; Cela-Conde et al., "Tribal love: the neural correlates of passionate engagement in football fans", Social Cognitive and Affective Neuroscience, 2017; Daniel Wann and S. Weaver, "Applying the Team Identification-Social Psychological Health Model", 2009; Wann, "Psychological Needs", University of Memphis Digital Commons, 2024; Inoue et al., social identification and fan well-being, University of Illinois, 2022; Harvard Divinity School, "Haka and Aotearoa/New Zealand Rugby", Religion and Public Life, 2024; All Blacks, "The Haka", 2025; Xu et al., "A study of cultural rituals in ultras supporters", Nature: Humanities and Social Sciences Communications, 2025; donations study at football stadiums, Journal of Behavioral and Experimental Economics, 2022; personality and team identification predict violent intentions, Frontiers in Sports and Active Living, 2021; "Is social identity theory enough to cover sports fans' behavior?", Frontiers in Psychology, 2025; Casper ter Kuile and Angie Thurston, How We Gather, Harvard Divinity School, 2015; Whiteman-Sandland et al., "The role of social capital and community belongingness for exercise adherence", Journal of Health Psychology, 2018; Sheridan et al., "CrossFit, Community, and Identity", Journal of Sport and Social Issues, 2024; Sheffield Hallam University, parkrun life satisfaction research, 2025; Stevinson and Hickson, "parkrun participation and perceived social inclusion among those with mental health conditions", 2023; Ordinary Runners Club, parkrun participation data, 2025; Alcoholics Anonymous, "A.A. Around the World", 2025; Alcoholics Anonymous, "The Twelve Steps", 2025; Kelly et al., "Alcoholics Anonymous and 12-Step Facilitation Treatments", Cochrane Review summary, Alcohol and Alcoholism, 2020; Tonigan et al., "The Relationship Between Perceived Alcoholics Anonymous Social Dynamics and Getting a Sponsor", Alcoholism Treatment Quarterly, 2019; Groh et al., "Social Network Variables in Alcoholics Anonymous: A Literature Review", Clinical Psychology Review, 2007; Alcoholics Anonymous UK, "The Serenity Prayer", 2024; "Affiliation to the Alcoholics Anonymous community", Journal of Substance Use, 2024; "The Value of New Parent Groups", The Journal of Perinatal Education, 2005; Parcel et al., "Is social capital durable?", PLOS ONE, 2024; BYU News, "More than money, family and community bonds prep teens for college success", 2024; "The influence of social support in the prevention and treatment of postpartum depression", Women's Health, 2024; Postpartum Support International, "The Power of Building a Supportive Community in Parenthood", 2025; Robert Putnam and David Campbell, American Grace: How Religion Divides and Unites Us, 2012.

Chapter 14

Building Without a Blueprint

The Saturday Morning Experiment

parkrun, examined in the previous chapter as perhaps the closest existing model of a secular congregation, raises a question that goes beyond its own Saturday morning rituals. What does its success require, structurally, that most secular communities lack? And what can that structural analysis tell us about the broader project of building moral community without the blueprint that religion has always provided?

The Structural Challenge

In 2003, the anthropologist Richard Sosis published a study that should haunt anyone trying to build lasting secular community. Examining 200 nineteenth-century American communal societies, he found that religious communes survived on average 35.6 years. Secular communes survived an average of 7.7 years. The religious communities were three times less likely to dissolve in any given year.

The reason wasn't simply that religious communes attracted more dedicated people. Sosis controlled for the number of costly requirements each commune imposed (dietary restrictions, dress codes, sexual regulation, communal labor, shared property). Religious communes imposed more than twice as many costly demands: an average of seven, compared to three for secular communes. Here's the finding that cuts deepest: costly demands predicted longevity only for religious communes. For secular communes, the number of sacrifices required had no effect whatsoever on how long the community survived.

The mechanism, Sosis argued, was costly signaling theory. In religious communities, the demands were embedded in the sacred. Fasting wasn't merely dietary discipline. It was an act of devotion to God. Shared property wasn't merely economic efficiency. It was obedience to a divine command. The sacred framing made the costs meaningful in a way that couldn't be disproven or debunked, because the claims they rested on were, by definition, unfalsifiable. You can't run an experiment to determine whether God wants you to share your possessions. You can only believe it or not. And that unfalsifiability, paradoxically, is what sustained commitment across decades of hardship, doubt, and interpersonal friction.

Secular communes lacked this anchor. Their ideologies (socialism, utopian philosophy, back-to-the-land romanticism) were falsifiable. They could be tested against reality, and reality often found them wanting. When the harvest failed, when members quarreled, when the original vision collided with the messiness of daily life, there was no sacred canopy to hold the community together. The costs felt arbitrary rather than meaningful. People left.

This is the structural challenge in its starkest form. The mechanism that makes religious communities so durable, costly signaling wrapped in the sacred, is precisely the mechanism that secular communities can't straightforwardly replicate without becoming, in some sense, religious.

Ara Norenzayan, in his 2013 book *Big Gods*, argued that moralizing gods weren't merely cognitive byproducts but cultural adaptations that enabled large-scale cooperation among strangers. If he's right, religion's community-building power is central to its design, which makes the secular replication challenge even more formidable.

Robert Bellah and his colleagues diagnosed a related problem in their landmark 1985 book *Habits of the Heart*. Bellah argued that communities sustain moral formation only when they combine four elements: shared practices, shared stories, shared accountability to something beyond self-interest, and face-to-face recurring encounter. When any of these is missing, the community drifts toward what he memorably called "Sheilaism," named after an interviewee who had constructed an entirely personal religion consisting of her own inner voice and a vague injunction to be gentle with herself and take care of others. Sheila's faith was sincere. It was also, Bellah observed, entirely private, entirely self-referential, and incapable of generating the communal moral formation that sustains a society across generations.

The Sheilaism problem isn't an argument against personal spirituality. It's an observation about structure. When spirituality becomes purely individualized, it loses the communal function. The inner voice may be wise, but it can't hold you accountable on a Tuesday afternoon when you'd rather not show up. It can't sit with you in a hospital waiting room or teach your children what you believe by modeling it in a community of practice.

The question, then, is whether secular communities can assemble the structural elements that Bellah identified (practices, stories, accountability, and face-to-face encounter) without the sacred framing that Sosis showed was so powerful.

The evidence from the communities examined in the previous chapter suggests a cautious yes. But only if the builders understand what they're actually building.

What the Successful Secular Communities Share

Not all secular communities are created equal. Some generate genuine belonging, prosocial behavior, and even something approaching moral formation. Others generate camaraderie that evaporates the moment circumstances change. The research reveals a pattern in what separates the two.

Consider the structural elements that distinguish communities capable of moral influence from those that produce only temporary connection:

An explicit moral code. Burning Man's 10 Principles (Radical Inclusion, Gifting, Decommodification, Communal Effort, Civic Responsibility, Leaving No Trace, among others) constitute one of the most explicit moral frameworks of any secular community. Alcoholics Anonymous has its 12 Steps. CrossFit gyms enforce a near-universal ethic: "leave your ego at the door." parkrun operates on an unstated but pervasive norm of radical welcome. These codes aren't sacred in the religious sense, but they function analogously: they provide a normative framework that goes beyond personal preference.

Costly ongoing demands. CrossFit members report significantly higher social capital than traditional gym members (a mean score of 51.6 versus 39.3, with a large effect size), partly because the workouts are genuinely difficult and endured together. Alcoholics Anonymous insists on lifelong meeting attendance, daily spiritual practice, and service to newcomers. The cost signals commitment. But Sosis's data warns us: cost alone isn't enough. It must be anchored in something that feels larger than individual benefit.

Regular, repeated face-to-face encounter. parkrun happens every Saturday, same time, same place. CrossFit classes run on weekly schedules. Alcoholics Anonymous meetings are daily. This regularity isn't incidental. Robert Putnam's research in *American Grace* found that more than 50 percent of American social capital is generated by faith communities, not because of what people believe but because of the repeated, face-to-face gathering that generates norms of reciprocity. The frequency is the mechanism.

Service orientation built in. Communities that turn outward develop moral muscles that inward-facing communities don't. Mutual aid networks during the COVID-19 pandemic provided shopping, prescriptions, and welfare checks for isolated neighbors, often within days of formation. At parkrun, volunteering nearly doubles the sense of community belonging. A meta-analysis in JAMA Network Open found that volunteering among older adults was associated with a 24 percent decrease in mortality. Serving others generates health and meaning that self-focused participation doesn't.

Accountability structures. Alcoholics Anonymous sponsors hold their sponsees to specific behavioral commitments. Cohousing communities maintain governance structures where neighbors must show up, negotiate, and account for their contributions. Research on cohousing found that 100 percent of residents would feel comfortable asking a neighbor for help if they fell ill, compared to only 40 percent in conventional housing. That gap is the gap between a community with accountability and one without it.

A narrative tradition. Religious communities are sustained by stories that connect the present moment to a larger arc of meaning. Secular communities are beginning to develop their own. CrossFit names its most grueling workouts after fallen soldiers and first responders, a practice called "Hero WODs" that transforms exercise into commemoration. Burning Man's origin story, the gathering of friends on a San Francisco beach in 1986 that grew into a city of 72,000 in the Nevada desert, functions as a founding myth. These narratives are young, but they're doing what narratives do: providing identity continuity across time.

The key finding is both encouraging and sobering. It's the structure, not the theology, that generates the benefits. The elements that make religious communities so effective at moral formation (regular gathering, shared practice, explicit norms, service, accountability, and narrative) aren't inherently sacred. They can be assembled in secular form. But assembling them requires deliberate effort. A church offers the full bundle on the first Sunday you walk through the door. A secular community must build it piece by piece, and most build only one or two pieces before declaring victory.

The Spiritual but Not Religious Gap

There's a population for whom this structural challenge isn't abstract but personal. They're the largest underserved community in the modern moral landscape, and they're growing every year.

The Pew Research Center's 2023 survey found that 22 percent of Americans identify as spiritual but not religious. They believe in transcendence. They practice centering and meditation. They spend time in nature seeking something beyond the material. They're not hostile to the sacred. They're hungry for it.

But they're overwhelmingly alone in their seeking.

Only 11 percent of spiritual but not religious Americans belong to a religious community. Only 13 percent belong to a spiritual one. Their most common practices are solitary by design. The Barna Group found that spiritual but not religious individuals are "very unlikely to take part in groups or retreats," with only 2 to 3 percent doing so. They crave transcendence but experience it privately. The congregation function is largely absent from their lives.

Meanwhile, 54 percent of Americans aged 18 to 29 never attend religious services. Another 21 percent attend only once or twice a year. For three-quarters of young adults, the weekly gathering that has been the backbone of moral community for millennia simply doesn't exist in their lives.

This isn't a story of people who have rejected meaning. It's a story of people who have rejected institutions but kept the hunger. They're speaking the moral language, often beautifully, but speaking it to themselves. And when moral practice becomes purely private, it atrophies. The inner voice, however sincere, can't substitute for the accountability, the shared story, and the face-to-face encounter that sustained moral formation requires.

The spiritual but not religious population isn't a problem to be solved. They're people to be invited. But the invitation must be to something real: a community with structure, with recurring encounter, with demands that go beyond showing up when you feel like it. The communities described in the previous chapter are beginning to provide this. Meditation groups that meet weekly. Running communities that expect consistent participation. Volunteer networks that ask for ongoing commitment rather than one-off service. These are the early forms of what the spiritual but not religious population needs: secular congregations worthy of the name.

The Embodiment Problem

One of the most common responses to the decline of in-person community is the suggestion that online communities can fill the gap. The evidence says otherwise, but it also says something more nuanced than a simple dismissal.

A 2023 study published in *Scientific Reports* found that face-to-face interactions were consistently superior to all digital alternatives for reducing loneliness and sadness and for increasing affection, support, and happiness. Even video calls produced significantly worse outcomes than sitting in the same room with another person. A 2024 study confirmed that while voice calls, group calls, and online messaging all increased social connection and positive affect, "the benefits of face-to-face interactions consistently eclipsed those of all virtual surrogates." A review in *Nature Mental Health* documented the mechanisms: online communities are prone to echo chambers, deindividuation, and the reinforcement of in-group identity at the expense of genuine moral encounter with difference.

In the language of social capital theory, online communities readily produce bridging capital, the loose, diverse connections between relative strangers that enable information flow and broad networks. They struggle to produce bonding capital, the deep, emotionally supportive relationships that sustain people through crisis and hold them accountable in daily life. Bridging capital is valuable. But bonding capital is what does the moral work.

This doesn't mean online communities are worthless. Far from it. A rapid review of online bereavement support in *Palliative Medicine* found that online grief communities were feasible, acceptable, and effective at reducing grief intensity and depression, with participant retention typically above 70 percent. Eighty-six percent of bereaved parents said it helped to meet others with similar experiences. These communities provide something irreplaceable for isolated and stigmatized individuals: connection at 2:00 a.m. when no one in their physical world is awake, the normalization of experiences that feel abnormal, and access to others who have survived what they're enduring.

Research on Reddit mental health communities found that members develop a genuine sense of community, addressing the platform itself as a "safe space" and identifying with other users who share an understanding of their conditions. The emotional and social functions of these communities may be even more impactful than informational guidance.

The honest synthesis: online communities are a lifeline for people who have no other option. They're a supplement for people who do. They're not a replacement for embodied gathering. The handshake, the shared meal, the silence held together in a room: these aren't sentimental luxuries. They're the foundation on which bonding capital is built, and bonding capital is what turns a network into a community.

Any serious attempt to build secular moral community must begin with a room. Not a feed, not a livestream. A room with people in it, returning to it, week after week.

Thriving, Not Just Surviving

There's a pattern in how people relate to community that may be the most important insight in this chapter, and one the research literature rarely states directly: people lean on community in hard times, but to thrive, they need community in good times and bad.

Religious congregations solve this automatically. The expectation is weekly attendance, regardless of personal circumstance. You go to church when your marriage is falling apart, and you go when your marriage is flourishing. The practice doesn't depend on need. It depends on commitment. Because it does, the community is already in place when the crisis arrives. The relationships are already deep enough to bear the weight.

Secular communities tend to operate on a different logic: opt-in when needed, opt-out when not. A parent group forms around the shared emergency of new parenthood, and attendance is perfect for the first six months. Then the acute need passes. Sleep returns. Routines stabilize. People stop coming. By the time the next crisis arrives, the community has dispersed. The people who understood your situation best are no longer in the room.

The parent groups that last are the ones where people keep showing up after the acute need passes. They come because they've built relationships that matter independent of the original need, because the group has developed its own identity and rituals, because showing up has become a habit rather than a response to crisis.

Alcoholics Anonymous illustrates this principle with unusual clarity. The program insists on continued meeting attendance even after sobriety is established, often for years, sometimes for life. Research from Stanford found Alcoholics Anonymous to be the most effective path to alcohol abstinence after evaluating 27 studies involving more than 10,000 participants. A longitudinal study tracking Alcoholics Anonymous attendance over seven years found that the group maintaining modest but steady attendance (about one meeting per week at each follow-up) achieved stable abstinence rates of 60 percent by year seven. The community isn't merely the crisis intervention. The community is the treatment. Continued participation isn't a failure to graduate. It's the ongoing practice that sustains the transformation.

This is the challenge for secular communities in its most practical form: creating the habit of regular attendance without the theological obligation that religion provides. A church doesn't ask you to evaluate, each Sunday morning, whether you feel like going. It assumes you will go, and the assumption does the work. Every secular gathering that depends on people choosing to attend, week after week, without institutional expectation or sacred obligation, is fighting against the gravitational pull of the couch, the inbox, the errands, and the entirely reasonable feeling that one week off won't matter.

One week off never matters. It's the accumulation of one-week-offs that dissolves a community.

The communities that resist this dissolution have found secular equivalents to the theological obligation. parkrun uses simple behavioral design: the barcode system means your attendance is recorded, your personal history is tracked, your milestones are celebrated publicly. CrossFit uses the small-group dynamic: when your class is only twelve people, your absence is noticed. Alcoholics Anonymous uses the sponsor relationship: someone specific is expecting you, and letting them down feels personal rather than abstract. Cohousing uses shared governance: if you don't show up to the monthly meeting, decisions get made without you.

None of these mechanisms invokes God. All of them create the felt expectation that keeps people returning when returning is inconvenient. And it's in the inconvenient returns, the Saturdays when it's raining and you'd rather stay in bed, the meetings when you feel fine and can't see the point, the volunteer shifts when you have better things to do, that the habit of community becomes the character of community. You're no longer someone who goes to parkrun when the weather is nice. You're a parkrunner. The identity has shifted from consumer to participant, from visitor to member. And that shift, invisible and undramatic, is where the moral formation actually happens.

What Is Still Missing

Let's be honest about the limits of what has been built so far.

No secular community has yet solved the problem of moral formation at scale comparable to what the world's religious traditions have achieved across centuries. The deficit isn't belonging. It's integration. Christianity has 2.4 billion adherents, Islam nearly 2 billion, Hinduism over 1.2 billion. Each provides a comprehensive package: moral code, communal practice, narrative tradition, rites of passage, care for the dying, education of the young, mutual aid in crisis, and a cosmic story that locates individual suffering within a framework of meaning. The package has been tested by famine, war, persecution, and the slow erosion of time. It's survived because it works, in the structural sense that Sosis and Bellah and Putnam have documented, at generating communities that endure.

The secular experiments described in this book are young. The oldest (civic organizations like Rotary, founded in 1905) are facing serious membership challenges, particularly among younger generations. The newer ones (parkrun, CrossFit boxes, meditation communities, mutual aid networks, psychedelic healing circles) are often brilliant at one or two structural elements and missing the rest. CrossFit generates powerful belonging but doesn't straightforwardly produce moral formation. Sports fandom creates identity and collective effervescence, but its moral direction is conditioned entirely on the norms of the specific fan community. Music festivals produce Turner's communitas in its most vivid form, but the communitas is transient by design; you go home, and the ordinary world reasserts itself.

What's still missing, most acutely, is integration. Religious traditions bundle everything together: moral code, rites of passage, mutual aid, cosmic story, all of it available in a single institution on a single day of the week. The secular landscape, by contrast, is fragmented. You might find belonging at parkrun, accountability in a therapy group, service through a volunteer organization, narrative in a book club, and transcendence on a solo hike. Each of these is real.

None provides the full bundle alone. The fragmentation itself is exhausting: it requires you to be your own curator of moral community, assembling from a dozen sources what a single religious tradition once provided.

This curation is possible for the educated, the energetic, the socially skilled, and the economically secure. It's much harder for those without those advantages. And here the equity dimension becomes urgent. Religious congregations, at their best, have always served as the social safety net of last resort for people at the margins: the poor, the elderly, the isolated, the recently immigrated, the grieving. Putnam found that religious Americans are two to three times more likely than matched secular Americans to belong to neighborhood associations, volunteer organizations, and civic groups. Over a third of all volunteering in America is carried out for or through religious organizations. When religious participation declines without a secular replacement, it's the most vulnerable who lose the most.

This isn't an argument for returning to religion. It's an argument for taking the structural challenge seriously. The ingredients are known: regular gathering, explicit moral norms, service to others, accountability, and narrative. What hasn't yet been built, at scale, is the secular institution that combines them all. That's not cause for despair. It's a description of the work.

An Invitation, Not a Conclusion

This book began with a hunt on the East African savanna, 70,000 years ago, and a simple observation: long before anyone had conceived of God or prayer or scripture, human beings were already sharing meat with the injured, caring for the elderly, and punishing those who took more than their share. The moral language was already being spoken. It was spoken in the body, in the gut feeling that fairness matters and that cruelty is wrong, in the urge to help and the fury at betrayal. It wasn't invented by religion. It was inherited by religion, shaped by religion, amplified by religion, and transmitted across generations by religion with extraordinary effectiveness.

Throughout these chapters, we've returned to the same image. Morality is the language. Religion is one of the accents in which that language is spoken. The accent is real and powerful. It carries the weight of centuries, the resonance of sacred stories, the comfort of belonging to something ancient and larger than any individual life. No serious person should dismiss what that accent has meant, and continues to mean, to billions of people.

But the language is older than any accent. And new accents are forming.

The secular communities described in these final chapters are developing new ways of pronouncing the universal moral language. Some of these accents are tentative, still searching for the right inflection. Some are confident, spoken by communities that have been practicing for decades. All of them are experiments. None has yet achieved what the great religious traditions have achieved. All of them are trying.

The structural ingredients are known. Regular gathering. Shared practice. Explicit moral commitment. Service to others. Accountability to someone beyond yourself. A story that connects your small life to something larger. These aren't religious inventions. They're human inventions that religion has deployed with remarkable skill, and they're available to anyone willing to do the work of assembling them.

The work is harder without a blueprint. Religion provides the blueprint: the schedule, the liturgy, the text, the community, the expectations, all of it waiting for you when you walk through the door. Building secular moral community requires constructing the blueprint as you go, and the construction never feels as elegant or as certain as what the traditions have polished over centuries. There will be awkward beginnings. There will be failed experiments. There will be Saturday mornings when only four people show up and you wonder whether any of this matters.

It matters.

It matters because the alternative isn't a world of liberated individuals, free from the constraints of community, pursuing their own private flourishing. The alternative, as the loneliness research has made devastatingly clear, is a world of isolated people dying younger, suffering more, and struggling to transmit moral values to the next generation without the communal structures that have always done that work. The question isn't whether we need moral community. The question is what form it will take.

For some people, the answer will continue to be a religious congregation, and that answer deserves respect. The accents of faith aren't going silent. They continue to provide, for billions, exactly what the research says communities need: regular gathering, shared practice, moral commitment, service, accountability, and a story vast enough to hold a human life. Nothing in this book has argued that this should stop. Everything in this book has argued that it should be understood, appreciated for what it does well, challenged where it does harm, and recognized as one accent among many rather than the only way the moral language can be spoken.

For other people, the 22 percent who are spiritual but not religious, the 54 percent of young adults who never attend services, the growing millions who have left religious institutions but haven't stopped asking the questions those institutions exist to address, the answer will need to be built. Not from nothing. From the same human materials that religion has always used: the need to belong, the capacity for sacrifice, the hunger for meaning, the deep, evolutionarily ancient pull toward caring for others and being cared for in return.

The moral language is already in you. It was there before you learned any particular accent for speaking it. It was there in your first act of sharing, your first fury at unfairness, your first impulse to comfort someone in pain. It's as old as the species and as immediate as your next encounter with another human being.

The question isn't whether you have the language. The question is where you'll choose to practice speaking it. In what room, with what people, on what recurring day, with what shared commitment, in service to what vision of how life together might be lived.

The accent you develop will be your own. It will be shaped by where you live and whom you love and what you've suffered and what you've been given. It will sound different from your neighbor's accent, and different from your parents'. That's as it should be. The moral language has always been spoken in many accents. The richness is in the variety.

But the language must be spoken aloud. It must be spoken in the company of others. It must be spoken not only when you need it but when you don't, not only in crisis but in the ordinary weeks when nothing is wrong and nothing is transcendent and the only reason to show up is that you said you would.

That's where community lives. Not in the dramatic moments but in the ordinary ones. Not in the peak experiences but in the Tuesday evenings and the Saturday mornings. Not in the theology but in the showing up.

The door is open. The room isn't yet full. There are people inside who came before you and people who will come after. What they share isn't a creed but a commitment: to keep practicing the language, to keep speaking it to one another, to keep showing up.

On a Saturday morning in March, in a park in south London, it's raining. Not dramatically, not the kind of rain that gives you an excuse. Just the grey, steady, English kind that makes the bed feel like a more rational choice. At the start line, a woman in a yellow vest is calling out the pre-run briefing to approximately 300 people, some of whom are stretching, some of whom are talking to friends, some of whom are standing alone with the particular expression of someone who got out of bed without quite knowing why.

The briefing ends. The group moves forward. The fast runners disappear into the trees. The walkers settle into their rhythm. The volunteers at the first marshal point wave and call encouragement to every single person who passes, regardless of speed, regardless of whether they're smiling or grimacing or simply putting one foot in front of the other.

Forty-five minutes later, when the last walker crosses the finish line, a volunteer scans her barcode and says, "Well done, see you next week." She nods. She doesn't look transformed. She doesn't look like she has found God or meaning or the answer to anything in particular. She looks like someone who showed up, which is what she did.

That's what showing up looks like. It's not dramatic. It's not transcendent. It's the most ordinary thing in the world, and it's the thing that holds communities together: the willingness to be present, again, on a morning when it would have been easier not to be.

The moral language belongs to all of us. It always has. The only question left is whether we'll speak it together.

Afterword: The Fire That Burns the House

I want to end this book by confronting something I've been dancing around for two hundred and some pages. Every tradition we've looked at, every thread of moral instinct, every convergence of ethics across cultures that shouldn't logically have talked to each other, all of it points in a hopeful direction. It suggests that human beings have a deep, shared foundation underneath all the religious differences.

And then you open the news.

Christian nationalists storming the United States Capitol holding wooden crosses. ISIS fighters filming executions and posting them online as religious duty. Jewish settlers attacking Palestinian shepherds with impunity in the West Bank. Buddhist monks in Myanmar cheering the displacement of 700,000 Rohingya Muslims. Hindu mobs lynching men accused of transporting cattle.

It's not just one tradition. It's all of them. And it demands an answer.

No One Gets a Pass

Let's go through it directly, because I think it matters to name it without flinching.

In the United States, Christian nationalism has become one of the most powerful predictors of support for political violence. A study published in Political Behavior found that the combination of Christian nationalist identity, white identity, perceived victimhood, and QAnon belief produced the most volatile mix. About 17.7% of white weekly churchgoers fell into the highest quartile on both violence justification and Christian nationalism scores. That's not a tiny fringe. And the January 6th Capitol attack didn't happen in a vacuum. Wooden crosses, flags reading "Jesus Saves," and prayers on the Senate floor were part of the same afternoon as the assault. Western terrorism fatalities rose 280% between 2024 and 2025, driven by antisemitism, Islamophobia, and far-right political violence.

In India, the BJP government that came to power in 2014 has been associated with a steady rise in communal violence targeting Muslims. India's own National Crime Records Bureau recorded over 2,900 religious violence cases between 2017 and 2021. Cow protection vigilante groups, loosely tolerated by state governments in several regions, have carried out lynchings. During the 2020 Delhi pogroms, supremacist mobs publicly attacked Muslim neighborhoods. USCIRF, the United States Commission on International Religious Freedom, has recommended India for its Country of Particular Concern list for multiple consecutive years. And this is happening in a country whose founding tradition, Hinduism, produced the concept of ahimsa, nonviolence, that Gandhi turned into a force that shook an empire.

In Myanmar, an organization called Ma Ba Tha, the Association for the Protection of Race and Religion, ran a years-long dehumanization campaign against the Rohingya Muslim minority. Multiple investigators concluded Ma Ba Tha was established and controlled by the military as a front organization. The 2017 scorched-earth campaign displaced more than 700,000 people, the UN called it a textbook case of ethnic cleansing, and Buddhist monks participated in and blessed the violence. This is the tradition of the Buddha. The teacher who said, "If you truly loved yourself, you could never hurt another."

In Sri Lanka, a group called the Bodu Bala Sena, the Buddhist Power Force, organized anti-Muslim violence including attacks on mosques and Muslim-owned businesses. Buddhist monks have attacked peace demonstrations. The country that gave the world some of the most beautiful writing on compassion has also produced monks who throw rocks through windows.

In Israel's West Bank, the IDF itself recorded 867 settler violence incidents in 2024, up 27% from 2023. Severe incidents including shootings and arson rose more than 50%. Israeli security agencies classify the most extreme settler attacks as terrorism. ACLED, the Armed Conflict Location and Event Data Project, has documented more than 5,350 violent settler incidents since 2016. And the people doing this often understand themselves as fulfilling divine covenant with the land.

And then there's the Islamic State, which remained the deadliest terrorist organization on the planet according to the 2025 and 2026 Global Terrorism Indices, responsible for 1,805 deaths in 2025 alone. The cruelest irony: the vast majority of ISIS's victims are Muslim. The scholars at the Yaqeen Institute have documented how extremist groups selectively quote fragments of the Quran, stripping context completely. Quran 9:29, for example, is the verse extremists cite as a universal command to fight non-believers. But the Treaty of Hudaybiyyah had just been broken when it was written. It's a response to a specific military situation, not a standing order for all time. Selective quotation divorced from context is exactly how this works.

Every single major religion. Not a coincidence.

They've Got It Exactly Backwards

Here's the thing I keep coming back to. The whole argument of this book is that morality is older than religion. The moral instinct, the revulsion at cruelty, the pull toward fairness, the impulse to protect the vulnerable, all of that predates any scripture, any prophet, any temple. Religion didn't create morality. It inherited it. It gave it language, structure, ritual, and community. The moral sense is the language. Religion is the accent.

Extremists have this perfectly inverted.

They use the accent to destroy the language. They take the framework that was built to transmit and protect human moral instincts and turn it into a weapon against those same instincts. An ISIS fighter killing a Yazidi woman isn't enacting Islam. He's murdering someone. The murder came first. The religious justification was layered on top afterward, found in selectively quoted fragments, filtered through years of political indoctrination, and packaged by leaders who found the whole arrangement convenient. A Christian nationalist who beat a Capitol police officer with a flagpole bearing Jesus's name wasn't performing Christianity. He was performing violence, with a religious costume on.

I think this distinction matters more than it might seem.

Because if we say religious extremism is caused by religion, we're actually doing the extremists a favor. We're accepting their framing. We're agreeing that the violence flows naturally from the faith. It doesn't. The research is actually quite consistent on this: the religion itself is never sufficient to cause mass violence. What you need is political power seeking an instrument. Perceived victimhood that can be amplified. An identity under threat, or one that can be made to feel that way. And then elite cues, conspiracy theories, and the systematic dehumanization of whoever gets cast as the enemy. The religion is the costume, not the cause.

That pattern repeats across every case. Myanmar's military used Ma Ba Tha to do what militaries do: identify an enemy, build public support for eliminating them, and outsource the moral legitimacy problem to the monks. The BJP has found communal violence politically useful in ways that have nothing to do with theology. Christian nationalist violence in the US follows the same playbook: victimhood narrative ("Christians are under attack"), elite cues from politicians who profit from the tension, conspiracy theories (QAnon, replacement theory), and a chosen enemy. The faith tradition gets conscripted into a political project that was always about power.

The extremists aren't more faithful than the moderates. They're more politically radicalized. And someone decided that was useful.

How Hate Travels Through Time

There's a phrase from Rwanda I haven't been able to shake since I first encountered it. It's a Kinyarwanda proverb: "A calf cannot fail to pick a colour from its mother."

In the spring of 1994, in 100 days, more than one million people were killed. Most of them were Tutsi. Most of the killers were Hutu. The genocide didn't come from nowhere. It was the result of decades of deliberate identity construction. Belgian colonial administrators imposed ethnic classification systems and put Tutsi and Hutu on identity cards. Radio broadcasts called Tutsis "cockroaches." Years of accumulated grievance, fear, and political manipulation did the rest. The killing was done neighbor by neighbor, often with machetes, often in churches where people had fled for sanctuary. And then it stopped.

But the hate didn't stop. It got inherited.

The children born to Hutu perpetrators grew up with one version of what happened. The children born to Tutsi survivors grew up with another. And those stories, those wounds, those dehumanizing frameworks that made the killing possible, they traveled forward in time through the same mechanism that transmits language and preference and cooking: family, community, story. Intergenerational trauma is real, and so is intergenerational hatred. You don't have to teach a child to hate explicitly. You just have to live with hatred in your house, and children absorb it the way they absorb everything else, without knowing they're doing it.

In Kaduna, Nigeria, Christians and Muslims have been fighting intermittently for decades. Hundreds of people have died in cycles of violence that started before most of the current fighters were born. Each new round of killing becomes the justification for the next round. The wound becomes the reason. And the children who grow up in communities shaped by that violence are handed a framework for understanding the world that starts with "they are dangerous to us." It's not a choice they made. It was made for them, years before they were born.

This is why the standard response to religious extremism, "that's not the real Islam" or "those aren't true Christians," is true but insufficient. It's true that the violent fringe doesn't represent the tradition accurately. But it doesn't account for how people actually come to hold extremist views. It's not usually a matter of bad theology. It's a matter of community, identity, and inherited fear. You believe what the people you love believe. And if the people you love were shaped by violence, the beliefs they hand you will carry that shape.

And it compounds. Pew Research found that 45 countries had high or very high social hostilities involving religion in 2022. That's nearly a quarter of the world. Government restrictions on religion were at near-peak levels globally. But here's the other number: 153 countries, 77%, had low to moderate levels of religious hostility. The extremism is real and serious and it demands our attention. But it's not the whole picture. Most of the world, most of the time, isn't on fire. That matters too.

What Actually Works

I don't want to end on hopelessness, because I don't think hopelessness is earned here. There are things that work. We know some of them.

The most important finding in the research on prejudice reduction is one that's been replicated so many times across so many contexts that it's hard to dismiss. Gordon Allport proposed it in 1954 in The Nature of Prejudice: contact between groups reduces prejudice. Not always. Not automatically. But consistently, across cultures and contexts, when people from different groups actually meet and interact as individuals rather than as representatives of enemy categories, the fear and hostility tend to diminish.

The research has been updated and tested in harder conditions since Allport. Jasper Van Assche at the University of Ghent led a meta-analysis of 34 studies covering nearly 64,000 people across 19 countries, specifically in contexts with active conflict and high discrimination. His conclusion: contact still reduces prejudice, even under those conditions. In fact, contact worked as much or more under high discrimination and threat as under low discrimination and threat. "Contact theory survived another test," Van Assche said. And importantly, it didn't have to be structured or deliberate. Accidental encounters, people from opposing groups who just happened to share space, reduced prejudice too.

This is genuinely good news. It means the solution isn't complicated in principle, even if it's hard in practice. People need to meet each other.

The most striking story I came across while writing this chapter belongs to two men in Nigeria. Pastor James Wuye and Imam Muhammad Ashafa were leaders of opposing armed militias in Kaduna in the early 1990s. They didn't just disagree with each other politically. They fought. Pastor Wuye lost his hand in the violence. Both men were radicalized, both had blood on their hands, and both viewed the other as an enemy of God.

In 1995, they founded the Interfaith Mediation Centre together.

I don't entirely know how that happens. But it happened. And the Centre has been doing conflict resolution work in Nigeria ever since, including in some of the most volatile regions in the country. "Before we started, this never would have happened," Wuye said of the now-routine meetings between leaders of Nigeria's Christian Association and Muslim leadership groups. "There has been a great improvement." Their story became a documentary called The Imam and the Pastor. Two men who'd been trying to kill each other decided that wasn't the story they wanted to be in.

I think about that choice a lot. Because it wasn't just a personal decision. It was a political act. Every time someone from one group treats someone from the other group as a full human being, they quietly dismantle the framework that made the violence possible. The dehumanization that enables mass atrocity requires constant maintenance. It requires that people never actually meet. Wuye and Ashafa broke that maintenance agreement. And then they spent the next three decades making sure other people could break it too.

Rwanda tried something harder. After a genocide in which the killers and the survivors were literal neighbors, the government had to figure out how a country rebuilds. They did several things that I think deserve more attention than they get.

The Gacaca courts, which ran from 2002 to 2012, were community-based justice proceedings that processed cases across the country, allowing truth-telling and accountability at a local level. They weren't perfect. But they were real. They put perpetrators and survivors in the same room and required something honest to happen between them. The government also made a decision that sounds small but I think was significant: they removed Hutu, Tutsi, and Twa ethnic labels from official documents and public life and replaced them with a single national identity. Rwandan. Just Rwandan. The label that had been used to sort people for killing was retired.

They also built what they called Multifamily Healing Spaces, structured gatherings that brought together families of perpetrators and families of survivors. Not for confrontation, but for something harder: the kind of dialogue where you have to look at the other person as a person. And intergenerational dialogues specifically addressed the wound that travels through time, the way that children who weren't alive for the genocide still carry its shape.

The key insight that came out of the Rwandan process is that reconciliation requires both sides. It requires perpetrators who genuinely accept moral responsibility, not just legal responsibility, for their individual role. And it requires survivors who are eventually willing to offer something like forgiveness, which is one of the hardest things one human being can do for another. Neither is sufficient without the other.

Similar programs have been tried in Burundi and Somalia through Interpeace, using community psychotherapy processes that let people share their stories of hardship. The documented results: challenging harmful stereotypes, building empathy, developing trust across lines that had been defined by violence. These aren't small things. They're the actual work of not repeating the past.

In the Bay Area, an organization called Building Bridges has been doing interfaith dialogue work for years. The participants tend to describe the same thing: they came in as strangers and left as something more like friends. That's not naive. That's the contact hypothesis in action.

And the Healing Hatred methodology, which has been applied in several conflict zones, makes a point that I think is underrated: the programs that actually reduce prejudice tend to target laypeople, not clergy. The clergy already know the theology. They can cite texts about peace and reconciliation all day. But the violence happens in communities, not seminaries. The change has to happen at the level where the hatred lives.

None of these programs is a silver bullet. None of them is fast. Reconciliation in Rwanda is still incomplete. The Kaduna region of Nigeria still sees periodic violence. The West Bank isn't healed. But the programs that work share something: they get people into the same room, force some kind of honest encounter, and trust that the moral instinct, the one that's older than any of the conflict, will do some of the work from there. I think that trust is warranted. The research says so, and so does the record of people like Wuye and Ashafa.

The Language and the Accent

I've been writing this book as a Catholic school kid who became an agnostic. I was an altar boy. I rang the bells during the Consecration. I believed the bread became the body. I believed the wine became the blood. I genuflected, I confessed, I tried, for years, to feel what I was supposed to feel.

And then, somewhere in my late teens and early twenties, I stopped believing it. Not all at once. It was more like a tide going out than a wall falling down. The doctrine faded. The certainty dissolved. What stayed, what I didn't lose along with the rest of it, was something harder to name. A sense that cruelty matters. That people deserve dignity. That the suffering of a stranger is real and it's yours to care about. That fairness isn't arbitrary.

I think that's what this book has been trying to say all along. That thing I kept when I lost the faith, that's not the religion's invention. That's older than any religion. It's the moral instinct, the deep human sense of what we owe each other, that predates every scripture and survives every loss of faith. Religion gave it structure. It gave it language, ritual, community, and the weight of the sacred. That's not nothing. That's an enormous gift. But the moral sense itself came first.

So when I watch someone light a church on fire in the name of Jesus, or post an execution video in the name of Allah, or burn a Palestinian farmer's olive trees in the name of divine covenant, or lynch a man for transporting cattle in the name of religious duty, I want to say: you have it exactly backwards.

The moral instinct is the language. Religion is the accent. And killing someone for having a different accent is the most profound misunderstanding of what faith was ever supposed to do.

Every religious tradition I've read about, seriously read about, has people in it who understood that. The Buddhist monk who shelters the Muslim refugee. The imam and the pastor who lost a limb fighting each other and then chose to build something instead. The

Rwandan survivor who sat across a table from the family of the man who killed her husband and decided that the story wasn't over yet. The Jewish voices in Israel, many of them, who look at settler violence and call it what it is: a desecration.

Those people aren't the exception to their traditions. I think they're the point.

The extremists who weaponize religion aren't more faithful. They're less so. They've traded the hard work of living out a moral vision, the actual daily discipline of treating people as they deserve to be treated, for the much easier work of identifying an enemy. That's always easier. It always feels righteous. And it always, eventually, burns the house down.

The fire doesn't care whose name it was started in.

We care. Or we're supposed to. And I think that caring, that refusing to let the fire win, is something that lives underneath every religion and outside of all of them. It's what we share when we share nothing else.

That's the foundation. It was there before any of us arrived.

It'll be there after.

Sources for this chapter:

- PMC Study on Christian Nationalism and Political Violence: https://pmc.ncbi.nlm.nih.gov/articles/PMC8724742/ - Global Terrorism Index 2026 (Vision of Humanity): https://www.visionofhumanity.org/global-terrorism-index/ - India National Crime Records Bureau: https://ncrb.gov.in/ - U.S. Commission on International Religious Freedom (India): https://www.uscirf.gov/countries/india - Crisis Group: Myanmar's Buddhist Monk Problem (Ma Ba Tha): https://www.crisisgroup.org/as ia/south-east-asia/myanmar/b116-myanmar-buddhist-monk-problem - Haaretz: IDF Data on Settler Violence 2024-2025: https://www.haaret

z.com/israel-news/2025-01-26/ty-article/settler-violence-rose-27-in-20 24-according-to-idf-data/ - Yaqeen Institute (Quran 9:29 context): https://yaqeeninstitute.org/ - Council on Foreign Relations: Nigeria Religious Conflict: https://www.cfr.org/blog/nigeria-religious-conflict -and-path-reconciliation - Gordon Allport, The Nature of Prejudice (1954): https://www.hup.harvard.edu/books/9780201001778 - Van Assche Meta-Analysis (contact hypothesis under conflict): https://www.tandfonline.com/doi/full/10.1080/01419870.2022.2146697 - UN Chronicle: Interfaith Mediation Centre Nigeria: https://www.un. org/en/chronicle/article/interfaith-mediation-centre-nigeria - The Imam and the Pastor (documentary): https://www.frrme.org/resources/the-imam-and-the-pastor - Interpeace: Intergenerational Dialogue for Reconciliation (Rwanda): https://www.interpeace.org/resource/intergenerational-dialogue-for-reconciliation/ - Building Bridges (Bay Area interfaith program): https://buildingbridgesproject.org/ - Healing Hatred methodology: https://www.healinghatred.org/

Epilogue: What You Can Do with What You Know

We've covered a lot of ground. We've walked through the archaeological record and the brain scans and the field notes of anthropologists who've spent their careers in communities very different from yours. We've looked at what happens when researchers stick electrodes on meditating monks and hook rosary-praying Catholics up to respiratory monitors. We've followed the sociologists into the church basements and the choir rehearsals and the volunteer rosters.

The argument this book has tried to make is simple, even if the evidence for it is complicated: morality didn't come from God. It came from us. From the long, slow, brutal process of human beings figuring out how to live together. Religion didn't invent that process. It inherited it, organized it, wrapped it in story and music and architecture, and handed it down. The accent isn't the language. But the accent kept the language alive.

So here's the question that matters now. If you accept any of this, what do you do with it?

That's what this chapter is for. Not a summary. Not a list of takeaways. Something more practical: a set of things you can actually do, drawn directly from what the research in these pages found, and from what the great traditions independently converged on over thousands of years. That convergence is the point. When Buddhist monks in the Himalayas and Catholic nuns in medieval Spain and practitioners of pranayama in ancient India all landed on the same technique without talking to each other, that's not coincidence. That's evidence. Millennia of human trial and error, conducted across every culture on earth, pointing at the same answers.

You don't have to believe in anything to use what they found.

Breathe

This is where to start, because it costs nothing and takes ten minutes and the evidence for it is about as solid as anything in this book.

In 2001, Luciano Bernardi and his colleagues at the University of Pavia published a study in the British Medical Journal that stopped a lot of people cold. They took healthy adults and had them recite the Ave Maria in Latin and chant the yoga mantra "om mani padme hum." Both practices, with no contact between their originating traditions, had converged on a breathing rate of roughly 5.5 to 5.7 breaths per minute. That's about half the rate of normal resting breathing. At that specific rate, the breath synchronizes with the body's Mayer wave, a ten-second cardiovascular rhythm that governs blood pressure and oxygen delivery to the brain. Rosary. Mantra. Same frequency. Same physiological effect. Two traditions, separated by thousands of miles and centuries of time, running the same experiment and arriving at the same result.

Herbert Benson at Harvard called this the relaxation response, and he spent decades documenting what happens when you engage it: cortisol drops, blood pressure drops, inflammation markers drop. A 2015 study out of Massachusetts General found a 43% reduction in healthcare utilization for stress-related conditions among people who practiced regularly. And Roderik Gerritsen and Guido Band's 2018 review traced much of the mechanism to the vagus nerve, which runs from the brainstem down through the heart and gut. Slow exhalation, specifically, stimulates that nerve. Long exhale. Parasympathetic response. Every major tradition figured this out.

Here's what you do. Sit comfortably. Breathe in for about four counts. Breathe out for six. Do that for ten minutes. That's it. You don't need a mantra. You don't need a rosary. You don't need to believe anything. If you want the mantra anyway, because rhythm helps you stay focused, use any phrase that takes about eleven seconds to say at a comfortable pace. The traditions that developed those phrases weren't performing magic. They were engineering breath.

The religious versions have real advantages. The rosary is said in community, which adds the synchrony effects we'll get to. The mantra comes embedded in a tradition that offers guidance on posture, timing, and what to do with the mind when it wanders. If those resources are available to you, use them. But the physiological core of the practice is accessible without any of that. Ten minutes of slow breathing, once a day, is a real intervention with real effects. Start there.

Express Gratitude

Not all prayer is the same, and this turns out to matter quite a bit.

Research on the different types of prayer consistently shows that petitionary prayer, asking God (or the universe, or whatever) to give you something or fix something, tends to correlate with *higher* anxiety, not lower. This makes sense when you think about it. If your prayer life is organized around what's missing and what might go wrong, you're spending your contemplative time rehearsing lack and fear.

Gratitude prayer is different. Across multiple studies, it's associated with improved mood, reduced depression, and higher self-esteem. And it doesn't require religious belief to work. The mechanism isn't theological. It's attentional. You're deliberately directing your attention toward what exists and is good rather than what doesn't exist and might be bad. The brain follows attention. Where you point your focus regularly, neural pathways strengthen.

The practice: before you sleep each night, write down three specific things that happened that day that you're glad happened. Not "my family" or "my health," which are categories. Specific things. The coffee was good. The meeting ended early. Your kid said something funny. A stranger held a door. Specificity is what makes this work. You're training the brain to notice good things as they happen, because you know you'll be asked to report on them later.

Do this for eight weeks. Studies of this practice consistently show measurable changes by that point. After that, some people find daily writing becomes repetitive. That's fine. Drop to a few times a week. The habit of attention is what you're building. The notebook is just scaffolding.

If you have a religious practice already, this is an argument for making gratitude the center of it rather than petitionary prayer. The traditions have always had both, but the evidence suggests one of them is doing more good.

Tell the Truth About Yourself

Confession is one of the oldest religious technologies there is. Catholicism formalized it into a sacrament. Jewish liturgy structures it into the Days of Awe. Many Protestant traditions have some version of "testimony." Indigenous healing ceremonies often involve public acknowledgment of wrongdoing. The form varies. The mechanism seems to be the same.

James Pennebaker at the University of Texas has spent his career studying what happens when people write or speak honestly about painful experiences. The findings are consistent enough to have generated something of an industry: disclosure works. Writing about traumatic or troubling experiences for fifteen to twenty minutes a day over three or four days reduces anxiety, strengthens immune function, and improves mood. The effect is specific to honest engagement with meaning. Just venting, or just describing events without trying to make sense of them, doesn't produce the same results. The benefit comes from the narrative work, from trying to understand what happened and what it means.

Religious confession, at its best, is exactly that. It's a structured opportunity to be honest about where you fell short, why, and what you might do differently. The priest or the rabbi or the community circle provides accountability and witness. Those things matter. But the core mechanism doesn't require a confessional booth.

Here's a secular version: take fifteen minutes. Write about something you did that you're not proud of, or something that happened that you've been carrying. Don't perform it for an imagined reader. Be accurate. Try to understand it. What were you actually feeling? What were you actually afraid of? What story were you telling yourself that made the action seem reasonable at the time?

Do this with difficult things, not trivial ones. Pennebaker found that people who wrote about genuinely painful or embarrassing material got more benefit than those who wrote about minor upsets. The research suggests the threshold is roughly: if you've never told anyone about it, it's probably worth writing about.

If you have someone you trust enough to tell, telling them out loud is more powerful than writing. Pennebaker compared oral and written disclosure and found both worked, but the social version added something. The traditions knew this. They built the witness in.

Move with Others

Here's something that gets left out of most conversations about religion and wellbeing: the body.

When people in religious communities describe feeling the presence of something larger than themselves, it often happens during collective physical practice. The congregation rising and sitting together. The kneeling. The singing. The swaying. The Catholic Mass choreographs the body over an hour in ways that are not random. Neither does the Friday prayer. Neither does the haka, the Maori ceremonial dance that opens this book's chapter on ritual.

Scott Wiltermuth and Chip Heath at Stanford ran a series of experiments in 2009 showing that people who walked or sang in synchrony with others subsequently cooperated more, even with strangers, even in economic games where defection would have been rational. The effect was specific to synchrony. Walking at different paces didn't produce it. Synchronized movement released something, some combination of endorphins and felt connection, that made people more generous and more trusting.

Robin Dunbar's research at Oxford found that group singing specifically raises pain thresholds, one measure of endorphin release, more than singing alone, and that the effect scales with group size. Larger choir, more endorphins. The churches that survived and grew figured this out empirically. They built it into their weekly practice.

You don't need a religious context to access this. Team sports do it. Group exercise classes do it. Choir does it. Dancing with people you know does it. The research doesn't care whether you're synchronized to a hymn or a rowing stroke or a fitness instructor counting to eight. The body doesn't know the difference.

What the research suggests is that you need physical, synchronized movement with other humans on a regular basis, and that most modern lives don't include it. Sitting in a meeting doesn't count. Watching sports doesn't count. The body has to be moving, and the movement has to be coordinated with others.

If you're looking for somewhere to start: join a choir, or a rowing club, or a weekly group fitness class with consistent membership. The "consistent membership" part matters. The benefit comes partly from the synchrony in the moment and partly from the repeated contact with the same people over time. Both are doing work.

Seek Awe

Dacher Keltner and Jonathan Haidt gave the field a working definition of awe in 2003: the experience of encountering something vast that challenges your current understanding of the world. Vastness can be physical (the Grand Canyon, a cathedral ceiling, the night sky) or conceptual (a mathematical proof, an act of extraordinary courage, the age of the universe). What defines awe is the feeling that your ordinary frame of reference is too small for what you're encountering.

That might sound like a luxury, an aesthetic experience for people with time on their hands. The research suggests it's considerably more than that. Jennifer Stellar and her colleagues at Berkeley found in 2015 that awe was the emotion most consistently associated with reduced levels of interleukin-6, a cytokine associated with inflammation and a marker of chronic stress. Not joy. Not contentment. Awe. The experience of being temporarily small in the face of something large seems to do something specific to the body's inflammatory response.

Keltner's work also consistently shows that awe increases prosocial behavior. People who've just experienced awe give more, help more, and report feeling more connected to others. The mechanism appears to involve what he calls "the small self," the quieting of the ego and its habitual self-focus. Religions have been engineering awe for as long as they've existed. The cathedral isn't just decoration. The pilgrimage to Mecca isn't just geography. These are awe delivery systems, and they work.

Nature produces the same effect as sacred architecture. Mountains, oceans, old forests, the open sky at night. Stellar's research found that nature-induced awe produced the same cytokine effects as built spaces. You don't need the cathedral if you have access to the outdoors.

The practice is simpler than most: spend time, regularly, in the presence of something much larger than yourself. Not scrolling through images of it. Actually in its presence. Standing under a sky full of stars without your phone. Walking in old-growth forest. Sitting in a building that was built to make you feel small. The research suggests even twenty minutes of this, once a week, produces measurable effects on mood and inflammation over time.

If you can't get to nature easily, go to the largest, oldest building you can find and sit in it. Museum of natural history. Cathedral. Library with a vaulted ceiling. The effect is real even if you don't share the building's theology.

Show Up

This is the one that may be hardest to sell, because it's the most countercultural advice in an era of digital everything.

Robert Putnam's research, documented in detail in chapter eight, found that religious Americans do volunteer more, donate more, and report being happier than their secular counterparts. The thing that most people miss about that finding is what Putnam and his colleagues found when they tried to isolate the variable that was doing the work. It wasn't the theology. It wasn't the prayer. It was the community. Specifically: regular, face-to-face contact with the same group of people over time.

"Secular friends," as Putnam's research distinguishes them, people you like and spend time with but don't share an organizational commitment with, don't produce the same civic effects as congregation members. There's something about a group that gathers around a shared commitment, shows up weekly regardless of how they feel, and has structures that make them accountable to each other. The church provides that. The synagogue provides that. Most secular social arrangements don't.

The Holt-Lunstad meta-analysis of 148 studies, covering more than 300,000 people, found that social isolation is associated with a 50% increase in mortality risk. That's roughly equivalent to smoking fifteen cigarettes a day. We don't treat loneliness like a health crisis. The evidence says we should.

The practice isn't "make friends." That's too vague. The specific prescription from the research is: find a group that gathers in person, regularly, around something you care about, and commit to showing up. Not when you feel like it. On schedule. The regularity is part of the mechanism. The early awkwardness passes. The trust builds in the showing up, not in the feeling ready to show up.

A book club, a team sport, a volunteer organization, a musical group, a community garden, a religious congregation if that's available to you. The religious version has accumulated wisdom about how to structure this kind of group for longevity and mutual accountability. If you have access to that and it fits, use it. If it doesn't fit, find the secular equivalent and treat the commitment seriously.

Your phone cannot do this for you. Video calls cannot do this for you. The body needs to be in the room with other bodies on a regular basis. This is not a preference. It's a biological requirement that we have, in recent decades, started treating as optional.

Meet a Stranger

Gordon Allport proposed in 1954 that prejudice decreases when members of different groups have direct contact, under conditions of equal status and common purpose. The contact hypothesis, as it became known, spent decades being debated and tested. A meta-analysis by Lemmer and Wagner, and a separate one by Louk Hagendoorn and Jost Massey, found that the core hypothesis holds up across a wide range of conditions. Jasper Van Assche's synthesis of thirty-four studies across nineteen countries found it even holds under high-conflict conditions, including in areas with active ethnic or religious tension. Contact with people who are different from you, over time, reduces the fear response and the negative attribution that drives prejudice.

Religious traditions understood this imperfectly and inconsistently. They built strong in-group bonds, which is part of what made them survive. But the better strands of every tradition have also pushed toward the stranger: the stranger is sacred, hospitality to the outsider is a religious duty, the other is made in the same image as you. These weren't just ethical flourishes. They were observations about what actually happens to human beings when they extend their circle.

The practice here requires some intentionality, because modern life is increasingly sorted. Neighborhoods are sorted. Online spaces are sorted. Your social feed shows you people who think what you think. You have to choose to go somewhere the sorting doesn't apply.

The research suggests that the contact needs to be sustained and personal to work. Not a rally or a demonstration, where groups face each other as groups. Actual individual contact, over time, where you learn someone's name and their specific situation and the particular way their life is different from yours, and also the ways it isn't.

This might mean joining a civic organization rather than an affinity group. Volunteering somewhere that brings you into regular contact with people outside your usual social world. Taking seriously the acquaintances at work or in your neighborhood who come from different backgrounds. It takes longer than a conversation to do what the research says contact can do. But the research says it does it.

There's a sentence that runs underneath everything in this book, and it's time to say it plainly: the great traditions were working with real data.

They didn't have randomized controlled trials. They didn't have cytokine assays or vagal nerve monitors or longitudinal surveys of 300,000 people. What they had was time and attention and the accumulated observation of millions of human lives. They watched what made people less anxious and what made them more connected and what made communities last. They kept what worked and discarded what didn't, often without knowing they were doing it, across generations and centuries and continents.

We now have the tools to see what they found. The breath rate that syncs with the cardiovascular system. The mechanism by which synchrony builds trust. The specific type of attention that reduces inflammation. The structural features of a community that translate belief into behavior that persists across decades.

You don't have to share their cosmology to inherit what they learned. The language of morality is older than any god, and the practices that support it belong to the whole species. What these traditions developed, across all their differences, is a set of tools for being human together. The tools are real. They work on you even if you don't believe in the framework that produced them.

Use them. The evidence is strong enough to act on. The cost of trying is low. And the alternative, deciding that because you're not religious none of this applies to you, is one of the more expensive mistakes a modern person can make.

The Accents of Faith is dedicated to the idea that we understand each other better than we think, that the apparently vast differences in our religious lives mask a shared grammar of human experience. If the book has done its job, you're leaving it with a different relationship to the traditions that aren't yours. Not agreement. Not conversion. Curiosity. The recognition that something real was being worked on in all those temples and churches and mosques and kivas and fire circles. And the knowledge that you don't have to choose any accent to speak the language.

Speak it anyway. Breathe slowly. Say what you're grateful for. Tell the truth about where you fell short. Move with people. Sit in the presence of something immense. Show up, even when you don't feel like it. Extend your hand to someone different from you.

The research supports all of this. So does most of what humans have held sacred across every culture in history.

That's not a coincidence. Act accordingly.

Acknowledgments

This book began as a question I couldn't stop asking, and it became a book because of the people who took the question seriously.

Paul taught me how to sit still long enough to listen. Tom was the first person to show up when I couldn't. Allen walked me through the parts I didn't want to look at. Dan showed me what it looks like to live with both rigor and gentleness. Claire reminded me to get involved and always be open. The members of my home group, SS, and the wider fellowship of the rooms taught me that moral seriousness does not require a theology, and that community is not a concept but a practice.

My parents drove me to serve 7 a.m. Mass on school mornings and sent me to Catholic school for thirteen years. They gave me the tradition this book examines. I would not have written it without that foundation, and I would not have written it honestly without eventually stepping outside of it.

Mr. Bosley, my high school math teacher, taught me that the point of a hard question is not the answer but the willingness to follow it wherever it goes. He also said to follow a problem until it is solved, not just until a page is full of notes. That disposition is underneath every chapter of this book.

Iszy encouraged me to write it, heard about early versions without a complaint, and never once suggested I was spending too much time on a book about religion. That is a kind of faith in itself.

Hannah and Dan showed me what AI can do, which reshaped how I thought about building this book and much else besides.

Whatever is clear in these pages, I owe to the people named here. Whatever is muddled, I managed on my own.

Bibliography

Alcoholics Anonymous World Services. *The Twelve Steps of Alcoholics Anonymous.* AA.org. https://www.aa.org/the-twelve-steps

Alcoholics Anonymous World Services. "AA Around the World." AA.org. https://www.aa.org/aa-around-the-world

Alcoholics Anonymous World Services. "The Serenity Prayer." Alcoholics-Anonymous.org.uk. https://www.alcoholics-anonymous.org.uk/magazines/the-serenity-prayer/

All Blacks. "The Haka." AllBlacks.com. https://www.allblacks.com/the-haka

American Psychological Association. "Why sports fandom may be good for mental health." *Speaking of Psychology* (podcast). APA.org. https://www.apa.org/news/podcasts/speaking-of-psychology/sports-fans

Archdiocese of Saint Paul and Minneapolis. "Why Don't Catholics Eat Meat on Fridays?" ArchSPM.org. https://www.archspm.org/why-dont-catholics-eat-meat-on-fridays/

Aristotle. *Nicomachean Ethics.* Translated by W. D. Ross. MIT Classics Archive. https://classics.mit.edu/Aristotle/nicomachaen.1.i.html

Armaly, Miles T., David T. Buckley, and Adam M. Enders. "Christian Nationalism and Political Violence: Victimhood, Racial Identity, Conspiracy, and Support for the Capitol Attacks." *Political Behavior*, vol. 44, no. 2 (2022): 937-960. https://pmc.ncbi.nlm.nih.gov/articles/PMC8724742/

Ashdown-Franks, Garcia, Catherine M. Sabiston, Brendon Stubbs, Michael Atkinson, Helen Quirk, Alice Bullas, and Steve Haake.

"parkrun participation, impact and perceived social inclusion among runners/walkers and volunteers with mental health conditions." *Psychology, Health and Medicine*, vol. 28, no. 9 (2023): 2621-2634. https://pubmed.ncbi.nlm.nih.gov/36881438/

Barnas, Thaddeus J. "The Effectiveness of Interfaith Dialogue in Countering Religious Intolerance: A Phenomenological Study of Interfaith Youth Program Alumni." *Journal of Security, Intelligence, and Resilience Education*, vol. 13, no. 2 (2022): 1-29. https://jsire.org/wp-content/uploads/sites/661/2022/10/jsire-v13_2-barnas-F-10.23.22.pdf

Barna Group. "Meet the 'Spiritual but Not Religious.'" Barna.com. https://www.barna.com/research/meet-spiritual-not-religious/

Barrett, Justin L. "Hyperactive Agency Detection Device (HADD)." *The Secular Frontier* (Infidels.org), 2011. https://secularfrontier.infidels.org/2011/10/justin-barretts-hyperactive-agency-detection-device-hadd/

Becker, Ernest. *The Denial of Death*. Free Press, 1973. (Referenced in Chapter 6; Terror Management Theory.)

Bellah, Robert N., Richard Madsen, William M. Sullivan, Ann Swidler, and Steven M. Tipton. *Habits of the Heart: Individualism and Commitment in American Life*. University of California Press, 1985. https://books.google.com/books/about/Habits_of_the_Heart.html?id=-S2OaJrgmUwC

Benson, Herbert. *The Relaxation Response*. William Morrow, 1975. (Referenced in Chapter 5; see also Benson-Henry Institute at Massachusetts General Hospital.)

Bermudez, Julio. "Empirically Validating the Effects of Sacred/Significant Architecture on Human Experience." (Referenced in Chapter 7; research at Catholic University of America, School of Architecture.)

Bernardi, Luciano, Peter Sleight, Gabriele Bandinelli, Simone Cencetti, Lamberto Fattorini, Johanna Wdowczyc-Szulc, and Alfonso Lagi. "Effect of rosary prayer and yoga mantras on autonomic cardiovascular rhythms: comparative study." *BMJ (British Medical Journal)*, vol. 323 (2001): 1446-1449. (Referenced in Chapter 5.)

Boyd, Robert, and Peter J. Richerson. "Culture and the evolution of human cooperation." *Philosophical Transactions of the Royal Society B: Biological Sciences*, vol. 364, no. 1533 (2009): 3281-3288. https://pmc.ncbi.nlm.nih.gov/articles/PMC2781880/

British Museum. "Papyrus of Ani (Book of the Dead), 4th-3rd century BCE." British Museum Collection, object EA10508. https://www.britishmuseum.org/collection/object/Y_EA10508

Building Bridges Project. BuildingBridgesProject.org. https://buildingbridgesproject.org/

Bulumac, Adriana Lavinia. "Affiliation to the Alcoholics Anonymous (AA) community: A qualitative study on differences between highly affiliated and low/non-affiliated individuals." *Nordic Studies on Alcohol and Drugs* (2024). https://journals.sagepub.com/doi/10.1177/14550725241278089

Burning Man Project. "The 10 Principles of Burning Man." BurningMan.org. https://burningman.org/about-us/10-principles/

Byrne, Margaret, Rayner Kay Jin Tan, Dan Wu, Gifty Marley, Takhona Grace Hlatshwako, Yusha Tao, Jennifer Bissram, Sophie Nachman, Weiming Tang, Rohit Ramaswamy, and Joseph D. Tucker. "Prosocial Interventions and Health Outcomes: A Systematic Review and Meta-Analysis." *JAMA Network Open*, vol. 6, no. 12 (2023). https://pmc.ncbi.nlm.nih.gov/articles/PMC10709779/

Campbell, Joseph. *The Hero with a Thousand Faces*. Princeton University Press, 1949. https://en.wikipedia.org/wiki/The_Hero_with_a_Thousand_Faces

Carrere, Juli, Alexia Reyes, Laura Oliveras, Anna Fernandez, Andres Peralta, Ana M. Novoa, Katherine Perez, and Carme Borrell. "The effects of cohousing model on people's health and wellbeing: a scoping review." *Public Health Reviews*, vol. 41 (2020): 22. https://pmc.ncbi.nlm.nih.gov/articles/PMC7539375/

Carstensen, Nils, Mandeep Mudhar, and Freja Schurmann Munksgaard. "'Let communities do their work': the role of mutual aid and self-help groups in the Covid-19 pandemic response." *Disasters*, vol. 45, Suppl. 1 (2021): S146-S173. https://pmc.ncbi.nlm.nih.gov/articles/PMC8653332/

Cofnas, Nathan. "The Golden Rule: A Naturalistic Perspective." *Utilitas*, vol. 34 (2022): 262-274. https://www.cambridge.org/core/servi ces/aop-cambridge-core/content/view/23D7AAC2FCA9B09DD64F2679 94F0722A/S0953820822000073a.pdf/golden_rule_a_naturalistic_persp ective.pdf

Collins, Randall. "The Elementary Forms of Sports Fandom." See: Serazio, Michael.

Corfield, Penelope J. "Egalitarian greetings: the social spread of the handshake in urbanizing Britain, 1700-1850." *Urban History*, vol. 52, no. 3 (2025): 498-517. https://www.cambridge.org/core/journals/ur ban-history/article/egalitarian-greetings-the-social-spread-of-the-han dshake-in-urbanizing-britain-17001850/4E9E162C09AA3E93DE6595AF 0B47510B

Council on Foreign Relations. "Nigeria: Religious Conflict and Path to Reconciliation." CFR.org. https://www.cfr.org/blog/nigeria-re ligious-conflict-and-path-reconciliation

Crisis Group. "Myanmar's Buddhist Monk Problem." International Crisis Group, Report B116. https://www.crisisgroup.org/asia/south-ea st-asia/myanmar/b116-myanmar-buddhist-monk-problem

Anderson, Craig L., Maria Monroy, and Dacher Keltner. "Awe in nature heals: Evidence from military veterans, at-risk youth, and college students." *Emotion*, vol. 18, no. 8 (2018): 1195-1202. (Referenced in Chapter 7.)

Dastghaib, Sanaz, Morvarid Siri, Nasim Rahmani-Kukia, Seyed Taghi Heydari, Mehdi Pasalar, Mozhdeh Zamani, Pooneh Mokaram, and Kamran Bagheri-Lankarani. "Effect of 30-day Ramadan fasting on autophagy pathway and metabolic health outcome in healthy individuals." *Molecular Biology Research Communications*, vol. 14, no. 2

(2025): 115-127. https://pmc.ncbi.nlm.nih.gov/articles/PMC11865935/

"Decline of ancient Egyptian religion." *Wikipedia.* https://en.wikipedia.org/wiki/Decline_of_ancient_Egyptian_religion

De Waal, Frans B. M. *Good Natured: The Origins of Right and Wrong in Humans and Other Animals.* Harvard University Press, 1996. https://books.google.com/books/about/Good_Natured.html?id=VMYPAQAAIAAJ

De Waal, Frans B. M., and Malini Suchak. "Prosocial primates: selfish and unselfish motivations." *Philosophical Transactions of the Royal Society B: Biological Sciences*, vol. 365, no. 1553 (2010): 2711-2722. https://www.emory.edu/LIVING_LINKS/publications/articles/deWaal_Suchak_2010.pdf

Dialogue Institute. "The Significance of Interfaith Dialogue in the Contemporary World." DialogueInstitute.org, September 2024. https://dialogueinstitute.org/diablogue-blog/2024/9/20/the-significance-of-interfaith-dialogue-in-the-contemporary-world

Doctors Without Borders / Medecins Sans Frontieres. "Humanitarian Responsibility." MSF.org. https://www.doctorswithoutborders.org/latest/humanitarian-responsibility

Duarte, Isabel C., Sonia Afonso, Helena Jorge, Ricardo Cayolla, Carlos Ferreira, and Miguel Castelo-Branco. "Tribal love: the neural correlates of passionate engagement in football fans." *Social Cognitive and Affective Neuroscience*, vol. 12, no. 5 (2017): 718-728. https://pmc.ncbi.nlm.nih.gov/articles/PMC5460049/

Dufur, Mikaela J., Toby L. Parcel, David B. Braudt, and John P. Hoffmann. "Is social capital durable?: How family social bonds influence college enrollment and completion." *PLOS ONE*, vol. 19, no. 3 (2024): e0298344. https://pmc.ncbi.nlm.nih.gov/articles/PMC10936839/

Dunbar, Robin I. M. "Gossip in Evolutionary Perspective." *Review of General Psychology*, vol. 8, no. 2 (2004): 100-110. https://allegatifac.unipv.it/ziorufus/Dunbar%20gossip.pdf

Dunbar, Robin I. M. *Grooming, Gossip and the Evolution of Language.* Harvard University Press, 1996. https://en.wikipedia.org/wiki/Grooming,_Gossip_and_the_Evolution_of_Language

Durkheim, Emile. *The Elementary Forms of Religious Life.* Translated by Karen Fields. Free Press, 1995. (Original French edition 1912. Referenced throughout Chapter 6.)

Etymonline. "Thank." Online Etymology Dictionary. https://www.etymonline.com/word/thank

Faria, Miguel A. "Religious morality (and secular humanism) in Western civilization as precursors to medical ethics: A historic perspective." *Surgical Neurology International*, vol. 6 (2015): 105. https://pmc.ncbi.nlm.nih.gov/articles/PMC4476139/

Fehr, Ernst, and Simon Gachter. "Altruistic punishment in humans." *Nature*, vol. 415, no. 6868 (2002): 137-140. https://pubmed.ncbi.nlm.nih.gov/11805825/

Finucane, Anne, Anne Canny, Ally Pax Arcari Mair, Emily Harrop, Lucy E. Selman, Brooke Swash, Donna Wakefield, and David Gillanders. "A rapid review of the evidence for online interventions for bereavement support." *Palliative Medicine*, vol. 39, no. 1 (2025): 31-52. https://pmc.ncbi.nlm.nih.gov/articles/PMC11673319/

Friends Journal. "The End of the Quaker Handshake." (Referenced in Chapter 10, discussing *Albion's Seed*.) https://www.friendsjournal.org/the-end-of-the-quaker-handshake/

FRRME (Foundation for Relief and Reconciliation in the Middle East). "The Imam and the Pastor." FRRME.org. https://www.frrme.org/resources/the-imam-and-the-pastor

Gerritsen, Roderik J. S., and Guido P. H. Band. "Breath of Life: The Respiratory Vagal Stimulation Model of Contemplative Activity." *Frontiers in Human Neuroscience*, vol. 12 (2018): 397. (Referenced in Chapter 5.)

George Mason University, Osher Lifelong Learning Institute. "Zoroastrianism, Judaism, and Christianity." OLLI.GMU.edu. https://

olli.gmu.edu/docstore/600docs/1403-651-3-Zoroastrianism,%20Judais
m,%20and%20Christianity.pdf

Gilligan, Carol. *In a Different Voice: Psychological Theory and Women's Development.* Harvard University Press, 1982. Referenced in: Internet Encyclopedia of Philosophy, "Care Ethics." https://iep.utm.edu/care-ethics/

Gottschall, Jonathan. "The Storytelling Animal: A Conversation with Jonathan Gottschall." *Scientific American* (blog), 2012. https://www.scientificamerican.com/blog/literally-psyched/the-storytelling-animal-a-conversation-with-jonathan-gottschall/

Graeber, David. *Debt: The First 5,000 Years.* Melville House, 2011. https://davidgraeber.org/books/debt-the-first-5000-years/

Greene, Joshua D. "The Secret Joke of Kant's Soul." In Walter Sinnott-Armstrong (ed.), *Moral Psychology*, vol. 3. (Cited as a study in *Science*; see also: Greene, J. D. 2009, PDF.) https://www.antoniocasella.eu/dnlaw/Greene_2009.pdf

Groh, D. R., L. A. Jason, and C. B. Keys. "Social Network Variables in Alcoholics Anonymous: A Literature Review." *Clinical Psychology Review*, vol. 28, no. 3 (2008): 430-450. https://pmc.ncbi.nlm.nih.gov/articles/PMC2289871/

Guest, Eileen Mary, and Diana R. Keatinge. "The Value of New Parent Groups in Child and Family Health Nursing." *Journal of Perinatal Education*, vol. 18, no. 3 (2009): 12-22. https://pmc.ncbi.nlm.nih.gov/articles/PMC2730910/

Haaretz. "Settler Violence Rose 27% in 2024 According to IDF Data." Haaretz.com, January 26, 2025. https://www.haaretz.com/israel-news/2025-01-26/ty-article/settler-violence-rose-27-in-2024-according-to-idf-data/

Hamlin, J. Kiley, Karen Wynn, and Paul Bloom. "Social evaluation by preverbal infants." *Nature*, vol. 450 (2007): 557-559. https://www.nature.com/articles/nature06288

Harris, Marvin. "India's Sacred Cow." *Human Nature* (1978). Reprinted at UNCW. https://people.uncw.edu/ricej/intro/indiasacredcow.pdf

Harvard Religion and Public Life Project. "The Haka and Aotearoa New Zealand Rugby." Harvard Divinity School, Religion in Context series. https://rpl.hds.harvard.edu/religion-context/case-studies/sports-and-society/haka-and-aotearoa-new-zealand-rugby

Healing Hatred. HealingHatred.org. https://www.healinghatred.org/

Interpeace. "Intergenerational Dialogue for Reconciliation." Interpeace.org. https://www.interpeace.org/resource/intergenerational-dialogue-for-reconciliation/

Interpeace. Interpeace.org. https://www.interpeace.org/

Irfan, Bilal, Ahmad Khleif, Jad Badarneh, Jana Abutaqa, Ali Allam, Shueib Kweis, Basel Tarab, Abdallah Abu Shammala, Elias Nasser, Sameeha Shweiki, Muaaz Wajahath, and Aasim Padela. "Considering Islamic Frameworks to Infectious Disease Prevention." *Open Forum Infectious Diseases*, vol. 12, no. 10 (2025): ofaf011. https://pmc.ncbi.nlm.nih.gov/articles/PMC12548785/

James, William. *The Varieties of Religious Experience: A Study in Human Nature*. Longmans, Green, and Co., 1902. https://www.religion-online.org/book/the-varieties-of-religious-experience-a-study-in-human-nature/

Jeffrey, David. "Books: Against Empathy: the Case for Rational Compassion." *British Journal of General Practice*, vol. 67, no. 663 (2017): 468. https://pmc.ncbi.nlm.nih.gov/articles/PMC5604819/

Kabat-Zinn, Jon. *Full Catastrophe Living: Using the Wisdom of Your Body and Mind to Face Stress, Pain, and Illness*. Delacorte Press, 1990. (Referenced in Chapter 5; originator of Mindfulness-Based Stress Reduction, 1979.)

Kaskutas, Lee Ann, Jason Bond, and Lyndsay Ammon Avalos. "7-year trajectories of Alcoholics Anonymous attendance and associations with treatment." *Addictive Behaviors*, vol. 34, no. 12 (2009): 1029-1035. https://pmc.ncbi.nlm.nih.gov/articles/PMC2739250/

Kelly, John F., Alexandra Abry, Marica Ferri, and Keith Humphreys. "Alcoholics Anonymous and 12-Step Facilitation Treatments for Alcohol Use Disorder: A Distillation of a 2020 Cochrane Review for Clinicians and Policy Makers." *Alcohol and Alcoholism*, vol. 55, no. 6 (2020): 641-651. https://pubmed.ncbi.nlm.nih.gov/32628263/

Keltner, Dacher, and Jonathan Haidt. "Approaching awe, a moral, spiritual, and aesthetic emotion." *Cognition and Emotion*, vol. 17, no. 2 (2003): 297-314. https://greatergood.berkeley.edu/dacherkeltner/docs/keltner.haidt.awe.2003.pdf

Koo, Taeyeon, Hyungi Harry Kwon, Jaeeun Shin, and Juhae Baeck. "Is social identity theory enough to cover sports fans' behavior?: additional perspective from identity fusion theory." *Frontiers in Psychology*, vol. 16 (2025): 1574520. https://pmc.ncbi.nlm.nih.gov/articles/PMC12188543/

Lim, Chaeyoon, and Robert D. Putnam. "Religion, Social Networks, and Life Satisfaction." *American Sociological Review*, vol. 75, no. 6 (2010): 914-933. (Referenced in Chapter 8.)

Liebst, Lasse Suoninen, Marie Rosenkrantz Lindegaard, and Peter Philpot. "Collective effervescence in crowd gatherings." *Sociological Science* (2019). (Referenced in Chapter 6.)

Lindstrom, Joanna. "Personality and Team Identification Predict Violent Intentions Among Soccer Supporters." *Frontiers in Sports and Active Living*, vol. 3 (2021): 741277. https://pmc.ncbi.nlm.nih.gov/articles/PMC8573121/

Lucca, Kelsey, Francis Yuen, Yiyi Wang, Nicolas Alessandroni, and 80+ co-authors including J. Kiley Hamlin. "Infants' Social Evaluation of Helpers and Hinderers: A Large-Scale, Multi-Lab, Coordinated Replication Study." *Developmental Science*, vol. 28, no. 1 (2025): e13581. https://pubmed.ncbi.nlm.nih.gov/39600132/

Murthy, Vivek H. *Our Epidemic of Loneliness and Isolation: The U.S. Surgeon General's Advisory on the Healing Effects of Social Connection and Community.* U.S. Department of Health and Human Services, 2023. (Referenced in Chapter 8.)

Metropolitan Museum of Art. "Mesopotamian Deities." MetMuseum.org. https://www.metmuseum.org/essays/mesopotamian-deities

Meyer-Rochow, Victor Benno. "Food taboos: their origins and purposes." *Journal of Ethnobiology and Ethnomedicine*, vol. 5, no. 18 (2009). https://pmc.ncbi.nlm.nih.gov/articles/PMC2711054/

"Moral foundations theory." *Wikipedia.* https://en.wikipedia.org/wiki/Moral_foundations_theory

Newberg, Andrew, Eugene d'Aquili, and Vince Rause. *Why God Won't Go Away: Brain Science and the Biology of Belief.* Ballantine Books, 2001. (Referenced in Chapter 5; SPECT brain imaging of prayer.)

National Crime Records Bureau (India). NCRB.gov.in. https://ncrb.gov.in/

National Geographic. "Longevity: Blue Zones Research." NationalGeographic.com. https://www.nationalgeographic.com/health/article/longevity-blue-zones-dan-buettner-archival

New Scientist. "70,000-year-old remains suggest Neanderthals buried their dead." NewScientist.com. https://www.newscientist.com/article/2233918-70000-year-old-remains-suggest-neanderthals-buried-their-dead/

Norenzayan, Ara. "A Precis of Big Gods: How Religion Transformed Cooperation and Conflict." Cognition and Culture.net. https://www.cognitionandculture.net/webinars/big-gods-book-club/a-preacutecis-of-big-gods-how-religion-transformed-cooperation-and-conflict/

Norazman, Camilla Wahida, and Lai Kuan Lee. "The influence of social support in the prevention and treatment of postpartum depression: An intervention-based narrative review." *Women's Health (London)*, vol. 20 (2024): 17455057241275587. https://pmc.ncbi.nlm.nih.gov/articles/PMC11378223/

Nowak, Martin A. "Five rules for the evolution of cooperation." *Science*, vol. 314, no. 5805 (2006): 1560-1563. https://pmc.ncbi.nlm.nih.gov/articles/PMC3279745/

Nowak, Martin A., and Karl Sigmund. "Evolution of indirect reciprocity." *Nature*, vol. 437, no. 7063 (2005): 1291-1298. https://pubmed.ncbi.nlm.nih.gov/16251955/

Otto, Rudolf. *The Idea of the Holy* (*Das Heilige*). Oxford University Press, 1923. (Original German 1917. Referenced throughout Chapter 7.)

O'Sickey, A. J., Jacob Hanes, and J. Scott Tonigan. "The Relationship Between Perceived Alcoholics Anonymous Social Group Dynamics and Getting an AA Sponsor." *Alcoholism Treatment Quarterly*, vol. 38, no. 1 (2020): 21-31. https://pmc.ncbi.nlm.nih.gov/articles/PMC7394485/

Otto, Rudolf. *The Idea of the Holy* (*Das Heilige*). Oxford University Press, 1923. (Original German 1917. Referenced throughout Chapter 7.)

Ordinary Runners. "How Many People Do parkrun Each Week?" OrdinaryRunners.co.uk. https://ordinaryrunners.co.uk/parkruns/how-many-people-do-parkrun-each-week/

Pearce, Eiluned, Jacques Launay, and Robin I. M. Dunbar. "The ice-breaker effect: singing mediates fast social bonding." *Royal Society Open Science*, vol. 2 (2015): 150221. (Referenced in Chapter 6.)

Pennebaker, James W. *Opening Up: The Healing Power of Expressing Emotions*. Guilford Press, 1990. (Referenced in Chapter 5; disclosure mechanism research.)

Pageis, Michal. Review of *Society Without God: What the Least Religious Nations Can Tell Us About Contentment*, by Phil Zuckerman. *Journal of the American Academy of Religion*, vol. 79, no. 1 (2011):

264-267. https://academic.oup.com/jaar/article-abstract/79/1/264/835199

Patheos. "Is Religion Anthropomorphism?" Science on Religion blog, December 2013. https://www.patheos.com/blogs/scienceonrelig ion/2013/12/is-religion-anthropomorphism/

Paul, Gregory S. "Cross-National Correlations of Quantifiable Societal Health with Popular Religiosity and Secularism in the Prosperous Democracies: A First Look." *Journal of Religion and Society*, vol. 7 (2005). https://pnhp.org/news/correlating-societal-health-with-r eligiosity-and-secularism/

Paul, Gregory. "The Chronic Dependence of Popular Religiosity upon Dysfunctional Psychosociological Conditions." *Evolutionary Psychology*, vol. 7 (2009). https://journals.sagepub.com/doi/10.1177/147470490900700305

PBS NewsHour. "Ancient but Small in Number, Zoroastrians Confront Depletion of Their Faith." PBS.org. https://www.pbs.org/ne wshour/arts/ancient-but-small-in-number-zoroastrians-confront-depl etion-of-their-faith

Peoples, Hervey C., Pavel Duda, and Frank W. Marlowe. "Hunter-Gatherers and the Origins of Religion." *Human Nature*, vol. 27 (2016): 261-282. https://pmc.ncbi.nlm.nih.gov/articles/PMC4958132/

Pew Research Center. "Religious Nones in America: Who They Are and What They Believe." January 24, 2024. https://www.pewresea rch.org/religion/2024/01/24/religious-nones-in-america-who-they-are -and-what-they-believe/

Pew Research Center. "Around 4 in 10 Americans Have Become More Spiritual over Time, Fewer Have Become More Religious." January 17, 2024. https://www.pewresearch.org/short-reads/2024/01/1 7/around-4-in-10-americans-have-become-more-spiritual-over-time-f ewer-have-become-more-religious/

Pew Research Center. "Religious Restrictions Around the World, 2022." August 22, 2024. https://www.pewresearch.org/religion/2024/08/22/religious-restrictions-around-the-world-2022/

Pew Research Center. "Who Are 'Spiritual but Not Religious' Americans?" December 7, 2023. https://www.pewresearch.org/religion/2023/12/07/who-are-spiritual-but-not-religious-americans/

Piff, Paul K., Pia Dietze, Matthew Feinberg, Daniel M. Stancato, and Dacher Keltner. "Awe, the small self, and prosocial behavior." *Journal of Personality and Social Psychology*, vol. 108, no. 6 (2015): 883-899. (Referenced in Chapter 7.)

Pizarro, Jose J., Nekane Basabe, Itziar Fernandez, Pilar Carrera, Pedro Apodaca, Carlos I. Man Ging, Olaia Cusi, and Dario Paez. "Self-Transcendent Emotions and Their Social Effects: Awe, Elevation and Kama Muta Promote a Human Identification and Motivations to Help Others." *Frontiers in Psychology*, vol. 12 (2021): 709859. https://pmc.ncbi.nlm.nih.gov/articles/PMC8473748/

Postpartum Support International. "The Power of Building a Supportive Community in Parenthood." Postpartum.net. https://postpartum.net/the-power-of-building-a-supportive-community-in-parenthood/

Price, Max D. *Evolution of a Taboo: Pigs and People in the Ancient Near East.* Oxford University Press, 2021. Reviewed in *European Journal of Archaeology.* https://www.cambridge.org/core/journals/european-journal-of-archaeology/article/max-d-price-evolution-of-a-taboo-pigs-and-people-in-the-ancient-near-east-oxford-oxford-university-press-2021-320-pp-bw-illustr-hbk-isbn-9780197543276/7AABD6BD3A97E332BACBF4D5C67AC3CE

Prindle Institute for Ethics. "Ethics and Peter Singer's Effective Altruism." Prindleinstitute.org, April 2017. https://www.prindleinstitute.org/2017/04/ethics-peter-singer-effective-altruism/

Purzycki, Benjamin Grant, Coren Apicella, Quentin D. Atkinson, Emma Cohen, Rita Anne McNamara, Aiyana K. Willard, Dimitris Xygalatas, Ara Norenzayan, and Joseph Henrich. "Moralistic gods, supernatural punishment and the expansion of human sociality." *Nature*, vol. 530 (2016): 327-330. https://www2.psych.ubc.ca/~ara/Man uscripts/Purzycki%20et%20al%202016%20Moralistic%20Gods%20Su pernatural%20Punishment%20and%20the%20Expansion%20of%20H uman%20Sociality.pdf

Putnam, Robert D. *Bowling Alone: The Collapse and Revival of American Community.* Simon and Schuster, 2000. (Referenced throughout Chapters 8 and 14.)

Putnam, Robert D., and David E. Campbell. *American Grace: How Religion Divides and Unites Us.* Simon and Schuster, 2010. Referenced in: Mercatornet.com. https://www.mercatornet.com/putnam-social-capital

"Religion Explained." *Wikipedia.* https://en.wikipedia.org/wiki/Religion_Explained (referencing Boyer, Pascal. *Religion Explained.* Basic Books, 2001.)

Rickard, W. R., and colleagues. Psychological Needs and community. *Memphis Digital Commons*, vol. 4, no. 1. https://digitalcommons.memphis.edu/finsheem/vol4/iss1/5/

Riksbankens Jubileumsfond (RJ). "Twilight of the Gods: On the Disintegration and Demise of Old Norse Religion." RJ.se, 2020. https:/ /www.rj.se/en/grants/2020/twilight-of-the-gods.-on-the-disintegration -and-demise-of-old-norse-religion-

Sartre, Jean-Paul. "Existentialism Is a Humanism." Lecture delivered 1945. Available via Marxists.org. https://www.marxists.org/ reference/archive/sartre/works/exist/sartre.htm

Serazio, Michael. "The Elementary Forms of Sports Fandom." *Communication and Sport,* vol. 1 (2013). https://journals.sagepub.com/doi/abs/10.1177/2167479512462017

Sheffield Hallam University. "Research: parkrun and Life Satisfaction." SHU.ac.uk. https://www.shu.ac.uk/news/all-articles/lat est-news/parkun-life-satisfaction-research

Singer, Peter. "Famine, Affluence, and Morality." *Philosophy and Public Affairs*, vol. 1, no. 3 (1972): 229-243. Reprinted at CU Boulder. https://rintintin.colorado.edu/~vancecd/phil308/Singer2.pdf

Smarthistory. "Temple of Amun-Re and the Hypostyle Hall, Karnak." Smarthistory.org. https://smarthistory.org/temple-of-amun-re-and-the-hypostyle-hall-karnak/

Social Work Today. "Higher Rates of Anxiety, Depression, and Neurotic Disorder Among 'Spiritual but Not Religious.'" SocialWorkToday.com. https://www.socialworktoday.com/news/pp_100517_2.htm

Solomon, Sheldon, Jeff Greenberg, and Tom Pyszczynski. "A terror management theory of social behavior: The psychological functions of self-esteem and cultural worldviews." *Advances in Experimental Social Psychology*, vol. 24 (1991): 93-159. (Referenced in Chapter 6.)

Sosis, Richard, and Eric R. Bressler. "Cooperation and Commune Longevity: A Test of the Costly Signaling Theory of Religion." *Cross-Cultural Research*, vol. 37, no. 2 (2003): 211-239. https://www.cog nitionandculture.net/wp-content/uploads/Sosis_2003_CommuneLon gevity.pdf

Stanford Medicine. "Alcoholics Anonymous Most Effective Path to Alcohol Abstinence." Stanford.edu, March 2020. https://med.stanford .edu/news/all-news/2020/03/alcoholics-anonymous-most-effective-pa th-to-alcohol-abstinence.html

Stark, Rodney. "Why Religious Movements Succeed or Fail: A Revised General Model." *Journal of Contemporary Religion*, vol. 11 (1996): 133-146. https://www.semanticscholar.org/paper/Why-religio us-movements-succeed-or-fail:-A-revised-Stark/ea4f71f09e3d8713bbc 0f51a02e7250489c764ca

Stieger, S., D. Lewetz, and D. Willinger. "Face-to-face more important than digital communication for mental health during the pandemic." *Scientific Reports*, vol. 13 (2023): 8022. https://pmc.ncbi.nlm.nih.gov/articles/PMC10191089/

Tedeschi, Richard G., Bret A. Moore, and Taryn C. Greene. "Posttraumatic Growth as a Pathway to Wellness for Individuals and Organizations." *Behavioral Sciences*, vol. 15, no. 12 (2025): 1653. https://pmc.ncbi.nlm.nih.gov/articles/PMC12729839/

Tedeschi, Richard G., and Lawrence G. Calhoun. "Clinical Applications of Posttraumatic Growth." In Stephen Joseph (ed.), *Positive Psychology in Practice*. Wiley, 2015. https://ptgi.uncc.edu/wp-content/uploads/sites/9/2015/01/Tedeschi-et-al-Joseph-Ch-30-Clinical-applications-of-PTG.pdf

The Historian's Hut. "A Sneeze Was Seen as a Good Omen in Ancient Greece." TheHistoriansHut.com, December 2018. https://thehistorianshut.com/2018/12/09/a-sneeze-was-seen-as-a-good-omen-in-ancient-greece/

The Springer Institute for Clinical Research. "Stanford Evolution of Cooperation Tournament." (See also Axelrod, Robert.) https://ee.stanford.edu/~hellman/Breakthrough/book/pdfs/axelrod.pdf

Till, Chris, and Joseph Ibrahim. "CrossFit, Community, and Identity: A Gemeinschaft in a Liquid Modern World?" *Sociological Research Online* (2025). https://journals.sagepub.com/doi/10.1177/13607804241258626

Tobian, Aaron A. R., and Ronald H. Gray. "The Medical Benefits of Male Circumcision." *JAMA*, vol. 306, no. 13 (2011): 1479-1480. https://pmc.ncbi.nlm.nih.gov/articles/PMC3684945/

Trivers, Robert L. "The Evolution of Reciprocal Altruism." *The Quarterly Review of Biology*, vol. 46, no. 1 (1971): 35-57. https://www.journals.uchicago.edu/doi/10.1086/406755

"UCLA Encyclopedia of Egyptology." Entry on Egyptian religion. eScholarship.org. https://escholarship.org/uc/item/07s1t6kj

United Nations. "Interfaith Mediation Centre, Nigeria." UN.org Chronicle. https://www.un.org/en/chronicle/article/interfaith-mediation-centre-nigeria

University of Illinois at Urbana-Champaign. "Social Identification with a Team Boosts Fans' Social Well-Being." Illinois.edu. https://news.illinois.edu/social-identification-with-a-team-boosts-fans-social-well-being/

Upenieks, Laura, and Joanne Ford-Robertson. "Changes in Spiritual but Not Religious Identity and Well-Being in Emerging Adulthood in the United States: Pathways to Health Sameness?" *Journal of Religion and Health*, vol. 61, no. 6 (2022): 4635-4673. https://pubmed.ncbi.nlm.nih.gov/35301635/

Upton, Shelley R., Tyler L. Renshaw, and Amanda Morice. "Sacred vs. secular mindfulness meditation: the influence of presentation priming on therapeutic effectiveness." *Mental Health, Religion and Culture*, vol. 25 (2022). https://www.tandfonline.com/doi/abs/10.1080/13674676.2022.2106199

USCIRF (United States Commission on International Religious Freedom). "India." USCIRF.gov. https://www.uscirf.gov/countries/india

VanderWeele, Tyler J. "Religious Service Attendance and Major Health Outcomes." (Multiple studies, Harvard T.H. Chan School of Public Health, 2016-2020. Referenced throughout Chapter 8.)

VanderWeele, Tyler J. "Association of Religious Service Attendance with Mortality Among Women." *JAMA Internal Medicine*, vol. 176, no. 6 (2016): 777-785. (Referenced in Chapter 8.)

Vital Choice. "What Began the Tradition of Fish on Fridays?" VitalChoice.com. https://www.vitalchoice.com/articles/food-facts/what-began-the-tradition-of-fish-on-fridays

Vision of Humanity. *Global Terrorism Index 2025*. VisionofHumanity.org. https://www.visionofhumanity.org/global-terrorism-index/

Wann, Daniel L., Kelly Rogers, Keith Dooley, and Mary Foley. "Applying the Team Identification-Social Psychological Health Model to older sport fans." *International Journal of Aging and Human*

Development, vol. 72, no. 4 (2011): 303-315. https://pubmed.ncbi.nlm.nih.gov/21977676/

Whitehouse, Harvey. *Modes of Religiosity: A Cognitive Theory of Religious Transmission.* AltaMira Press, 2004. (Referenced throughout Chapter 6.)

Whiteman-Sandland, Jessica, Jemma Hawkins, and Debbie Clayton. "The role of social capital and community belongingness for exercise adherence: An exploratory study of the CrossFit gym model." *Journal of Health Psychology*, vol. 23, no. 12 (2018): 1545-1556. https://pubmed.ncbi.nlm.nih.gov/27553606/

Willard, Aiyana K., and Connair Russell-Wilks. "Belief as explanation: a motivation-based theory of agency and anthropomorphism in religious belief." *Religion, Brain and Behavior* (2025). https://www.tandfonline.com/doi/full/10.1080/2153599X.2025.2584792

Wiltermuth, Scott S., and Chip Heath. "Synchrony and Cooperation." *Psychological Science*, vol. 20, no. 1 (2009): 1-5. (Referenced in Chapter 6.)

Xygalatas, Dimitris. *Ritual: How Seemingly Senseless Acts Make Life Worth Living.* Little, Brown Spark, 2022.

Xygalatas, Dimitris, and colleagues. "Extreme Rituals Promote Prosociality." *Psychological Science*, vol. 24, no. 8 (2013): 1602-1605. (Referenced in Chapter 6, Kavadi festival and fire-walking studies.)

Yaqeen Institute for Islamic Research. Yaqeeninstitute.org. https://yaqeeninstitute.org/

Zarina, Daria, Adi Berger, Pavel Fishbein, Vadim Tkachev, and Maria Korman. "Living by the clock of the book: religious observance enhances circadian stability and reduces social jetlag in older adults, a cross-sectional study." *BMC Public Health*, vol. 25 (2025): 2607. https://pmc.ncbi.nlm.nih.gov/articles/PMC12315278/

Zeffren, Noam, Tova Chein, and Robert Stern. "Public health measures derived from the Jewish tradition: II. Washing and

Cleaning." *Hektoen International Journal*, vol. 9, no. 1 (2017). https://touroscholar.touro.edu/cgi/viewcontent.cgi?article=1033&context=tcomny_pubs

"Zoroastrianism." *Wikipedia.* https://en.wikipedia.org/wiki/Zoroastrianism

Zuckerman, Phil. *Living the Secular Life: New Answers to Old Questions.* Penguin Press, 2014. Reviewed in *The New York Times*, December 21, 2014. https://www.nytimes.com/2014/12/21/books/review/living-the-secular-life-by-phil-zuckerman.html

Zuckerman, Phil. *Society Without God: What the Least Religious Nations Can Tell Us About Contentment.* New York University Press, 2008.

"Ancient Egyptian religion." *Wikipedia.* https://en.wikipedia.org/wiki/Ancient_Egyptian_religion

Archaeology Magazine. "The World's Oldest Writing: Cuneiform Tablets." May-June 2016. https://archaeology.org/issues/may-june-2016/collection/cuneiform-last-tablets/the-worlds-oldest-writing/

Archaeology Magazine. "On the Origin of the Pork Taboo." March-April 2025. https://archaeology.org/issues/march-april-2025/letters-from/on-the-origin-of-the-pork-taboo/

A Collection of Outside Scholarship (ACOUP). "Fireside Friday, March 29, 2024, on Roman Values." ACOUP.blog. https://acoup.blog/2024/03/29/fireside-friday-march-29-2024-on-roman-values/

Axelrod, Robert. "The Evolution of Cooperation." Computer tournament results. Referenced in Chapter 10. https://ee.stanford.edu/~hellman/Breakthrough/book/pdfs/axelrod.pdf

BYU News. "More Than Money: Family and Community Bonds Prep Teens for College Success." News.BYU.edu. https://news.byu.edu/intellect/more-than-money-family-and-community-bonds-prep-teens-for-college-success

Cambridge University. "The Shanidar Cave Flower Burial." Cam.ac.uk. https://www.cam.ac.uk/stories/shanidarz

Christianity Today. "Pew Study: America Spiritual but Not Religious, Young Adult Revival." February 2025. https://www.christianitytoday.com/2025/02/pew-study-america-spiritual-but-not-religious-young-adult-revival/

Cooney Classics. "The History of the Handshake." CooneyClassics.org. https://www.cooneyclassics.org/blog/the-history-of-the-handshake

Crown School, University of Chicago. "Ethics of Mindfulness-Based Interventions." CrownSchool.UChicago.edu. https://crownschool.uchicago.edu/student-life/advocates-forum/ethics-mindfulness-based-interventions

"Christianization of Iceland." *Wikipedia.* https://en.wikipedia.org/wiki/Christianization_of_Iceland

"Decline of the Aztec Empire." *Encyclopaedia Britannica.* https://www.britannica.com/summary/Decline-of-the-Aztec-Empire

"Diego de Landa." *Encyclopaedia Britannica.* https://www.britannica.com/biography/Diego-de-Landa

"Hamilton's Rule." *Encyclopaedia Britannica.* https://www.britannica.com/science/Hamiltons-rule

"Mesopotamian Religion." *Encyclopaedia Britannica.* https://www.britannica.com/topic/Mesopotamian-religion

"Why Do Catholics Eat Fish on Fridays?" *Encyclopaedia Britannica.* https://www.britannica.com/topic/Why-Do-Catholics-Eat-Fish-on-Fridays

Hoover Institution. "Religious Faith and Charitable Giving." Social Capital Community Benchmark Survey analysis. Hoover.org. https://www.hoover.org/research/religious-faith-and-charitable-giving

ICNL (International Center for Not-for-Profit Law). "Religious Organizations and Social Capital." ICNL.org. https://www.icnl.org/res

ources/research/ijnl/religious-organizations-and-social-capital

Internet Sacred Text Archive. "Popular Superstitions and the Old Customs of England." Sacred-Texts.com. https://sacred-texts.com/neu/eng/osc/osc60.htm

JSTOR. "Sacred Cow, India." (Academic article via JSTOR.) https://www.jstor.org/stable/40736128

Lilly School of Philanthropy / Philanthropy Roundtable. "Less God, Less Giving?" PhilanthropyRoundtable.org. https://www.philanthropyroundtable.org/magazine/less-god-less-giving/

Mercatornet. "Putnam on Social Capital." MercatorNet.com. https://www.mercatornet.com/putnam-social-capital

Olli, George Mason University. "Zoroastrianism, Judaism, and Christianity." OLLI.GMU.edu. https://olli.gmu.edu/docstore/600docs/1403-651-3-Zoroastrianism,%20Judaism,%20and%20Christianity.pdf

Religion Unplugged. "How Many Americans Are Actually 'Spiritual but Not Religious'?" ReligionUnplugged.com, May 2025. https://religionunplugged.com/news/2025/5/15/how-many-americans-are-actually-spiritual-but-not-religious

Social Work Today. "Higher Rates of Anxiety, Depression, and Neurotic Disorder." SocialWorkToday.com. https://www.socialworktoday.com/news/pp_100517_2.shtml

Weizenbaum Journal. "Reddit Mental Health Communities." WJds (Weizenbaum Institute). https://ojs.weizenbaum-institut.de/index.php/wjds/article/view/5_3_3/197

"Do Fans' Emotions Influence Charitable Donations? Evidence from monetary and returnable cup donations in German soccer stadiums." *Journal of Behavioral and Experimental Economics*, 2022. https://www.sciencedirect.com/science/article/abs/pii/S2214804321001476

Yaqeen Institute. Yaqeeninstitute.org. https://yaqeeninstitute.org/

Note: Sources from Chapters 5, 6, 7, and 8 were extracted from the chapter text, as those chapters contained no inline hyperlinks. These sources are included as full entries in the bibliography above. For sources without a publicly accessible URL, the citation reflects the information available in the chapter text.

Index

Key Concepts and Terms

Studies and Experiments

About the Author

Michael Carroll grew up in the Catholic tradition. He attended Catholic grade school and high school, served as an altar boy, and later as a Eucharistic minister. Carroll studied finance and statistics at Carnegie Mellon University in Pittsburgh. He has identified as Catholic, an atheist, and now an agnostic. He lives in Williamsburg, Brooklyn, with his partner.

www.ingramcontent.com/pod-product-compliance
Lightning Source LLC
Chambersburg PA
CBHW021806130726
47987CB00010B/3033